From Passion to Resurrection

The Conclusion of a Celtic Journey
through
The Spiritual Exercises of Saint Ignatius of Loyola

Timothy J. Ray

To
James L. Connor, SJ

who never ceased encouraging me
to live as a companion of Jesus

Table of Contents

Magis and the Pilgrimage into the Unknown

Abiding in the Domains of Love

Textual Resources

A commitment to the spiritual life involves a journey of unfolding possibilities and new awarenesses. Each new discovery in our relationship with God reveals a deeper experience of divine love as well as further opportunities to serve God through our involvement with other people and various causes in our world, which in turn invites further prayer and reflection about these new expressions of God's activity in our lives. This is a journey into ever-deepening awareness of God's love for us and our need to respond in kind – a love that invites a reciprocal response of love. It is an unending pilgrimage into the mystery of creation that does not end until we find our rest within God's loving consciousness.

For the ancient Celtic saints, this pilgrimage is a journey towards the individual's "place of resurrection" – that place in the world where a person discovers his or her relationship to God and their purpose in life. For the ancient Celts, this was an actual location a man or woman sought out through prayer (and often quite dangerous travel) where he or she would wait for death and subsequent resurrection while committing themselves to rigorous spiritual disciplines and prayers. In the modern world, this "place of resurrection" might better be understood as an earthly situation or type of ministry where a person feels closest to God through prayerful and social activities intended to foster the renewal of God's creation (both human and nonhuman) and the establishment of the kingdom of God.

Centuries later, Saint Ignatius of Loyola would create in his *Spiritual Exercises* an ordered set of meditations designed to help men and women open themselves with ever-increasing generosity to the love God demonstrates towards them and the world around them. At the heart of these Ignatian exercises lies an ideal that Ignatius called *"magis"*, "the more" by which God invites an individual – through an incremental and ongoing process of revelation and invitation – to greater and more challenging opportunities to become instruments of God's love in the world. Like the Celtic saints before him, Ignatius understood the spiritual life as an unfolding journey of possibilities to be embraced in response to the individual's tangible experience of God's love in his or her life.

i

The recognition of this shared vision between the ancient Celtic saints and St. Ignatius of Loyola forms the foundation for the books in this series. Each book presents a self-directed retreat addressing a portion of *The Spiritual Exercises of Saint Ignatius of Loyola* accompanied by materials by or about a particular Celtic saint whose vision complements Ignatius' exercises. Each book in the series also provides resources from both the Celtic and Ignatian spiritual traditions to facilitate further prayer and reflection as well as exercises developed from Celtic spiritual practices related to the themes of each retreat. Used together, these retreats and their companion materials cultivate habits of prayer and action intended to nurture a holistic spirituality embracing spiritual discipline, sacred citizenship, and articulate witness in the world.

So, as you begin this pilgrimage of faith and love, you should walk with confidence in the knowledge that many have walked before you and others will follow after you. You are being invited into an intimate relationship with God through which your faults and failings are forgiven as you become an instrument of love and reconciliation in a world often bereft of hope. The examples of the ancient Celtic saints and the followers of the Ignatian spiritual tradition offer you a supportive companionship as you strive to find your own "place of resurrection" – embracing the increasingly wonderful gifts God presents to you and expressing your gratitude through generous acts of self-giving service to God's other children and creatures.

Through the prayers and reflections of this final book in the "Finding your Place of Resurrection" series, you will experience the fullness of your love for God and your need to reciprocate the love God has expressed toward you through your own concrete (and emotionally unreserved) actions. During the retreat presented in *From Passion to Resurrection*, you will witness the human suffering of Jesus as he is abandoned by his disciples and crucified for your sake. This should evoke deep sorrow in you, both because you are witnessing a friend's agony and because it reveals the fragility of the ideals you have expressed in your earlier travels through this series. Yet, at the end of this experience of pain, you also will experience the joy and hope that comes from recognizing the power of God through Jesus' resurrection.

At the end of this journey through the dark night of Jesus' passion to the morning of his resurrection (and building upon your earlier experiences in *From Loss to Love* and *From Disciple to Friend*), you will be invited to make in oblation of love – a complete offering of yourself and your abilities to the service of God in the restoration of creation. While you may still find this self-offering challenging, your journey through the retreats and reflections of this "Finding your Place of Resurrection" series will empower you to recognize that you can (if only eventually) make this offering freely and without reservation. This new knowledge of yourself and your capacity to love will direct you toward the people, places, and types of activities where you most clearly find the restorative presence of God and wish to participate in that redemptive work – your "place of resurrection".

Once you achieve this awareness of your capacity to offer yourself in love and service to God where you are most needed, you will be transformed into an instrument of God's love for humanity and all of creation. Still, this transformation is a reflection and demonstration of your willingness to accept Ignatius' ideal of *magis*. Through opening yourself to the activity of God within and through you, you will continually experience new possibilities and invitations to serve God with love and absolute generosity. This is the fruit of the seeds you planted in your earlier retreats in this series and which you will harvest during your upcoming retreat. So, once again pray for the grace of openness to God's desires as you approach the prayers and reflections of these final portions of *The Spiritual Exercises of Saint Ignatius of Loyola*.

From Passion to Resurrection presents the two final movements in Ignatius' *Spiritual Exercises* – the third and fourth 'weeks' dealing with the passion and resurrection of Jesus – but it also represents the culmination of your journey toward the oblation of love you will be invited to make at the end of the retreat. Because this book concludes a journey of prayer and reflection, you may find yourself more impatient than at the end of the earlier books in the series. So, you need to remember that the retreat is not an ending. Instead, it offers a new beginning and you need to remain especially attentive to the reflections and exercises offered in this book (drawing upon the stories and prayers of Saint Columba of Iona [known as Colmcille in Ireland] and other resources which Columba would find familiar) so that the seeds of this retreat may mature in the same manner as those from your earlier experiences in prayer.

So, as in your previous retreats, you again should pray for the patience to learn the disciplines of prayer and to persevere as the seeds planted in this book mature and bear fruit over time – carrying with you the promise offered by God through Isaiah 55:10-11:

> *For as the rain and the snow come down from heaven,*
> *and do not return there until they have watered the earth,*
> *making it bring forth and sprout,*
> *giving seed to the sower and bread to the eater,*
> *so shall my word be that goes out from my mouth;*
> *it shall not return to me empty,*
> *but it shall accomplish that which I purpose,*
> *and succeed in the thing for which I sent it.*

Acknowledgements

This book represents a personal journey that would not have been possible without the companionship of the many friends and spiritual companions who, to varying degrees and for different lengths of time, supported and encouraged me to persevere in this pilgrimage.

Among these friends, I remain especially grateful to Kathleen Deignan, Edward Egros, Rosalyn Knowles Ferrell, Douglas Galbraith, Patrick Henry, Susan Rakoczy, Jim Swonger and George Theodoridis.

In addition, I am very grateful for:
* the permission of *The Capuchin Annual* and the King estate to reproduce Richard King's image of Saint Colmcille (Columba) on the cover of this book.
* the permission of Johnston McMaster to excerpt "Columba – The Ambivalent Peacemaker" from his *A Passion for Justice: Social Ethics in the Celtic Tradition* (Edinburgh: Dunedin Academic Press Ltd., 2008) in this book.
* the permission of T. M. Moore to include his translation of Saint Columba's "The Aid of All Workers" (*Adiutor Laborantium*) in this book.

The prayer sequences presented in this book were developed using material from the following public domain books, all of which are available on the Internet Archive:
* *Early Christian Hymns; translations of the verses of the most notable Latin writers of the early and middle ages* (1908) by Daniel Joseph Donahoe.
* *Early Christian Hymns, Series II: translations of the verses of the early and middle ages* (1911) by Daniel Joseph Donahoe.
* *Hymns of the Early Church* (1896) by John Brownlie.
* *The Irish "Liber hymnorum", Volume 2* (1908) by John Henry Bernard Robert Atkinson.
* *The Religious Songs of Connacht: A collection of poems, stories, prayers, satires, ranns, charms, etc., Volume One* (1906) by Douglas Hyde.
* *The Religious Songs of Connacht: A collection of poems, stories, prayers, satires, ranns, charms, etc., Volume Two* (1906) by Douglas Hyde.
* *The Story of Iona* (1909) by Edward Craig Trenholme.

These prayer sequences are adaptations of these sources – not transcriptions or translations – so any fault in their literary quality lies with the author.

Finally, excerpts from the following public domain books have been included in this retreat, its reflection materials, and its resources:
- *The life of Saint Columba, founder of Hy* by Saint Adamnan (1874), edited by William Reeves.
- *The Spiritual Exercises of Saint Ignatius of Loyola* (1847), edited by Charles Seager.
- *Three Middle-Irish homilies on the lives of Saints Patrick, Brigit and Columba* (1877), edited by Whitley Stokes.

All these books are available on the Internet Archive.

Embracing the Fullness of Jesus' Friendship

The greatest test to a friendship usually comes amidst adversity since it is in these times that the full cost of friendship must be either accepted or rejected. In the days or weeks ahead, you will be with Jesus in Jerusalem. This is the culmination of Jesus' earthly mission, a time of sorrow and pain when the opposition to Jesus – both human and cosmic – becomes most evident and recognizable. As a friend to Jesus, you will ask during this time "for grief with Christ and grief, to be broken with Christ broken, for tears and interior suffering on account of the great suffering that Christ endured for [you] (*Sp.Ex.* #203)" as you share in his Passion. As you see Jesus abandoned by his earthly friends, you will come to understand the cost of befriending Jesus.

In Jerusalem during his Passion, Jesus demonstrates his humanity at its fullest and invites you to embrace your intrinsic human weakness. This invitation challenges your desire to be Jesus' friend since it demands that you honor the promises you made to Jesus during the earlier moments of your relationship. You may feel the temptation to walk – or run – away from Jesus as his disciples did, leading you to feel the shame they experienced when they abandoned Jesus in his moment of need. Blessed by greater knowledge than these early disciples, you will experience the liberation of remaining a steadfast friend of the king of heaven. Still, you cannot recognize the joy of this moment until you have remained faithful to Jesus during his sorrow and pain.

Witnessing the death of friend is always painful, but watching the death of Jesus remains an essential part of your friendship with him. Among the ancient Celtic saints, soul friends often wanted to see each other before death, and there are stories of saints who died and refused to go to heaven until their friend arrived. This was not about closure. Instead, it expressed the desire to be present at the moment of a friend's glorification and journey to heaven. So, while it is tempting to rush through the suffering of Jesus to arrive at the joy of his resurrection, this denies the intrinsic unity of Jesus' passion and resurrection as well as the subsequent invitation of the Risen Jesus to participate in his continuing redemptive mission.

Your prayerful encounters with the suffering Jesus will deepen your friendship with him and make it possible for you to embrace the wonder of his resurrection. Witnessing Jesus' willingness to suffer and die on our behalf will help heal your own sense of woundedness. Also, your desire to share in Jesus' moments of loneliness, self-doubt, and physical pain will free you from the limitations of a narrowly defined sense of self and awaken in you an empathy for the solitary pain of God's other creatures (both human and nonhuman). These evocations of healing, generosity and love will be sanctified through Jesus' resurrection and allow you to fully embrace the fullness of your friendship with Jesus and the sacrifices this relationship entails.

A Contemplation of the Friendship of Jesus Christ

So, through the following exercise, consider the qualities you present to Jesus Christ that would lead him to embrace you as a friend:

This exercise is an adaptation of the "Consideration of Christ's Kingdom" in The Spiritual Exercises of Saint Ignatius. *You may want to read the text of this exercise as Ignatius presented it (see page 295) since this might offer different perspectives on various aspects of this exercise, illuminate your reflections, and open you to a broader awareness of God's activity during your prayers. However, you should feel free to ignore this suggestion if it distracts you from your prayers.*

[1]   Focus on this specific time and place as you allow all other concerns to fall away. As you become still, become aware of your desires during this moment of prayer. Ask of Jesus Christ that you may not be deaf to his offer of friendship but alert and eager to fulfill his most holy will to the best of your ability. Ask also that you might fully understand the qualities of Jesus, the King of Heaven, which attract you to him as a friend.

As these desires fill your consciousness, let all other concerns fall aside as you focus on this specific time and place of prayer.

[2]   Then, slowly and deliberately, consider the invitation of Jesus Christ to become his friend.

•   In your imagination, allow yourself to see the generosity and love you have shown toward your closest friends. Take a moment to see your inner circle of friends, making a mental note of their physical

4

appearance and demeanor. Watch and listen as you see them dealing with sadness, illness, or emotional confusion. See the sacrifices you make to comfort or help them in these difficult times, putting aside your needs or desires to support them. Listen to the love expressed in your voice as you care for your friends. Experience your pain when they suffer and your pleasure when they begin to feel better.

Linger for a time in this moment, becoming aware of all the emotions and thoughts evoked in you. Then, allow this moment to fade from your consciousness while retaining an awareness of the feelings evoked in you by this invitation and the challenges opposed to accepting this invitation through your frail human nature.

• When you are ready, allow yourself to see Jesus Christ standing in front of you. Note his physical appearance and demeanor. In your imagination, visualize the various ways Jesus has suffered – especially for you. Watch and listen as Jesus feels pain and suffers for you. See your response as you try to console or comfort Jesus, even sacrificing your needs or desires to alleviate Jesus' pain. Listen to the love in your voice as you speak with Jesus in these moments. Experience your pain as you feel unable to do enough for Jesus and your pleasure when Jesus acknowledges your efforts.

Again, linger in this moment and become aware of all the emotions and thoughts evoked in you. Then, allow this moment to fade from your consciousness while retaining an awareness of the liberation you have been offered in this moment.

• Afterward, allow the various words and images of your prayer to flow freely in your consciousness without being controlled. Become aware of those aspects of your prayer that arouse holy desires in you, toward God and toward others (including nonhuman creatures). Become aware of those aspects of your prayer that make you feel shame for those times you fall short of these holy aspirations.

• Gradually allow these thoughts and images to fade from your consciousness and become aware of the return of Jesus, standing, or sitting with you in this moment. Then, have open and informal conversation about your experiences during this meditation. Speak about how these experiences express your own desires and fears, giving space for Jesus to explain the love at the heart of your relationship. At the end of this conversation, ask Jesus to help you reform those aspects of your personality and life that impede your ability to respond to his friendship.

• Then, gradually allow your thoughts to recede as you focus on Jesus' continuing presence in your life and in the world around you.

[3]   Conclude by offering this prayer adapted from a Christian song collected in Daniel Joseph Donahoe's *Early Christian Hymns (Series II)*:

O Christ, my everlasting Light,
You the glory of the starry sky,
Illume the darkness of my night,
Quicken my breast and purify.
O, save me from insidious snares,
Protect me from the dangerous foe,
Guard, lest I stumble unawares,
And let my sleep no evil know.
Keep you my heart forever pure,
Increase my faith, my will with you combine.
Be with me, your protection sure,
Save by your power and love divine. Amen.

[4]   Afterward, take 10-15 minutes in a quiet space to reflect on the most significant moments from your prayer and record your reflections in your journal.

From Passion to Resurrection

As with your retreats in *From Loss to Love* and *From Disciple to Friend*, you need to consider the requirements of your upcoming retreat. You will need to decide whether you will approach this retreat in the same manner as the previous one or change your process during this part of your journey. You again need to decide whether you will conduct this retreat in daily life or in seclusion and whether you will invite others to join you in your upcoming journey prayer or travel that path alone. You will need to carefully review your experiences during your previous prayers in order to properly prepare yourself for the needs of this retreat

So, by again considering the following questions, you can build upon the successes of your previous retreat sand learn from the challenges you faced during your earlier experiences:

If a previous retreat was in daily life:

• **How might you improve the quality and consistency of your prayer?** To answer this question… Reflect upon the times that were most consoling during your previous retreats and those times you found most challenging. If it is not clear to you why these moments have these qualities, ask God in prayer to illuminate your heart and mind so that you may better be present to the spiritual leadings of your upcoming retreat.

• **How might you better preserve the sacred character of the place where you pray?** To answer this question… Consider the aspects of your prayer space that were most comforting and those which were most distracting during your previous retreats. Think about ways to adjust the place in which you pray to alleviate or enhance these various experiences and ask God to confirm your decisions.

• **How successful were you in avoiding distractions while praying at or near your home?** To answer this question… Examine the record of your previous retreats in your journal and try to determine any commonalities in those situations which were either most prayerful or most distracting. As with the previous question, think about ways to adjust the habits of your prayer to alleviate or enhance these various experiences and ask God to confirm your insights.

If a previous retreat was in seclusion:

• **What were the most affirming and challenging aspects of your experience?** To answer this question… Visualize the good and bad experiences of your time in seclusion. Try to find commonalities within each type of experience and ask God to help you understand the ways through which you might be able to alleviate the negative and enhance the positive aspects of your experience.

• **How successful were you in maintaining a calm environment for your prayer throughout the day?** To answer this question… Think about those moments when you were most distracted and contemplate the commonalities of these different times during your previous retreat before asking God how you might better preserve a calm atmosphere in your upcoming retreat.

• **What issues or distractions diminished the quality of your prayer during your retreat?** To answer this question… Visualize the good and bad experiences of your time in seclusion as well as review your journal notes from the previous retreat. Then, isolate those moments when you were most distracted and determine whether they were movements of prayer that you found difficult emotionally or external distractions that took you away from prayer. Finally, ask God to help you improve your spiritual focus and stamina when you approach these types of moments during your upcoming prayer.

• **How successful were you and avoiding distractions either at your home or away from home during your retreat?** To answer this question… Consider the activities that surrounded your prayer during your retreat and determine those which disrupted the prayerful environment you hope to create. Again, consider the adjustments you need to make in your environment to reduce these problems and ask God to help you remain focused when new distractions come during your upcoming retreat.

If you were alone during a previous retreat:

• **What were the liberating aspects of being in solitude with God during your retreat?** To answer this question… Visualize the good and bad experiences of your retreat and review your retreat journal, finding those moments when you found pleasure in being alone with God and express your gratitude for these times.

• **What aspects of being in solitude left you feeling alone or easily distracted during your retreat?** To answer this question… Again visualize the good and bad experiences of your retreat and review your retreat journal, finding those moments when you felt completely alone and ask God to illuminate the reasons for these feelings as well as the loving presence you failed to recognize during these times.

If a previous retreat was with companions:

• **What aspects of your retreat were improved by the presence of others praying with you?** To answer this question… Through visualization and a consideration of your memories, become aware of these special moments and express your gratitude for them to God.

• **What aspects of your retreat were diminished by the presence of others praying with you?** To answer this question… Again, through visualization and a consideration of your memories, become aware of these moments and ask God to help you understand the emotional and spiritual dynamics that shaped these times.

• **If any, which activities with your companions during your previous retreat brought you joy?** To answer this question… Again, through visualization and a consideration of your memories, become aware of these special moments and express your gratitude for them to God.

• **If any, which activities with your companions during your previous retreat brought you sorrow or sadness?** To answer this question… Again, through visualization and a consideration of your memories, become aware of these special moments and ask God to help you understand the emotional and spiritual dynamics that shaped these times.

Note: If your previous retreat was with companions and away from home, you should repeat the previous set of questions focusing on the logistical and practical matters you encountered during your time together.

Finally, after making this review and addressing the issues raised by these questions, take some time to reaffirm your desire to walk with God once again with the confidence that comes from your experiences of God's love, guidance, and protection during your previous retreat. As with your earlier retreat, you may face spiritual and emotional challenges during your upcoming time of prayer, which you now know from direct experience that God is traveling with you and instilling in you holy desires that will transform you into an instrument of divine love.

Remember the words of the prophet Jeremiah:
> *Blessed are those who trust in the Lord,*
> *whose trust is the Lord.*
> *They shall be like a tree planted by water,*
> *sending out its roots by the stream.*
> *It shall not fear when heat comes,*
> *and its leaves shall stay green;*
> *in the year of drought it is not anxious,*
> *and it does not cease to bear fruit.*
> *(Jeremiah 17:7-8)*

Prelude

Praying with Jesus and Saint Columba

During the days or weeks of this retreat, you will be accompanied by two companions: Jesus and Saint Columba. So, it is important for you to have a clear image in your mind of how they look, speak and act.

Note: *It is important to remember that these images are not intended to be historically accurate. Instead, they provide you with an image of how you perceive these two individuals and how you think they will act while you are with them.*

Begin by calming yourself and putting aside all other concerns.

Then, when you are ready, allow an image of Jesus to come into your mind. He is alone, either standing or sitting. Look at him carefully, noting his physical features and demeanor as he looks back at you. Take your time with this first encounter and become aware of the love and care Jesus radiates toward you. After a short while, watch as a person approaches Jesus and observe how he interacts with that individual. Then, watch and listen as a crowd gathers around Jesus. Observe any nuances of his behavior that seem particularly unexpected and hear his voice as he speaks to different people.

Take as long as you need to make these observations. Then, remaining in your imagination, listen as Jesus instructs you, "Pray then in this way… Our Father in heaven, hallowed be your name. Your kingdom come. Your will be done, on earth as it is in heaven. Give us this day our daily bread. And forgive us our debts, as we also have forgiven our debtors. And do not bring us to the time of trial, but rescue us from the evil one." (Matthew 6: 9-13)

Take a moment to linger in the sounds and resonances of Jesus' voice, then allow this image to fade from your consciousness before summarizing your impressions, reactions, and observations in your workbook.

Then, read the description of Saint Columba presented on page 301.

Gradually, guided by the description, allow an image of Saint Columba to emerge in your mind. He also is alone, either standing or sitting. Note his physical features and demeanor while he looks back at you. Again, take your time with this first encounter and be aware of how you feel in Columba's presence. Consider power of his personality and how it manifests itself and his gaze toward you. Then, see other people approach Columba – first a few and then many. Watch and listen as he engages these different people and speaks with them, noting any nuances in Columba's behavior that seem unexpected while listening to the sound of his voice as he speaks with these different people.

As with your time with Jesus, take as long as you need to make these observations of Saint Columba. Then, while remaining in your imagination as much as possible, listen to Columba's voice as you read "Helper of All Workers" (found on page 305). Allow the rhythm and pace of your reading to be guided by Columba's voice.

Linger in the sounds and resonances of Saint Columba's voice for a moment. Then, allow this image to fade from your consciousness before summarizing your impressions, reactions, and observations in your workbook.

> _Note:_ It is important to remember that these impressions are intended as an aid to helping you imagine Jesus and Columba during your periods of prayer. If you find your images of Jesus and Columba changing during the retreat, you should embrace these transitions and record these new perceptions in your workbook as they occur.

1. Jesus Enters Jerusalem

a prayer of praise, gratitude, and victory

Take a moment to quiet your spirit, becoming completely present to this time and place. Allow all other thoughts and concerns to fall away as you come into the presence of God. Then, when you are ready, begin.

Dear God of mercy and of power,
Bowed at your feet in prayer and love
      I am; send down your heavenly dower,
      The Spirit's largess, from above.

As you have filled my life with light,
And oped my heart to your grace,
      So guide me ever in your might,
      And fit me for your dwelling-place.

A Hymn, sung or heard (optional)

Tell, my tongue, the glorious conflict,
Crowned with victory nobly won;
      More than all the spoils of battle,
      Praise the triumph of God's Son;
How by death the crown of conquest
      Graced Him when the strife was done.

Grieving sore o'er Eden's sorrow
When our race in Adam fell;
      And the fatal fruit he tasted,
      Welcomed sin, and death, and hell;
God ordained a tree in Zion,
      Eden's poison to dispel.

In the work of our Redemption
Wisdom met the tempter's foils;
      On the ground he claimed, the Victor
      Fought, and bore away the spoils;
And the bane became the blessing,
      Freedom sprang amid his toils.

From the bosom of the Father,
Where He shared the regal crown,
At the time by God appointed,
Came the world's Creator down
God incarnate, born of a Virgin,
Shorn of glory and renown.

Read or recite Psalm 21.

Holy Lord,
Under my thoughts may I God-thoughts find.
Half of my sins escape my mind.
For what I said, or did not say,
Pardon me, O Lord, I pray.

Read Matthew 21: 1-11, read aloud or quietly.

O Lord, Jesus the Christ,
If I were in Heaven my harp I would sound
With apostles and angels and saints all around,
Praising and thanking the Son who is crowned,
May the poor race of Eve for that heaven be bound!

All hail to you, Body of Christ,
All hail, King of Heaven's lights,
All hail, O Holy Trinity,
All hail to you you Right of Rights.

All hail to you, blood and flesh,
All hail to you, king of good,
No more be angry with my soul,
But wash it in your precious blood.

No more be angry with my soul,
But cleanse it by your gracious might,
A hundred welcomes, God and man,
Both now and when the Death shall smite.

O Holy Lord,

God with the Father and the Spirit,
For me is many a snare designed,
To fill my mind with doubts and fears;
Far from the land of holy saints,
I dwell within my vale of tears.
Let faith, let hope, let love –
Traits far above the cold world's way –
With patience, humility, and awe,
Become my guides from day to day.

I acknowledge, the evil I have done.
From the day of my birth till the day of my death,
Through the sight of my eyes,
Through the hearing of my ears,
Through the sayings of my mouth,
Through the thoughts of my heart,
Through the touch of my hands,
Through the course of my way,
Through all I said and did not,
Through all I promised and fulfilled not,
Through all the laws and holy commandments I broke.
I ask even now absolution of you,
For fear I may have never asked it as was right,
And that I might not live to ask it again,

O Holy Lord, my King in Heaven,
May you not let my soul stray from you,
May you keep me in a good state,
May you turn me toward what is good to do,
May you protect me from dangers, small and great.
May you fill my eyes with tears of repentance,
So I may avoid the sinner's awful sentence.
May the Grace of the God for ever be with me,
And whatever my needs, may the Triune God give me.

Select one of the following options for the Lord's Prayer.

Option A

O Jesus Christ,

Lord of heaven and earth,
Help me pray as you yourself taught:
> *"Our Father in heaven,*
> *hallowed be your name.*
> *Your kingdom come.*
> *Your will be done,*
> *on earth as it is in heaven.*
> *Give us this day our daily bread.*
> *And forgive us our debts,*
> *as we also have forgiven our debtors.*
> *And do not bring us to the time of trial,*
> *but rescue us from the evil one."*
> *(Matthew 6: 9-13)*

From the foes of my land,
from the foes of my faith,
From the foes who would us dissever,
> O Lord, preserve me, in life and in death,
> With the Sign of the Cross for ever.
> *For the kingdom, the power, and the glory*
> *are yours now and for ever. Amen.*

Please proceed with "I beseech you, O Lord…," found after Option B.

Option B

O Jesus Christ,
Lord of heaven and earth,
Help me pray as you yourself taught:
> *Our Father in heaven,*
> *hallowed be your name,*
> *your kingdom come,*
> *your will be done,*
> *on earth as in heaven.*
> *Give us today our daily bread.*
> *Forgive us our sins*
> *as we forgive those who sin against us.*
> *Lead us not into temptation*
> *but deliver us from evil.*

From the foes of my land,

from the foes of my faith,
From the foes who would us dissever,
>> O Lord, preserve me, in life and in death,
>> With the Sign of the Cross for ever.
>> *For the kingdom, the power, and the glory*
>> *are yours now and for ever. Amen.*

I beseech you, O Lord.
God in Heaven, unsurpassed in power and might;
>> Be behind me, Be on my left,
>> Be before me, Be on my right!
Against each danger, you are my help;
In distress, upon you I call.
>> In dark times, may you sustain me
>> And lift me up again when I fall.
Lord over heaven and of earth,
You know my offenses.
>> Yet, listening to my pleadings,
>> You guide me away from sinful pretenses.
Lord of all creation and the many creatures,
You bestow on me many earthly treasures.
>> Revealing love in each life and season,
>> You share with me heavenly pleasures.
May you arouse me
In moments both of joy and of strife;
>> Most holy Lord, bring me new life!

A Hymn, sung or heard (optional)

O Jesus Christ,
>> Lord of heaven and earth,
>> You are my riches, my store, my provision,
My star through the years
When troubles rend me,
>> Through times of strife and tears,
>> Sweet Jesus, defend me.

"Forevermore hosanna sing,
To David's Son, our conquering King;
>> To you be ever love and laud

Who earns in the name of God."

To you shall rise the song and psalm,
O Victim meek, O spotless Lamb,
>Whose blood has washed all earthly taints
>From the white vestments of the saints.

End this time of prayer by taking some time to bring to mind the various ways God shields you from harm or guides you through the world's tumult. Then, when you are ready, conclude by saying:

O Holy Lord, King in Heaven,
I place myself at the edge of your grace,
>On the floor of your house myself I place,
And to banish the sin of my heart away,
>I lower my knee to you this day.
Through life's torrents of pain may you bring me whole,
>And, O Lord Jesus Christ, preserve also my soul. Amen.

Consideration of the Readings

After reciting or prayerfully reading the prayer sequence for this day or week:
- Read about Jesus entering Jerusalem in Matthew 21:1-11. Make a mental note of each person's appearance and actions during the episode as well as the key elements of the story and its setting. Then, consider any aspects of this story that speak strongly to you before recording these observations in your workbook.
- Read about Jesus at the temple in Matthew 21:12-17. Again, note each person's appearance and actions during the episode as well as the key elements of the story and its setting, including the setting. Then, record in your workbook any aspects of this story that speak strongly to you.
- Read about the Greeks approaching Jesus in John 12:20-36. Again, note each person's appearance and actions during the episode as well as the key elements of the story and its setting before recording any aspects of this story that speak strongly to you.

Note: You also should take a moment to consider any aspect of the prayer sequence from this day or week that seemed particularly significant to you.

Contemplation of Your Needs

When you are ready, concentrating on your breath or an object near you, allow any distractions to fade from your consciousness as you become aware of your desire to live in God's goodness. Feel yourself yearning to properly use the many gifts God has given you, to experience God's continuing care, and to be open to the immense love God shows for you, then:
- Read "Columba Raises a Dead Cleric" (found on page 301). Allow yourself to linger on any thoughts, phrases or images that seem particularly meaningful or significant to your earlier preparations or prayer.
- Pray for your desires in the coming day or week. Ask that the divine presence all around you may be revealed, so you may feel deep

grief and confusion because it is for your sins that the Lord is going to his passion. Ask also that, in this day or week of prayer, you may feel joy and excitement as you watch Jesus interacting with the people of Jerusalem and with the Greek visitors.

   • Conclude by praying to become aware that this is the beginning of the passion – that there is an undercurrent of anger toward Jesus and even a hint of betrayal.
Then, take a moment record any significant thoughts, emotions, or reactions from these moments in your workbook.

   After this, put your notes aside. Without straining your memory, consider in turn each of the readings for the coming day or week and allow them to take shape in your imagination – even if all you remember are small fragments. Prayerfully ponder how each reading affects you emotionally without overtly thinking about their content, asking God to illuminate the spiritual gifts offered in each reading – quieting your mind and creating a receptive space in yourself to see or hear the response.

   Finally, conclude by allowing these desires to fade from your consciousness as you offer this traditional Irish prayer collected by Douglas Hyde in *The Religious Songs of Connacht*:

> *O God, I believe in you; strengthen my belief.*
> *I trust in you; confirm my trust.*
> *I love you; double my love.*
> *I repent that I angered you,*
> *Increase my repentance.*
> *Fill you my heart with awe without despair;*
> *With hope, without over-confidence;*
> *With piety without infatuation;*
> *And with joy without excess.*
> *My God, consent to guide me by your wisdom;*
> *To constrain me by your right;*
> *To comfort me by your mercy;*
> *And to protect me by your power. Amen.*

Allow these words to linger on your mind and in your heart for a few moments and then, while they are still fresh in your memory, write the most important thoughts, feelings, and desires from this preparatory time in your retreat journal.

In this contemplation of Matthew 21:1-11, you will see and hear Jesus entering Jerusalem with his disciples.

[1]   Begin by reading the biblical selection and reviewing your notes on it from your earlier preparations.

[2]   Then, focus on this specific time and place as you allow all other concerns to fall away. Then, when you are ready, consider the people and place in this moment of prayer.

• Allow an image of Jesus to emerge in your imagination, noting his physical characteristics and mannerisms. Look at what he is wearing or carrying, observing his clothing and any objects he is holding. Make a note of whether he is sitting, standing, or walking. Ponder this mental image, allowing any other observations about Jesus to form in your mind.

• Then, observe the men and women around Jesus. Note how many people are with Jesus, making a mental note of their appearance and demeanor. Look at Jesus' disciples, observing where they are standing and how they behave toward Jesus. Look at the crowd, noting their attitude and behavior toward Jesus. Observe whether the people are sitting, standing, or walking. Take a moment to ponder this mental image, allowing other impressions of these men and women to form. Become familiar with the men and women you will encounter during your prayer as well as their behavior.

• Gradually, allow yourself to become aware of the location of this moment of prayer. Pay attention to its physical characteristics and the arrangement of the people in it. As you ponder this mental image, look around the place and notice more details about it – noting if it is crowded or not, if it has an unusual smell or not, etc. Become familiar with the location of your upcoming prayer.

• Take a moment to remain in this place with these men and women, then allow these images to fade from your consciousness.

[3]   After you become still, become aware of your desires during this moment of prayer. Remember your desire to experience the divine presence all around you and to trust in God's plan for you, asking that you may feel deep grief and confusion because it is for your sins that the Lord is going to his passion. Recall your desire that, in this day or week of prayer, you may feel joy as you watch Jesus interacting with the people of Jerusalem and with the Greek visitors. However, ask that

you may always remain aware that there is an undercurrent of anger toward Jesus and a hint of betrayal as Jesus begins his passion.

As these desires fill your consciousness, let all other concerns fall aside as you focus on this specific time and place of prayer.

[4]   Again, when you are ready, allow the image of Jesus and his disciples to reemerge in your imagination.

• Watch as the Jesus enters Jerusalem with his disciples, surrounded by a large crowd. Listen to the sounds of this moment and become comfortable as you prepare to hear Jesus speak. Feel the anticipation of the people around you and share in that enthusiasm.

• Ask God to help you share in their experience – either by joining them or by listening quietly to them. Focus your attention on Jesus, noting his physical appearance and his emotional demeanor.

• Then, watch and listen as Jesus speaks to the crowd and see their response. You may want to quietly read the passage while remaining prayerfully aware of your mental image of Jesus or you may choose to stay completely within the imagined realm of your prayer. Whichever you choose, know that God will offer you the words from the biblical passage that you need to hear – even if only in fragments.

– Look around as Jesus speaks, see the reactions both of his disciples and the people in the crowd. Become aware of their feelings and how they behave toward Jesus and one another.

– Remember that Jesus is speaking to men and women living with the expectation that God will radically change their lives. Remember that he also is speaking to you.

• Afterward, allow this image to fade from your imagination as you become aware of the phrases and images from this moment which touched you most deeply. Recall the emotions and memories – including any sounds or smells – evoked during your prayer. Allow these seminal aspects of your meditation to linger on your mind and in your heart, noting any special feelings evoked by them.

[5]   When you are ready, become aware of Jesus' presence with you in this moment and have an open and informal conversation about this prayer period and how the passage from Matthew's gospel expresses your own needs or desires – giving space for Jesus to respond or to highlight different aspects from the biblical account and your experiences during this contemplation.

Note: Saint Ignatius says this conversational prayer (called a colloquy) should "be made similarly to the language of a friend to a *friend, or of a servant to his Lord; now by asking some favour, now by accusing myself of some fault; sometimes by communicating my own affairs of any kind, and asking counsel or help concerning them (Sp.Ex. #54)."*

After this conversation with Jesus, gradually allow your thoughts to recede as you focus on God's broader presence in your life and in the world around you.

[6]   Finally, conclude by allowing these desires to fade from your consciousness as you offer this traditional Irish prayer collected by Douglas Hyde in *The Religious Songs of Connacht*:

> *Confirm me in your love divine,*
> *Smooth for my feet life's rugged way;*
> *My will with yours entwine,*
> *Lest evil lead my steps astray.*
> *Be with my still as guard and guide,*
> *Keep me in holy sanctity,*
> *Let my firm faith on you abide,*
> *From fraud and error hold me free. Amen.*

[7]   Afterward, take 10-15 minutes in a quiet space to reflect on the most significant moments from this time of prayer and record your reflections in your retreat journal.

In this contemplation of Matthew 21:12-17, you will see and hear Jesus cleansing the temple in Jerusalem.

[1]   Begin by reading the biblical selection and reviewing your notes on it from your earlier preparations.

[2]   Then, focus on this specific time and place as you allow all other concerns to fall away. Then, when you are ready, consider the people and place in this moment of prayer.

• Allow an image of Jesus to emerge in your imagination, noting his physical characteristics and mannerisms. Look at what he is wearing or carrying, observing his clothing and any objects he is holding. Ponder this mental image, allowing any other observations about Jesus to form in your mind.

• Then, observe the people around Jesus. Note how many people are with Jesus, making a mental note of their appearance and demeanor. Look at Jesus' disciples, observing where they are standing and how they behave toward Jesus. Look at the crowd, noting their attitude and behavior toward Jesus. Observe whether the people are sitting, standing, or walking. Observe the temple officials and how they respond to Jesus. Take a moment to ponder this mental image, allowing other impressions of these men and women to form. Become familiar with the men and women you will encounter during your prayer as well as their behavior.

• Gradually, allow yourself to become aware of the location of this moment of prayer. Pay attention to its physical characteristics of the temple and the arrangement of the people in it. As you ponder this mental image, look around the place and notice more details about it – noting if it is crowded or not, if it has an unusual smell or not, etc. Become familiar with the location of your upcoming prayer.

• Take a moment to remain in this place with these men and women, then allow these images to fade from your consciousness.

[3]   After you become still, become aware of your desires during this moment of prayer. Remember your desire to experience the divine presence all around you and to trust in God's plan for you, asking that you may feel deep grief and confusion because it is for your sins that the Lord is going to his passion. Recall your desire that, in this day or week of prayer, you may feel joy as you watch Jesus interacting with the people of Jerusalem and with the Greek visitors. However, ask that

you may always remain aware that there is an undercurrent of anger toward Jesus and a hint of betrayal as Jesus begins his passion.

As these desires fill your consciousness, let all other concerns fall aside as you focus on this specific time and place of prayer.

[4]   Again, when you are ready, allow the image of Jesus and his disciples to reemerge in your imagination.

• Watch as Jesus and his disciples enter the temple. Listen to the sounds of this moment and become comfortable as you prepare to hear Jesus speak. Feel the anticipation of the people around you and share in that enthusiasm.

• Ask God to help you share in their experience – either by joining them or by listening quietly to them. Focus your attention on Jesus, noting his physical appearance and his emotional demeanor.

• Then, watch and listen as Jesus becomes angry and begins to overturn the tables of the money changers. You may want to quietly read the passage while remaining prayerfully aware of your mental image of Jesus or you may choose to stay completely within the imagined realm of your prayer. Whichever you choose, know that God will offer you the words from the biblical passage that you need to hear – even if only in fragments.

– Look around as Jesus speaks to the crowd and the temple officials, seeing and hearing the reactions of his disciples and the people in the crowd. Become aware of their feelings and how they behave toward Jesus and one another.

– Remember that Jesus is speaking to men and women struggling to reconcile their expectations of Jesus and the ways his actions and desires challenge their preconceptions. Remember that he also is speaking to you.

• Afterward, allow this image to fade from your imagination as you become aware of the phrases and images from this moment which touched you most deeply. Recall the emotions and memories – including any sounds or smells – evoked during your prayer. Allow these seminal aspects of your meditation to linger on your mind and in your heart, noting any special feelings evoked by them.

[5]   When you are ready, become aware of Jesus' presence with you in this moment and have an open and informal conversation about this prayer period and how the passage from Matthew's gospel expresses your own needs or desires – giving space for Jesus to respond or to highlight different aspects from the biblical account and your experiences during this contemplation. Then, gradually allow your

thoughts to recede as you focus on God's broader presence in your life and in the world around you.

[6]   Finally, conclude by allowing these desires to fade from your consciousness as you offer this traditional Irish prayer collected by Douglas Hyde in *The Religious Songs of Connacht*:

> *Confirm me in your love divine,*
> *Smooth for my feet life's rugged way;*
> *My will with yours entwine,*
> *Lest evil lead my steps astray.*
> *Be with my still as guard and guide,*
> *Keep me in holy sanctity,*
> *Let my firm faith on you abide,*
> *From fraud and error hold me free. Amen.*

[7]   Afterward, take 10-15 minutes in a quiet space to reflect on the most significant moments from this time of prayer and record your reflections in your retreat journal.

In this contemplation of John 12:20-36, you will see and hear Jesus speaking with Greeks while in Jerusalem.

[1]   Begin by reading the biblical selection and reviewing your notes on it from your earlier preparations.

[2]   Then, focus on this specific time and place as you allow all other concerns to fall away. Then, when you are ready, consider the people and place in this moment of prayer.

• Allow an image of Jesus to emerge in your imagination, noting his physical characteristics and mannerisms. Look at what he is wearing or carrying, observing his clothing and any objects he is holding. Make a note of whether he is sitting, standing, or walking. Ponder this mental image, allowing any other observations about Jesus to form in your mind.

• Then, observe the people around Jesus. Note how many people are with Jesus, making a mental note of their appearance and demeanor. Look at Jesus' disciples, observing where they are standing and how they behave toward Jesus. Look at the crowd, noting their attitude and behavior toward Jesus. See the Greek visitors, noting how they are different from the other men and women in the crowd. Observe whether the people are sitting, standing, or walking. Take a moment to ponder this mental image, allowing other impressions of these men and women to form. Become familiar with the men and women you will encounter during your prayer as well as their behavior.

• Gradually, allow yourself to become aware of the location of this moment of prayer. Pay attention to its physical characteristics of the temple and the arrangement of the people in it. As you ponder this mental image, look around the place and notice more details about it – noting if it is crowded or not, if it has an unusual smell or not, etc. Become familiar with the location of your upcoming prayer.

• Take a moment to remain in this place with these men and women, then allow these images to fade from your consciousness.

[3]   After you become still, become aware of your desires during this moment of prayer. Remember your desire to experience the divine presence all around you and to trust in God's plan for you, asking that you may feel deep grief and confusion because it is for your sins that the Lord is going to his passion. Recall your desire that, in this day or week of prayer, you may feel joy as you watch Jesus interacting with

the people of Jerusalem and with the Greek visitors. However, ask that you may always remain aware that there is an undercurrent of anger toward Jesus and a hint of betrayal as Jesus begins his passion.

As these desires fill your consciousness, let all other concerns fall aside as you focus on this specific time and place of prayer.

[4]   Again, when you are ready, allow the image of Jesus and his disciples to reemerge in your imagination.

• Watch as the Greeks approach one of Jesus' disciples and how that disciple responds. Listen to the sounds of this moment and become comfortable as you prepare to hear Jesus speak. Feel the anticipation of the people around you and share in that enthusiasm.

• Ask God to help you share in their experience – either by joining them or by listening quietly to them. Focus your attention on Jesus, noting his physical appearance and his emotional demeanor.

• Then, watch and listen as the Greeks are brought to Jesus and he speaks with them. You may want to quietly read the passage while remaining prayerfully aware of your mental image of Jesus or you may choose to stay completely within the imagined realm of your prayer. Whichever you choose, know that God will offer you the words from the biblical passage that you need to hear – even if only in fragments.

– Look around as Jesus speaks and see the reactions of his disciples, the Greeks, and the other people in the crowd. Become aware of their feelings and how they behave toward Jesus and one another.

– Remember that Jesus is speaking to men and women struggling to find and understand God's desires in their lives. Remember that he also is speaking to you.

• Afterward, allow this image to fade from your imagination as you become aware of the phrases and images from this moment which touched you most deeply. Recall the emotions and memories – including any sounds or smells – evoked during your prayer. Allow these seminal aspects of your meditation to linger on your mind and in your heart, noting any special feelings evoked by them.

[5]   When you are ready, become aware of Jesus' presence with you in this moment and have an open and informal conversation about this prayer period and how the passage from John's gospel expresses your own needs or desires – giving space for Jesus to respond or to highlight different aspects from the biblical account and your experiences during this contemplation. Then, gradually allow your thoughts to recede as

you focus on God's broader presence in your life and in the world around you.

[6]   Finally, conclude by allowing these desires to fade from your consciousness as you offer this traditional Irish prayer collected by Douglas Hyde in *The Religious Songs of Connacht*:

> *Confirm me in your love divine,*
> *Smooth for my feet life's rugged way;*
> *My will with yours entwine,*
> *Lest evil lead my steps astray.*
> *Be with my still as guard and guide,*
> *Keep me in holy sanctity,*
> *Let my firm faith on you abide,*
> *From fraud and error hold me free. Amen.*

[7]   Afterward, take 10-15 minutes in a quiet space to reflect on the most significant moments from this time of prayer and record your reflections in your retreat journal.

In this meditation on Matthew 21:12-17, Saint Columba preaches to a crowd about the need to preserve the purity of their faith and prayer.

[1]   Begin by reading the biblical selection and reviewing your notes on it from your earlier preparations.

[2]   Then, focus on this specific time and place as you allow all other concerns to fall away. Then, when you are ready, consider the people and place in this moment of prayer.

• Allow an image of Columba to emerge in your imagination, noting his physical characteristics and mannerisms. Look at what he is wearing or carrying, observing his clothing and any objects he is holding. Make a note of whether he is sitting, standing, or walking. Ponder this mental image, allowing any other observations about Columba to form in your mind.

• Then, observe the men and women around Saint Columba. Note how many people are with Columba, making a mental note of their appearance and demeanor. Look at Columba's disciples, observing where they are standing and how they behave toward Columba. Look at the crowd, noting their attitude and behavior toward Saint Columba. Observe whether the people are sitting, standing, or walking. Take a moment to ponder this mental image, allowing other impressions of these men and women to form. Become familiar with the men and women you will encounter during your prayer as well as their behavior.

• Gradually, allow yourself to become aware of the location of this encounter with Columba. Note its physical characteristics and the arrangement of the people in it. As you ponder this mental image, look around the place and notice more details about it – noting if it is in dim or bright light, if it is still and silent or filled with noise, if it has an unusual smell or not, etc. Become familiar with the location of your upcoming prayer.

• Take a moment to remain in this place with these men and women, then allow these images to fade from your consciousness.

[3]   After you become still, become aware of your desires during this moment of prayer. Remember your desire to experience the divine presence all around you and to trust in God's plan for you, asking that you may feel deep grief and confusion because it is for your sins that

the Lord is going to his passion. Recall your desire that, in this day or week of prayer, you may feel joy as you watch Jesus interacting with the people of Jerusalem and with the Greek visitors. However, ask that you may always remain aware that there is an undercurrent of anger toward Jesus and a hint of betrayal as Jesus begins his passion.

As these desires fill your consciousness, let all other concerns fall aside as you focus on this specific time and place of prayer.

[4]   Again, when you are ready, allow the image of Saint Columba and his disciples to reemerge in your imagination.

• Watch as the group assembles around Columba. Listen to the sounds of this moment and become comfortable as you prepare to hear Columba speak. Feel the anticipation of the people around you and share in that enthusiasm.

• Ask God to help you share in their experience – either by joining them or by listening quietly to them. Focus your attention on Columba, noting his physical appearance and his emotional demeanor.

• Then, watch and listen as Columba tells story of Jesus cleansing the temple and speaks to them about their need to cleanse themselves since they are living temples of God's love. You may want to quietly read the passage while remaining prayerfully aware of your mental image of Columba or you may choose to stay completely within the imagined realm of your prayer. Whichever you choose, know that God will offer you the words from the biblical passage that you need to hear – even if only in fragments.

– Look around as Columba speaks and see the reactions of his disciples and of the people in the crowd. Become aware of their feelings and how they behave toward Columba and one another.

– Remember that Columba is speaking to men and women struggling to remain faithful to God's desires and promises while living difficult lives which challenge their faith. Remember that he also is speaking to you.

• After Columba finishes speaking, allow this image to fade from your imagination as you become aware of the phrases and images from this moment of prayer which touched you most deeply. Recall the emotions and memories – including any sounds or smells – evoked during your prayer. Allow these seminal aspects of your meditation to linger on your mind and in your heart, making a mental note of any special feelings evoked by them.

[5]   When you are ready, become aware of Jesus' presence with you in this moment and have an open and informal conversation about this

prayer period and how the passage from Matthew's gospel expresses your own needs or desires – giving space for Jesus to respond or to highlight different aspects from the biblical account and your experiences during this contemplation. Then, gradually allow your thoughts to recede as you focus on God's broader presence in your life and in the world around you.

[6]   Finally, conclude by allowing these desires to fade from your consciousness as you offer this traditional Irish prayer collected by Douglas Hyde in *The Religious Songs of Connacht*:

> *Confirm me in your love divine,*
> *Smooth for my feet life's rugged way;*
> *My will with yours entwine,*
> *Lest evil lead my steps astray.*
> *Be with my still as guard and guide,*
> *Keep me in holy sanctity,*
> *Let my firm faith on you abide,*
> *From fraud and error hold me free. Amen.*

[7]   Afterward, take 10-15 minutes in a quiet space to reflect on the most significant moments from this time of prayer and record your reflections in your retreat journal.

1.6   An Application of the Senses

[1]   Become aware of your prayerful desires during this day or week. Bring to mind your desire to feel deep grief and confusion because it is for your sins that the Lord is going to his passion. Ask also that, in this day or week of prayer, you may feel joy and excitement as you watch Jesus interacting with the people of Jerusalem and with the Greek visitors.

[2]   When you are ready, in your imagination, call to mind the various prayers of the preceding day or days. Allow the images and words of these prayers to linger and then slowly fade from your consciousness.

• Remember your imaginative contemplation of Matthew 21:1-11. Consider the images and feelings evoked in you during your prayer, feeling God's presence in these memories and becoming aware of the specific sensations associated with each image.

• Recall your imaginative contemplation and meditation concerning Matthew 21:12-17, considering them in the same way as your earlier memories of Matthew 21.

• Review your imaginative contemplation of John 12:20-36 in the same manner as the previous prayers.

As these prayers enter your memory, make a mental note of which senses are most active. You may see an image or a color, hear a sound or a phrase, or smell a scent or a fragrance. You may even taste a flavor or feel a sensation on your skin.

[3]   Then, relax and allow these various memories and experiences to quietly enter and leave your consciousness without being controlled – whether they are clear or diffuse, whether they come quickly or slowly. Linger on the sensory images and memories being evoked in you – noticing any images or colors, any sounds or phrases, any scents or fragrances, any flavors or physical sensations associated with each prayer.

[4]   When you are ready, become completely still and clear your mind of all thoughts and concerns. Allow an image of a special personal space to form in your imagination, a place where you are completely comfortable and alone. Then, watch as God enters that place and forms a small image or object for you that expresses the thought or awareness that you most need to carry with you into your life.

Reverently pick up the object or image, a reflection of the most important gift you have been given during this time of prayer. Look at it carefully and become aware of the divine presence contained within it. Take a moment to register what it looks like and how it feels in your hand. Then, feel the joy and confidence that comes from touching the presence of God as you accept this gift, offering a short prayer of gratitude while you relax into the pleasure of this moment.

[5]   Then, conclude by allowing these images to fade from your consciousness as you offer this traditional Irish prayer collected by Douglas Hyde in *The Religious Songs of Connacht*:

> *Confirm me in your love divine,*
> *Smooth for my feet life's rugged way;*
> *My will with yours entwine,*
> *Lest evil lead my steps astray.*
> *Be with my still as guard and guide,*
> *Keep me in holy sanctity,*
> *Let my firm faith on you abide,*
> *From fraud and error hold me free. Amen.*

[6]   While your experiences are still fresh in your mind, record the most significant impressions or sensations from this time of prayer in your retreat journal.

[1]   Remember your desires during the preceding day or week of prayer. As you become aware of the divine presence all around you, ask that you may feel deep grief and confusion because it is for your sins that the Lord is going to his passion. Recall also your desire to feel joy and excitement as you watch Jesus interacting with the people of Jerusalem and with the Greek visitors.

After bringing these thoughts and desires into your consciousness, ask God once again to fulfill these desires in your own life and in your interactions with others.

[2]   Then, take a moment to allow the words, thoughts, and feelings from your prayers during the last day or week to linger – on your mind and in your heart – before asking God to reveal the fulfillment of your deepest desires in these various memories.

• Think about the prayer sequence at the beginning of this day or week. Make a mental note of any words, insights or images that remain particularly significant or meaningful to you.

• Ponder the story, "Columba Raises a Dead Cleric". Note any words, insights, or images from it that remain particularly significant or meaningful to you.

• Remember your imaginative contemplation of Matthew 21:1-11.

– Consider the most powerful images, phrases, or feelings from your prayer. Ask yourself what gifts God gave to you through these moments, perhaps offering you new insights or perhaps affirming an important aspect of your faith. Ask yourself how God may be calling you to change through these moments, being as specific as possible.

– Examine your disposition as you prayed, noting whether prayer came easily or with resistance. Recall the easiest moments in your prayer and any moments of joy you may have experienced. Remember also if you encountered any difficulty opening yourself to God or if you felt any sadness as you prayed. Ask God to help you understand why these feelings surfaced.

– Bring to mind any moments when you added personal elements (e.g., familiar places or people from your life) or connected your prayers to other scriptures or spiritual writings. Ask yourself how these additions helped or hindered you as you prayed. Again, if you do not know why this happened, ask God to help you understand.

• Recall your imaginative contemplation and meditation concerning Matthew 21:12-17. Then, review your prayer in the same way as your earlier reflection on Matthew 21.

• Review your imaginative contemplation of John 12:20-36 in the same manner as the previous prayers.

• Reflect on the ebb and flow of sensory impressions and feelings that marked your application of the senses. Isolate the most memorable moments and sensory impressions from your prayer and reflect on how God used these moments to give you a particular gift, perhaps offering you new insights or changing you in some way.

[3]   Finally, ponder the times when images or feelings from the readings of this day or week surfaced outside these prayer periods. Consider those moments or events in which God's presence or guidance was especially strong as well as any moments when you were struggling. Think about the most memorable aspects of these experiences, asking God to explain their significance.

[4]   Take a moment to allow the words, thoughts, and feelings of these prayers to linger on your mind and in your heart. Finally, conclude by allowing these desires to fade from your consciousness as you offer this traditional Irish prayer collected by Douglas Hyde in *The Religious Songs of Connacht*:

> *O God, I believe in you; strengthen my belief.*
> *I trust in you; confirm my trust.*
> *I love you; double my love.*
> *I repent that I angered you,*
> *Increase my repentance.*
> *Fill you my heart with awe without despair;*
> *With hope, without over-confidence;*
> *With piety without infatuation;*
> *And with joy without excess.*
> *My God, consent to guide me by your wisdom;*
> *To constrain me by your right;*
> *To comfort me by your mercy;*
> *And to protect me by your power. Amen.*

[5]   After finishing these prayers, summarize your reflections on the gifts or graces you received during the prayers of this last day or week and record these thoughts in your retreat journal.

2. The Last Supper

2.1a   Let Earth And Heaven Rejoice And Sing

a prayer on Jesus' Passion

Take a moment to quiet your spirit, becoming completely present to this time and place. Allow all other thoughts and concerns to fall away as you come into the presence of God. Then, when you are ready, begin.

Let earth and heaven rejoice and sing
The supper of our Lord and King,
         Who cleansed our souls from sin, and gave
         The living bread to heal and save.
Let earth and heaven rejoice and sing
         That supper of our Lord and King.

The Maker of the world, that night,
With wondrous mystery and might,
         Brought to the soul her heavenly meat,
         His blood to drink, his flesh to eat;
He cleansed our souls from sin and gave
         The living bread to heal and save.

A Hymn, sung or heard (optional)

Thus the work of our salvation
Was by law divine ordained,
         Thus by good to ill opposing,
         Was the tempter's power restrained;
Whence the evil, thence the healing,
         Whence came death true life is gained.

In his holy hour the Saviour
From the halls of heaven is come.
         Takes the flesh of human nature;
         So to save the flesh from doom;
Born as man, the world's Creator
         Issues from a virgin's womb.

In a stable poor and lowly,
He, a tender child is born,

With a manger for a cradle,
Our Redeemer lies forlorn;
Swathing him in bands, the mother
Shields the Babe from shame and scorn.

Thirty years are soon completed,
And the day of woe is nigh;
Comes the hour of man's redemption,
When the Christ is doomed to die;
On the cross, a lamb, uplifted,
Lo! the Lord of earth and sky!

With a crown of thorns they crown him,
And they nail him to the wood,
With a lance they pierce his body
Whence the water and the blood
Flow, till ocean, earth and heaven
Bathe in the redeeming flood.

Read or recite Psalm 113.

Holy Lord,
Under my thoughts may I God-thoughts find.
Half of my sins escape my mind.
For what I said, or did not say,
Pardon me, O Lord, I pray.

Read John 13: 1-30, aloud or quietly.

O Lord, Jesus the Christ,
If I were in Heaven my harp I would sound
With apostles and angels and saints all around,
Praising and thanking the Son who is crowned,
May the poor race of Eve for that heaven be bound!

O Jesus, sorely suffering
Rent by your Passion's pain,
And in un-torn offering,
Slain as among the slain,
Scoffed at, despised, neglected,

Tortured by cruel men,
      Trembling to be rejected
      I turn to you again.

O Holy Lord,
      God with the Father and the Spirit,
For me is many a snare designed,
To fill my mind with doubts and fears;
      Far from the land of holy saints,
      I dwell within my vale of tears.
Let faith, let hope, let love –
Traits far above the cold world's way –
      With patience, humility, and awe,
      Become my guides from day to day.

I acknowledge, the evil I have done.
From the day of my birth till the day of my death,
      Through the sight of my eyes,
Through the hearing of my ears,
      Through the sayings of my mouth,
Through the thoughts of my heart,
      Through the touch of my hands,
Through the course of my way,
      Through all I said and did not,
Through all I promised and fulfilled not,
      Through all the laws and holy commandments I broke.
I ask even now absolution of you,
      For fear I may have never asked it as was right,
      And that I might not live to ask it again,

O Holy Lord, my King in Heaven,
May you not let my soul stray from you,
May you keep me in a good state,
      May you turn me toward what is good to do,
      May you protect me from dangers, small and great.
May you fill my eyes with tears of repentance,
      So I may avoid the sinner's awful sentence.
May the Grace of the God for ever be with me,
      And whatever my needs, may the Triune God give me.

Select one of the following options for the Lord's Prayer.

Option A

O Jesus Christ,
Lord of heaven and earth,
Help me pray as you yourself taught:
> *"Our Father in heaven,*
> *hallowed be your name.*
> *Your kingdom come.*
> *Your will be done,*
> *on earth as it is in heaven.*
> *Give us this day our daily bread.*
> *And forgive us our debts,*
> *as we also have forgiven our debtors.*
> *And do not bring us to the time of trial,*
> *but rescue us from the evil one."*
> *(Matthew 6: 9-13)*

From the foes of my land,
from the foes of my faith,
From the foes who would us dissever,
> O Lord, preserve me, in life and in death,
> With the Sign of the Cross for ever.
> *For the kingdom, the power, and the glory*
> *are yours now and for ever. Amen.*

Please proceed with "I beseech you, O Lord…," found after Option B.

Option B

O Jesus Christ,
Lord of heaven and earth,
Help me pray as you yourself taught:
> *Our Father in heaven,*
> *hallowed be your name,*
> *your kingdom come,*
> *your will be done,*
> *on earth as in heaven.*
> *Give us today our daily bread.*

Forgive us our sins
as we forgive those who sin against us.
Lead us not into temptation
but deliver us from evil.
From the foes of my land,
from the foes of my faith,
From the foes who would us dissever,
       O Lord, preserve me, in life and in death,
       With the Sign of the Cross for ever.
       For the kingdom, the power, and the glory
       are yours now and for ever. Amen.

I beseech you, O Lord.
God in Heaven, unsurpassed in power and might;
       Be behind me, Be on my left,
       Be before me, Be on my right!
Against each danger, you are my help;
In distress, upon you I call.
       In dark times, may you sustain me
       And lift me up again when I fall.
Lord over heaven and of earth,
You know my offenses.
       Yet, listening to my pleadings,
       You guide me away from sinful pretenses.
Lord of all creation and the many creatures,
You bestow on me many earthly treasures.
       Revealing love in each life and season,
       You share with me heavenly pleasures.
May you arouse me
In moments both of joy and of strife;
       Most holy Lord, bring me new life!

A Hymn, sung or heard (optional)

O Jesus Christ,
       Lord of heaven and earth,
       You are my riches, my store, my provision,
My star through the years
When troubles rend me,
       Through times of strife and tears,

Sweet Jesus, defend me.

O Christ, our everlasting Light,
You the glory of the starry sky,
      Illume the darkness of our night,
      Quicken our breasts and purify.

O, save us from insidious snares,
Protect us from the dangerous foe,
      Guard, lest we stumble unawares,
      And let our sleep no evil know.

Keep you our hearts forever pure,
Increase our faith, our will with you combine.
      Be with us your protection sure,
      Save by your power and love divine.

End this time of prayer by taking some time to bring to mind the various ways God shields you from harm or guides you through the world's tumult. Then, when you are ready, conclude by saying:

O Holy Lord, King in Heaven,
I place myself at the edge of your grace,
      On the floor of your house myself I place,
And to banish the sin of my heart away,
      I lower my knee to you this day.
Through life's torrents of pain may you bring me whole,
    And, O Lord Jesus Christ, preserve also my soul. Amen.

Consideration of the Readings

After reciting or prayerfully reading the prayer sequence for this day or week:

• Read about the plot to kill Jesus in Luke 22:1-13. Again, make a mental note of each person's appearance and actions during the episode as well as the key elements of the story and its setting. Then, consider any aspects of this story that speak strongly to you before recording these observations in your workbook.

• Read about the Last Supper in Luke 22:14-27, noting the appearance of Jesus and the tempter while observing their actions during the episode as well as the key elements of the story. Then, record any aspects of this story that speak strongly to you.

• Read about Jesus washing the feet of his disciples in John 13:1-30. Again, note each person's appearance and actions during the episode as well as the key elements of the story and its setting before recording any aspects of this story that speak strongly to you.

Note: You also should take a moment to consider any aspect of the prayer sequence from this day or week that seemed particularly significant to you.

Contemplation of Your Needs

When you are ready, concentrating on your breath or an object near you, allow any distractions to fade from your consciousness as you become aware of your desire to live in God's goodness. Feel yourself yearning to properly use the many gifts God has given you, to experience God's continuing care, and to be open to the immense love God shows for you, then:

• Read "Columba and the Miracle of the Feast" (found on page 302). Allow yourself to linger on any thoughts, phrases or images that seem particularly meaningful or significant to your earlier preparations or prayer.

• Pray for your desires in the coming day or week. Ask that the divine presence all around you may be revealed, so you may feel deep grief and confusion because it is for your sins that the Lord is going to his passion. Ask also that, in this day or week of prayer, you experience the intimacy of being one of his friends while remaining aware of sadness Jesus feels when witnessing the bickering among the apostles and the betrayal of Judas Iscariot.

Then, take a moment record any significant thoughts, emotions, or reactions from these moments in your workbook.

After this, put your notes aside. Without straining your memory, consider in turn each of the readings for the coming day or week and allow them to take shape in your imagination – even if all you remember are small fragments. Prayerfully ponder how each reading affects you emotionally without overtly thinking about their content, asking God to illuminate the spiritual gifts offered in each reading – quieting your mind and creating a receptive space in yourself to see or hear the response.

Finally, conclude by allowing these desires to fade from your consciousness as you offer this traditional Irish prayer collected by Douglas Hyde in *The Religious Songs of Connacht*:

> *O God, I believe in you; strengthen my belief.*
> *I trust in you; confirm my trust.*
> *I love you; double my love.*
> *I repent that I angered you,*
> *Increase my repentance.*
> *Fill you my heart with awe without despair;*
> *With hope, without over-confidence;*
> *With piety without infatuation;*
> *And with joy without excess.*
> *My God, consent to guide me by your wisdom;*
> *To constrain me by your right;*
> *To comfort me by your mercy;*
> *And to protect me by your power. Amen.*

Allow these words to linger on your mind and in your heart for a few moments and then, while they are still fresh in your memory, write the most important thoughts, feelings, and desires from this preparatory time in your retreat journal.

2.2   A Contemplation of Luke 22:1-13

In this contemplation of Luke 22:1-13, you will see and hear various plots against Jesus while he is in Jerusalem.

[1]   Begin by reading the biblical selection and reviewing your notes on it from your earlier preparations.

[2]   Then, focus on this specific time and place as you allow all other concerns to fall away. Then, when you are ready, consider the people and place in this moment of prayer.

• Allow an image of Jesus to emerge in your imagination, noting his physical characteristics and mannerisms. Look at what he is wearing or carrying, observing his clothing and any objects he is holding. Ponder this mental image, allowing any other observations about Jesus to form in your mind.

• Observe the disciples around Jesus. Make a mental note of their appearance and how they behave toward Jesus. Take a moment to ponder this mental image, allowing other impressions of these people to form. Become familiar with the men and women you will encounter during your prayer as well as their behavior.

• Then, look at Judas Iscariot, noting his appearance and demeanor. Observe the priests and scribes around Judas, making a mental note of their appearance and demeanor. Notice how these people behave differently toward Jesus.

• Gradually, allow yourself to become aware of the locations of this moment of prayer. Pay attention to their physical characteristics and the arrangement of the people in them. As you ponder these mental images, look around the places and notice more details about them – noting if they are in dim or bright light, if they are still and silent or filled with noise, if they have an unusual smell or not, etc. Become familiar with these locations of your upcoming prayer.

• Take a moment to remain in this place with these men and women, then allow these images to fade from your consciousness.

[3]   After you become still, become aware of your desires during this moment of prayer. Remember your desire to experience the divine presence all around you and to trust in God's plan for you, asking that you may feel deep grief and confusion because it is for your sins that the Lord is going to his passion. Recall your desire that, in this day or week of prayer, you may experience the intimacy of being one of his

friends while remaining aware of sadness Jesus feels when witnessing the bickering among the apostles and the betrayal of Judas Iscariot.

As these desires fill your consciousness, let all other concerns fall aside as you focus on this specific time and place of prayer.

[4]   Again, when you are ready, allow the images of Judas and Jesus to reemerge in your imagination.

• Watch as the disciples assemble around Jesus, with Judas staying on the fringe of the group. Listen to the sounds of this moment and become comfortable in it. Feel the anticipation of the disciples and share in that enthusiasm while becoming aware of Judas' growing anger and resentment.

• Ask God to help you share in their experience – either by joining them or by listening quietly to them. Focus your attention on Jesus, noting his physical appearance and his emotional demeanor.

• Then, watch and listen as Judas leaves and speaks with the priests and scribes before seeing and hearing Jesus ask some disciples to prepare the Passover meal. You may want to quietly read the passage while remaining prayerfully aware of your mental image of Jesus or you may choose to stay completely within the imagined realm of your prayer. Whichever you choose, know that God will offer you the words from the biblical passage that you need to hear – even if only in fragments.

– Look around when Judas and Jesus speak and observe the different ways the different groups perceive Jesus. Become aware of their respective feelings and how they behave toward Jesus and one another.

– Remember that Jesus spoke often of the hostility of the worldly to his mission. Remember that he also was speaking to you in those moments and recall how these warnings affected you.

• Afterward, allow this image to fade from your imagination as you become aware of the phrases and images from this moment which touched you most deeply. Recall the emotions and memories – including any sounds or smells – evoked during your prayer. Allow these seminal aspects of your meditation to linger on your mind and in your heart, noting any special feelings evoked by them.

[5]   When you are ready, become aware of Jesus' presence with you in this moment and have an open and informal conversation about this prayer period and how the passage from Luke's gospel expresses your own needs or desires – giving space for Jesus to respond or to highlight different aspects from the biblical account and your experiences during

this contemplation. Then, gradually allow your thoughts to recede as you focus on God's broader presence in your life and in the world around you.

[6]   Finally, conclude by allowing these desires to fade from your consciousness as you offer this traditional Irish prayer collected by Douglas Hyde in *The Religious Songs of Connacht*:

> *Confirm me in your love divine,*
> *Smooth for my feet life's rugged way;*
> *My will with yours entwine,*
> *Lest evil lead my steps astray.*
> *Be with my still as guard and guide,*
> *Keep me in holy sanctity,*
> *Let my firm faith on you abide,*
> *From fraud and error hold me free. Amen.*

[7]   Afterward, take 10-15 minutes in a quiet space to reflect on the most significant moments from this time of prayer and record your reflections in your retreat journal.

In this contemplation of Luke 22:14-27, you will see and hear Jesus and his disciples at the Last Supper.

[1]   Begin by reading the biblical selection and reviewing your notes on it from your earlier preparations.

[2]   Then, focus on this specific time and place as you allow all other concerns to fall away. Then, when you are ready, consider the people and place in this moment of prayer.

• Allow an image of Jesus to emerge in your imagination, noting his physical characteristics and mannerisms. Look at what he is wearing or carrying, observing his clothing and any objects he is holding. Ponder this mental image, allowing any other observations about Jesus to form in your mind.

• Then, observe the disciples around Jesus, making a mental note of their appearance and demeanor. Observe how they behave toward Jesus and one another. Observe whether there are any other people in the room with Jesus and his disciples, noting their appearance and demeanor   Take a moment to ponder this mental image, allowing other impressions of these people to form. Become familiar with the men and women you will encounter during your prayer as well as their behavior.

• Gradually, allow yourself to become aware of the location of this moment of prayer. Pay attention to its physical characteristics of the room and the arrangement of the people in it. As you ponder this mental image, look around the place and notice more details about it – noting if it is in dim or bright light, if it is still and silent or filled with noise, if it has any unusual smells or not, etc. Become familiar with the location of your upcoming prayer.

• Take a moment to remain in this place with these people, then allow these images to fade from your consciousness.

[3]   After you become still, become aware of your desires during this moment of prayer. Remember your desire to experience the divine presence all around you and to trust in God's plan for you, asking that you may feel deep grief and confusion because it is for your sins that the Lord is going to his passion. Recall your desire that, in this day or week of prayer, you may experience the intimacy of being one of his friends while remaining aware of sadness Jesus feels when witnessing the bickering among the apostles and the betrayal of Judas Iscariot.

As these desires fill your consciousness, let all other concerns fall aside as you focus on this specific time and place of prayer.

[4]   Again, when you are ready, allow the image of Jesus and his disciples to reemerge in your imagination.

• Watch as the group assembles around Jesus. Listen to the sounds of this moment and become comfortable as you prepare to hear Jesus speak. Feel the anticipation of the disciples around you and share in that enthusiasm.

• Ask God to help you share in their experience – either by joining them or by listening quietly to them. Focus your attention on Jesus, noting his physical appearance and his emotional demeanor.

• Then, watch and listen as Jesus to the disciples and see their response to his words. You may want to quietly read the passage while remaining prayerfully aware of your mental image of Jesus or you may choose to stay completely within the imagined realm of your prayer. Whichever you choose, know that God will offer you the words from the biblical passage that you need to hear – even if only in fragments.

– Look around as Jesus speaks and see the reactions of his disciples and the people in the crowd. Become aware of their feelings and how they behave toward Jesus and one another.

– Remember that Jesus often challenged the expectations of his disciples. Remember that he also often challenges your expectations of him.

• Afterward, allow this image to fade from your imagination as you become aware of the phrases and images from this moment which touched you most deeply. Recall the emotions and memories – including any sounds or smells – evoked during your prayer. Allow these seminal aspects of your meditation to linger on your mind and in your heart, noting any special feelings evoked by them.

[5]   When you are ready, become aware of Jesus' presence with you in this moment and have an open and informal conversation about this prayer period and how the passage from Luke's gospel expresses your own needs or desires – giving space for Jesus to respond or to highlight different aspects from the biblical account and your experiences during this contemplation. Then, gradually allow your thoughts to recede as you focus on God's broader presence in your life and in the world around you.

[6]   Finally, conclude by allowing these desires to fade from your consciousness as you offer this traditional Irish prayer collected by Douglas Hyde in *The Religious Songs of Connacht*:

Confirm me in your love divine,
Smooth for my feet life's rugged way;
My will with yours entwine,
Lest evil lead my steps astray.
Be with my still as guard and guide,
Keep me in holy sanctity,
Let my firm faith on you abide,
From fraud and error hold me free. Amen.

[7]   Afterward, take 10-15 minutes in a quiet space to reflect on the most significant moments from this time of prayer and record your reflections in your retreat journal.

In this contemplation of John 13:1-30, you will see and hear Jesus washing the feet of his disciples.

[1]   Begin by reading the biblical selection and reviewing your notes on it from your earlier preparations.

[2]   Then, focus on this specific time and place as you allow all other concerns to fall away. Then, when you are ready, consider the people and place in this moment of prayer.

• Allow an image of Jesus to emerge in your imagination, noting his physical characteristics and mannerisms. Look at what he is wearing or carrying, observing his clothing and any objects he is holding. Ponder this mental image, allowing any other observations about Jesus to form in your mind.

• Then, observe the disciples around Jesus, making a mental note of their appearance and demeanor. Observe how they behave toward Jesus and one another. Observe whether there are any other people in the room with Jesus and his disciples, noting their appearance and demeanor   Take a moment to ponder this mental image, allowing other impressions of these men and women to form. Become familiar with the men and women you will encounter during your prayer as well as their behavior.

• Gradually, allow yourself to become aware of the location of this moment of prayer. Pay attention to its physical characteristics of the room and the arrangement of the people in it. As you ponder this mental image, look around the place and notice more details about it – noting if it is in dim or bright light, if it is still and silent or filled with noise, if it has any unusual smells or not, etc. Become familiar with the location of your upcoming prayer.

• Take a moment to remain in this place with these men and women, then allow these images to fade from your consciousness.

[3]   After you become still, become aware of your desires during this moment of prayer. Remember your desire to experience the divine presence all around you and to trust in God's plan for you, asking that you may feel deep grief and confusion because it is for your sins that the Lord is going to his passion. Recall your desire that, in this day or week of prayer, you may experience the intimacy of being one of his friends while remaining aware of sadness Jesus feels when witnessing the bickering among the apostles and the betrayal of Judas Iscariot.

As these desires fill your consciousness, let all other concerns fall aside as you focus on this specific time and place of prayer.

[4]   Again, when you are ready, allow the image of Jesus and his disciples to reemerge in your imagination.

• Watch as Jesus and his disciples eat their Passover meal. Listen to the sounds of this moment and become comfortable in it. Feel the joy of the people around you and share in their enthusiasm.

• Ask God to help you share in their experience – either by joining them or by listening quietly to them. Focus your attention on Jesus, noting his physical appearance and his emotional demeanor.

• Then, watch and listen as Jesus gets up from the meal, begins washing the feet of his disciples and speaks with the disciples afterward (including Judas Iscariot). You may want to quietly read the passage while remaining prayerfully aware of your mental image of Jesus or you may choose to stay completely within the imagined realm of your prayer. Whichever you choose, know that God will offer you the words from the biblical passage that you need to hear – even if only in fragments.

– Look around and see the reactions of his disciples, both while Jesus is washing their feet and when he speaks to them afterward. Become aware of their feelings and how they behave toward Jesus and one another.

– Remember that Jesus often challenged the expectations of his disciples. Remember that he also often challenges your expectations of him.

• Afterward, allow this image to fade from your imagination as you become aware of the phrases and images from this moment which touched you most deeply. Recall the emotions and memories – including any sounds or smells – evoked during your prayer. Allow these seminal aspects of your meditation to linger on your mind and in your heart, noting any special feelings evoked by them.

[5]   When you are ready, become aware of Jesus' presence with you in this moment and have an open and informal conversation about this prayer period and how the passage from John's gospel expresses your own needs or desires – giving space for Jesus to respond or to highlight different aspects from the biblical account and your experiences during this contemplation. Then, gradually allow your thoughts to recede as you focus on God's broader presence in your life and in the world around you.

[6]   Finally, conclude by allowing these desires to fade from your consciousness as you offer this traditional Irish prayer collected by Douglas Hyde in *The Religious Songs of Connacht*:

> *Confirm me in your love divine,*
> *Smooth for my feet life's rugged way;*
> *My will with yours entwine,*
> *Lest evil lead my steps astray.*
> *Be with my still as guard and guide,*
> *Keep me in holy sanctity,*
> *Let my firm faith on you abide,*
> *From fraud and error hold me free. Amen.*

[7]   Afterward, take 10-15 minutes in a quiet space to reflect on the most significant moments from this time of prayer and record your reflections in your retreat journal.

In this meditation on John 13:1-30, you will see and hear Saint Columba teach his disciples how they must emulate Jesus' courage and humility in their lives.

[1]   Begin by reading the biblical selection and reviewing your notes on it from your earlier preparations.

[2]   Then, focus on this specific time and place as you allow all other concerns to fall away. Then, when you are ready, consider the people and place in this moment of prayer.

• Allow an image of Columba to emerge in your imagination, noting his physical characteristics and mannerisms. Look at what he is wearing or carrying, observing his clothing and any objects he is holding. Make a note of whether he is sitting, standing, or walking. Ponder this mental image, allowing any other observations about Columba to form in your mind.

• Then, observe the disciples around Saint Columba. Note how many disciples are with Columba, making a mental note of their appearance and demeanor. Observe whether they are sitting, standing, or walking. Take a moment to ponder this mental image, allowing other impressions of these people to form. Become familiar with the men and women you will encounter during your prayer as well as their behavior.

• Gradually, allow yourself to become aware of the location of this encounter with Saint Columba. Observe whether it is inside or outside, paying attention to its physical characteristics and the arrangement of the people in it. As you ponder this mental image, look around the place and notice more details about it – noting if it is in dim or bright light, if it is still and silent or filled with noise, if it has an unusual smell or not, etc. Become familiar with the location of your upcoming prayer.

• Take a moment to remain in this place with these people, then allow these images to fade from your consciousness.

[3]   After you become still, become aware of your desires during this moment of prayer. Remember your desire to experience the divine presence all around you and to trust in God's plan for you, asking that you may feel deep grief and confusion because it is for your sins that the Lord is going to his passion. Recall your desire that, in this day or week of prayer, you may experience the intimacy of being one of his

friends while remaining aware of sadness Jesus feels when witnessing the bickering among the apostles and the betrayal of Judas Iscariot.

As these desires fill your consciousness, let all other concerns fall aside as you focus on this specific time and place of prayer.

[4]   Again, when you are ready, allow the image of Saint Columba and his disciples to reemerge in your imagination.

• Watch as the group assembles around Columba. Listen to the sounds of this moment and become comfortable as you prepare to hear Columba speak. Feel the anticipation of the people around you and share in that enthusiasm.

• Ask God to help you enter this moment – either by joining these events or by listening quietly to them. Focus your attention on Saint Columba, noting his physical appearance and his emotional demeanor.

• Then, relying on your earlier prayers, watch and listen as Columba tells the story of Jesus washing the feet of his disciples at the beginning of his Passion. You may want to quietly read the passage while remaining prayerfully aware of your mental image of Columba or you may choose to stay completely within the imagined realm of your prayer. Whichever you choose, know that God will offer you the words from the biblical passage that you need to hear – even if only in fragments.

– Look around as Columba speaks and see the reactions of his disciples. Become aware of their feelings and how they behave toward Columba and one another.

– Remember that Columba is speaking to men and women struggling to remain faithful to God's desires and promises. Remember that he also is speaking to you.

• After Saint Columba finishes speaking, allow this image to fade from your imagination as you become aware of the phrases and images from this moment of prayer which touched you most deeply. Recall the emotions and memories – including any sounds or smells – evoked during your prayer. Allow these seminal aspects of your meditation to linger on your mind and in your heart, making a mental note of any special feelings evoked by them.

[5]   When you are ready, become aware of Jesus' presence with you in this moment and have an open and informal conversation about this prayer period and how the passage from John's gospel expresses your own needs or desires – giving space for Jesus to respond or to highlight different aspects from the biblical account and your experiences during

this contemplation. Then, gradually allow your thoughts to recede as you focus on God's broader presence in your life and in the world around you.

[6]   Finally, conclude by allowing these desires to fade from your consciousness as you offer this traditional Irish prayer collected by Douglas Hyde in *The Religious Songs of Connacht*:

> *Confirm me in your love divine,*
> *Smooth for my feet life's rugged way;*
> *My will with yours entwine,*
> *Lest evil lead my steps astray.*
> *Be with my still as guard and guide,*
> *Keep me in holy sanctity,*
> *Let my firm faith on you abide,*
> *From fraud and error hold me free. Amen.*

[7]   Afterward, take 10-15 minutes in a quiet space to reflect on the most significant moments from this time of prayer and record your reflections in your retreat journal.

2.6   An Application of the Senses

[1]   Become aware of your prayerful desires during this day or week. Bring to mind your desire to feel deep grief and confusion because it is for your sins that the Lord is going to his passion. Ask also that, in this day or week of prayer, you experience he intimacy of being one of his friends as you participate in the last supper with Jesus and sadness as you see the bickering among the apostles – and the sadness this causes for Jesus.

[2]   When you are ready, in your imagination, call to mind the various prayers of the preceding day or days. Allow the images and words of these prayers to linger and then slowly fade from your consciousness.

• Remember your imaginative contemplation of Luke 22:1-13. Consider the images and feelings evoked in you during your prayer, feeling God's presence in these memories and becoming aware of the specific sensations associated with each image.

• Recall your imaginative contemplation of Luke 22:14-27, considering them in the same way as your earlier memories of Luke 22.

• Review your contemplation and meditation concerning John 13:1-30 in the same manner as the previous prayers.

As these prayers enter your memory, make a mental note of which senses are most active. You may see an image or a color, hear a sound or a phrase, or smell a scent or a fragrance. You may even taste a flavor or feel a sensation on your skin.

[3]   Then, relax and allow these various memories and experiences to quietly enter and leave your consciousness without being controlled – whether they are clear or diffuse, whether they come quickly or slowly. Linger on the sensory images and memories being evoked in you – noticing any images or colors, any sounds or phrases, any scents or fragrances, any flavors or physical sensations associated with each prayer.

[4]   When you are ready, become completely still and clear your mind of all thoughts and concerns. Allow an image of a special personal space to form in your imagination, a place where you are completely comfortable and alone. Then, watch as God enters that place and forms a small image or object for you that expresses the thought or awareness that you most need to carry with you into your life.

Reverently pick up the object or image, a reflection of the most important gift you have been given during this time of prayer. Look at it carefully and become aware of the divine presence contained within it. Take a moment to register what it looks like and how it feels in your hand. Then, feel the joy and confidence that comes from touching the presence of God as you accept this gift, offering a short prayer of gratitude while you relax into the pleasure of this moment.

[5]   Then, conclude by allowing these images to fade from your consciousness as you offer this traditional Irish prayer collected by Douglas Hyde in *The Religious Songs of Connacht*:

> *Confirm me in your love divine,*
> *Smooth for my feet life's rugged way;*
> *My will with yours entwine,*
> *Lest evil lead my steps astray.*
> *Be with my still as guard and guide,*
> *Keep me in holy sanctity,*
> *Let my firm faith on you abide,*
> *From fraud and error hold me free. Amen.*

[6]   While your experiences are still fresh in your mind, record the most significant impressions or sensations from this time of prayer in your retreat journal.

[1]   Remember your desires during the preceding day or week of prayer. As you become aware of the divine presence all around you, ask that you may feel deep grief and confusion because it is for your sins that the Lord is going to his passion. Recall your desire to experience the intimacy of being one of his friends as you participate in the last supper with Jesus and sadness as you see the bickering among the apostles – and the sadness this causes for Jesus.

After bringing these thoughts and desires into your consciousness, ask God once again to fulfill these desires in your own life and in your interactions with others.

[2]   Then, take a moment to allow the words, thoughts, and feelings from your prayers during the last day or week to linger – on your mind and in your heart – before asking God to reveal the fulfillment of your deepest desires in these various memories.

• Think about the prayer sequence at the beginning of this day or week. Make a mental note of any words, insights or images that remain particularly significant or meaningful to you.

• Ponder the story, "Columba and the Miracle of the Feast". Note any words, insights, or images from it that remain particularly significant or meaningful to you.

• Remember your imaginative contemplation of Luke 22:1-13

– Consider the most powerful images, phrases, or feelings from your prayer. Ask yourself what gifts God gave to you through these moments, perhaps offering you new insights or perhaps affirming an important aspect of your faith. Ask yourself how God may be calling you to change through these moments, being as specific as possible.

– Examine your disposition as you prayed, noting whether prayer came easily or with resistance. Recall the easiest moments in your prayer and any moments of joy you may have experienced. Remember also if you encountered any difficulty opening yourself to God or if you felt any sadness as you prayed. Ask God to help you understand why these feelings surfaced.

– Bring to mind any moments when you added personal elements (e.g., familiar places or people from your life) or connected your prayers to other scriptures or spiritual writings. Ask yourself how these additions helped or hindered you as you prayed. Again, if you do not know why this happened, ask God to help you understand.

• Recall your imaginative contemplations of Luke 22:14-27. Then, review your prayer in the same way as your earlier reflection on Luke 22.

• Review your contemplation and meditation concerning John 13:1-30 in the same manner as the previous prayers.

• Reflect on the ebb and flow of sensory impressions and feelings that marked your application of the senses. Isolate the most memorable moments and sensory impressions from your prayer and reflect on how God used these moments to give you a particular gift, perhaps offering you new insights or changing you in some way.

[3] Finally, ponder the times when images or feelings from the readings of this day or week surfaced outside these prayer periods. Consider those moments or events in which God's presence or guidance was especially strong as well as any moments when you were struggling. Think about the most memorable aspects of these experiences, asking God to explain their significance.

[4] Take a moment to allow the words, thoughts, and feelings of these prayers to linger on your mind and in your heart. Finally, conclude by allowing these desires to fade from your consciousness as you offer this traditional Irish prayer collected by Douglas Hyde in *The Religious Songs of Connacht*:

> *O God, I believe in you; strengthen my belief.*
> *I trust in you; confirm my trust.*
> *I love you; double my love.*
> *I repent that I angered you,*
> *Increase my repentance.*
> *Fill you my heart with awe without despair;*
> *With hope, without over-confidence;*
> *With piety without infatuation;*
> *And with joy without excess.*
> *My God, consent to guide me by your wisdom;*
> *To constrain me by your right;*
> *To comfort me by your mercy;*
> *And to protect me by your power. Amen.*

[5] After finishing these prayers, summarize your reflections on the gifts or graces you received during the prayers of this last day or week and record these thoughts in your retreat journal.

3. Jesus' Arrest

3.1a   From Out The Ancient Garden Came

a prayer on Jesus' Passion

Take a moment to quiet your spirit, becoming completely present to this time and place. Allow all other thoughts and concerns to fall away as you come into the presence of God. Then, when you are ready, begin.

From out the ancient garden came,
By disobedience, death and shame;
> But from the new come life and light
> Where Jesus prayed in the night.

The woe of all the world he feels,
While faint upon the ground he kneels;
> His great heart trembles with the pain,
> Till blood-drops ooze from every vein.

A Hymn, sung or heard (optional)

Thirty years by God appointed,
And there dawns the woeful day,
> When the great Redeemer girds Him
> For the tumult of the fray;
And upon the cross uplifted,
> Bears our load of guilt away.

Ah! 'tis bitter gall He drinks,
When His heart in anguish fails;
> From the thorns His life-blood trickles,
> From the spear wound and the nails;
But that crimson stream for cleansing,
> O'er creation wide prevails.

Faithful Cross! in all the woodland,
Stands not a nobler tree;
> In thy leaf, and flower, and fruitage,
> None can e'er thy equal be;
Sweet the wood, and sweet the iron,
Sweet the load hung upon you, holy tree.

Noble tree! unbend thy branches,
Let thy stubborn fibres bend,
        Cast your native rigour from you,
        Be a gentle, loving friend;
Bear Him in your arms, and softly,
        Christ, the King eternal, tend.

Only you could bear the burden
Of the ransom of our race;
        Only you could be a refuge,
        Like the ark, a hiding-place,
By the sacred blood anointed,
        Of the Covenant of Grace.

Read or recite Psalm 118.

Holy Lord,
Under my thoughts may I God-thoughts find.
Half of my sins escape my mind.
        For what I said, or did not say,
        Pardon me, O Lord, I pray.

Read Mark 14:26-42, aloud or quietly.

O Lord, Jesus the Christ,
If I were in Heaven my harp I would sound
With apostles and angels and saints all around,
        Praising and thanking the Son who is crowned,
        May the poor race of Eve for that heaven be bound!

O Jesus sore-suffering,
Martyr of pain,
        You were offered, an offering,
        Slain with the slain,
Despised and rejected,
To be mocked among men,
        May my soul be protected
        From sin and from stain.

O Holy Lord,
> God with the Father and the Spirit,
For me is many a snare designed,
To fill my mind with doubts and fears;
> Far from the land of holy saints,
> I dwell within my vale of tears.
Let faith, let hope, let love –
Traits far above the cold world's way –
> With patience, humility, and awe,
> Become my guides from day to day.

I acknowledge, the evil I have done.
From the day of my birth till the day of my death,
> Through the sight of my eyes,
Through the hearing of my ears,
> Through the sayings of my mouth,
Through the thoughts of my heart,
> Through the touch of my hands,
Through the course of my way,
> Through all I said and did not,
Through all I promised and fulfilled not,
> Through all the laws and holy commandments I broke.
I ask even now absolution of you,
> For fear I may have never asked it as was right,
> And that I might not live to ask it again,

O Holy Lord, my King in Heaven,
May you not let my soul stray from you,
May you keep me in a good state,
> May you turn me toward what is good to do,
> May you protect me from dangers, small and great.
May you fill my eyes with tears of repentance,
> So I may avoid the sinner's awful sentence.
May the Grace of the God for ever be with me,
> And whatever my needs, may the Triune God give me.

Select one of the following options for the Lord's Prayer.

Option A

O Jesus Christ,
Lord of heaven and earth,
Help me pray as you yourself taught:
  "Our Father in heaven,
  hallowed be your name.
  Your kingdom come.
  Your will be done,
  on earth as it is in heaven.
  Give us this day our daily bread.
  And forgive us our debts,
  as we also have forgiven our debtors.
  And do not bring us to the time of trial,
  but rescue us from the evil one."
  (Matthew 6: 9-13)
From the foes of my land,
from the foes of my faith,
From the foes who would us dissever,
  O Lord, preserve me, in life and in death,
  With the Sign of the Cross for ever.
  For the kingdom, the power, and the glory
  are yours now and for ever. Amen.

Please proceed with "I beseech you, O Lord…," found after Option B.

Option B

O Jesus Christ,
Lord of heaven and earth,
Help me pray as you yourself taught:
  Our Father in heaven,
  hallowed be your name,
  your kingdom come,
  your will be done,
  on earth as in heaven.
  Give us today our daily bread.
  Forgive us our sins
  as we forgive those who sin against us.
  Lead us not into temptation
  but deliver us from evil.

From the foes of my land,
from the foes of my faith,
From the foes who would us dissever,
> O Lord, preserve me, in life and in death,
> With the Sign of the Cross for ever.
> *For the kingdom, the power, and the glory*
> *are yours now and for ever. Amen.*

I beseech you, O Lord.
God in Heaven, unsurpassed in power and might;
> Be behind me, Be on my left,
> Be before me, Be on my right!
Against each danger, you are my help;
In distress, upon you I call.
> In dark times, may you sustain me
> And lift me up again when I fall.
Lord over heaven and of earth,
You know my offenses.
> Yet, listening to my pleadings,
> You guide me away from sinful pretenses.
Lord of all creation and the many creatures,
You bestow on me many earthly treasures.
> Revealing love in each life and season,
> You share with me heavenly pleasures.
May you arouse me
In moments both of joy and of strife;
> Most holy Lord, bring me new life!

A Hymn, sung or heard (optional)

O Jesus Christ,
> Lord of heaven and earth,
> You are my riches, my store, my provision,
My star through the years
When troubles rend me,
> Through times of strife and tears,
> Sweet Jesus, defend me.

O Soul of Christ bless me.
O Body of Christ save me.

O Blood of Christ satisfy me.
O Water of Christ's side wash me.
O Passion of Christ strengthen me.
O Jesus of the Elements, hear me O Lord.
Make a protection for me of your wounds.
Permit me not to be separated from you
Keep me from the attack of the Adversary.
I call me to you at the time of my death.
In hope that I may praise you
Along with the angels
For ever and ever. Amen.

End this time of prayer by taking some time to bring to mind the various ways God shields you from harm or guides you through the world's tumult. Then, when you are ready, conclude by saying:

O Holy Lord, King in Heaven,
I place myself at the edge of your grace,
On the floor of your house myself I place,
And to banish the sin of my heart away,
I lower my knee to you this day.
Through life's torrents of pain may you bring me whole,
And, O Lord Jesus Christ, preserve also my soul. Amen.

Consideration of the Readings

After reciting or prayerfully reading the prayer sequence for this day or week:

• Read about Jesus at the Garden of Gethsemane in Mark 14:26-42. Again, make a mental note of each person's appearance and actions during the episode as well as the key elements of the story and its setting. Then, consider any aspects of this story that speak strongly to you before recording these observations in your workbook.

• Read about Jesus' arrest in Mark 14:43-53. Again, note each person's appearance and actions during these episodes as well as the key elements of the story and its setting before recording any aspects of this story that speak strongly to you.

• Read about Peter's denial of Jesus in John 18:15-18,25-27. Again, note each person's appearance and actions during these episodes as well as the key elements of the story and its setting before recording any aspects of this story that speak strongly to you.

• Read about God's love in John 3:16-21. Again, pay careful attention to any phrases or images that seem particularly meaningful to you. Then, record these highlights in your workbook so you will remember them during this day or week of prayer.

Note: You also should take a moment to consider any aspect of the prayer sequence from this day or week that seemed particularly significant to you.

Contemplation of Your Needs

When you are ready, concentrating on your breath or an object near you, allow any distractions to fade from your consciousness as you become aware of your desire to live in God's goodness. Feel yourself yearning to properly use the many gifts God has given you, to experience God's continuing care, and to be open to the immense love God shows for you, then:

• Read "Columba Nears Death" (found on page 302). Allow yourself to linger on any thoughts, phrases or images that seem particularly meaningful or significant to your earlier preparations or prayer.

  • Pray for your desires in the coming day or week. Ask that the divine presence all around you may be revealed, so you may feel deep grief and confusion because it is for your sins that the Lord is going to his passion. Ask also that, in this day or week of prayer, you may go to the garden with Jesus and see his sadness as he is becoming completely alone.

  • Conclude by praying for a desire to join completely with Jesus during this difficult moment, experiencing his solitude and aloneness that his choices may cause while praying for the strength to follow through with it.

Then, take a moment record any significant thoughts, emotions, or reactions from these moments in your workbook.

After this, put your notes aside. Without straining your memory, consider in turn each of the readings for the coming day or week and allow them to take shape in your imagination – even if all you remember are small fragments. Prayerfully ponder how each reading affects you emotionally without overtly thinking about their content, asking God to illuminate the spiritual gifts offered in each reading – quieting your mind and creating a receptive space in yourself to see or hear the response.

Finally, conclude by allowing these desires to fade from your consciousness as you offer this traditional Irish prayer collected by Douglas Hyde in *The Religious Songs of Connacht*:

> *O God, I believe in you; strengthen my belief.*
> *I trust in you; confirm my trust.*
> *I love you; double my love.*
> *I repent that I angered you,*
> *Increase my repentance.*
> *Fill you my heart with awe without despair;*
> *With hope, without over-confidence;*
> *With piety without infatuation;*
> *And with joy without excess.*
> *My God, consent to guide me by your wisdom;*
> *To constrain me by your right;*
> *To comfort me by your mercy;*
> *And to protect me by your power. Amen.*

Allow these words to linger on your mind and in your heart for a few moments and then, while they are still fresh in your memory, write the most important thoughts, feelings, and desires from this preparatory time in your retreat journal.

In this contemplation of Mark 14:26-42, you will see and hear Jesus predicts Peter will deny him before praying alone in the garden of Gethsemane.

[1]   Begin by reading the biblical selection and reviewing your notes on it from your earlier preparations.

[2]   Then, focus on this specific time and place as you allow all other concerns to fall away. Then, when you are ready, consider the people and place in this moment of prayer.

• Allow an image of Jesus to emerge in your imagination, noting his physical characteristics and mannerisms. Look at what he is wearing or carrying, observing his clothing and any objects he is holding. Ponder this mental image, allowing any other observations about Jesus to form in your mind.

• Then, observe the people around Jesus. Look at Jesus' disciples, observing where they are standing and how they behave toward Jesus. Look at the crowd, noting their attitude and behavior toward Jesus. Observe whether the people are sitting, standing, or walking. Take a moment to ponder this mental image, allowing other impressions of these people to form. Become familiar with the men and women you will encounter during your prayer as well as their behavior.

• Gradually, allow yourself to become aware of the location of this moment of prayer in the garden of Gethsemane. Pay attention to its physical characteristics and the arrangement of the people in it. As you ponder this mental image, look around the place and notice more details about it – noting the sources of light, the sounds of animals, etc. Become familiar with the location of your upcoming prayer.

• Take a moment to remain in this place with these people, then allow these images to fade from your consciousness.

[3]   After you become still, become aware of your desires during this moment of prayer. Remember your desire to experience the divine presence all around you and to trust in God's plan for you, asking that you may feel deep grief and confusion because it is for your sins that the Lord is going to his passion. Ask for grief with Christ and grief to be broken with Christ broken for tears and interior suffering on account of the great suffering the Christ endured for you. Recall your desire that, in this day or week of prayer, to join completely with Jesus during this difficult moment, experiencing his solitude and aloneness that his

choices may cause while praying for the strength to follow through with it.

As these desires fill your consciousness, let all other concerns fall aside as you focus on this specific time and place of prayer.

[4]   Again, when you are ready, allow the image of Jesus and his disciples to reemerge in your imagination.

• Watch as Jesus and his disciples enter the garden of Gethsemane. Listen to the sounds of this moment and become comfortable as you prepare to hear Jesus speak. Feel the tension of the people around you and share in their concern.

• Ask God to help you share in their experience – either by joining them or by listening quietly to them. Focus your attention on Jesus, noting his physical appearance and his emotional demeanor.

• Then, watch and listen as Jesus speaks to his disciples before leaving them to pray privately. You may want to quietly read the passage while remaining prayerfully aware of your mental image of Jesus or you may choose to stay completely within the imagined realm of your prayer. Whichever you choose, know that God will offer you the words from the biblical passage that you need to hear – even if only in fragments.

– Look around as Jesus speaks and to his disciples. Become aware of their feelings and how they behave toward Jesus and one another.

– Remember that Jesus is speaking to men and women whose confidence in Jesus is easily shaken. Remember that he also is speaking to you.

• Afterward, allow this image to fade from your imagination as you become aware of the phrases and images from this moment which touched you most deeply. Recall the emotions and memories – including any sounds or smells – evoked during your prayer. Allow these seminal aspects of your meditation to linger on your mind and in your heart, noting any special feelings evoked by them.

[5]   When you are ready, become aware of Jesus' presence with you in this moment and have an open and informal conversation about this prayer period and how the passage from Mark's gospel expresses your own needs or desires – giving space for Jesus to respond or to highlight different aspects from the biblical account and your experiences during this contemplation. Then, gradually allow your thoughts to recede as you focus on God's broader presence in your life and in the world around you.

[6]   Finally, conclude by allowing these desires to fade from your consciousness as you offer this traditional Irish prayer collected by Douglas Hyde in *The Religious Songs of Connacht*:

> *Confirm me in your love divine,*
> *Smooth for my feet life's rugged way;*
> *My will with yours entwine,*
> *Lest evil lead my steps astray.*
> *Be with my still as guard and guide,*
> *Keep me in holy sanctity,*
> *Let my firm faith on you abide,*
> *From fraud and error hold me free. Amen.*

[7]   Afterward, take 10-15 minutes in a quiet space to reflect on the most significant moments from this time of prayer and record your reflections in your retreat journal.

**In this contemplation of Mark 14:43-53, you will see and hear
Jesus being betrayed by Judas Iscariot and arrested.**

[1]   Begin by reading the biblical selection and reviewing your
notes on it from your earlier preparations.

[2]   Then, focus on this specific time and place as you allow all
other concerns to fall away. Then, when you are ready, consider the
people and place in this moment of prayer.

   • Allow an image of Jesus to emerge in your imagination, noting
his physical characteristics and mannerisms. Look at what he is wearing
or carrying, observing his clothing and any objects he is holding. Make
a note of whether he is sitting, standing, or walking. Ponder this mental
image, allowing any other observations about Jesus to form in your
mind.

   • Then, observe the people around Jesus. Note how many
people are with Jesus, making a mental note of their appearance and
demeanor. Look at Jesus' disciples, observing where they are standing
and how they behave toward Jesus. Look at the Judas Iscariot and the
people with him, noting their attitude and behavior toward Jesus. Take
a moment to ponder this mental image, allowing other impressions of
these people to form. Become familiar with the men and women you
will encounter during your prayer as well as their behavior.

   • Gradually, allow yourself to become aware of the location of
this moment of prayer in the garden of Gethsemane. Pay attention to
its physical characteristics and the arrangement of the people in it. As
you ponder this mental image, look around the place and notice more
details about it – noting the sources of light, the sounds of animals, etc.
Become familiar with the location of your upcoming prayer.

   • Take a moment to remain in this place with these people,
then allow these images to fade from your consciousness.

[3]   After you become still, become aware of your desires during
this moment of prayer. Remember your desire to experience the divine
presence all around you and to trust in God's plan for you, asking that
you may feel deep grief and confusion because it is for your sins that
the Lord is going to his passion. Ask for grief with Christ and grief to be
broken with Christ broken for tears and interior suffering on account of
the great suffering the Christ endured for you. Recall your desire that,
in this day or week of prayer, to join completely with Jesus during this

difficult moment, experiencing his solitude and aloneness that his choices may cause while praying for the strength to follow through with it.

As these desires fill your consciousness, let all other concerns fall aside as you focus on this specific time and place of prayer.

[4]   Again, when you are ready, allow the image of Jesus and his disciples to reemerge in your imagination.

• Watch as Judas and a group of armed men approach Jesus. Listen to the sounds of this moment. Feel the tension of the people around you and share in their concern.

• Ask God to help you share in their experience – either by joining them or by listening quietly to them. Focus your attention on Jesus, noting his physical appearance and his emotional demeanor.

• Then, watch and listen as Judas kisses Jesus before Jesus is arrested. You may want to quietly read the passage while remaining prayerfully aware of your mental image of Jesus or you may choose to stay completely within the imagined realm of your prayer. Whichever you choose, know that God will offer you the words from the biblical passage that you need to hear – even if only in fragments.

– Look around as Jesus speaks and see the reactions of his disciples and the people with Judas Iscariot. Become aware of their feelings and how they behave toward Jesus and one another.

– Remember that Jesus is speaking to men and women with vary tenuous faith. Remember that he also is speaking to you.

• Afterward, allow this image to fade from your imagination as you become aware of the phrases and images from this moment which touched you most deeply. Recall the emotions and memories – including any sounds or smells – evoked during your prayer. Allow these seminal aspects of your meditation to linger on your mind and in your heart, noting any special feelings evoked by them.

[5]   When you are ready, become aware of Jesus' presence with you in this moment and have an open and informal conversation about this prayer period and how the passage from Mark's gospel expresses your own needs or desires – giving space for Jesus to respond or to highlight different aspects from the biblical account and your experiences during this contemplation. Then, gradually allow your thoughts to recede as you focus on God's broader presence in your life and in the world around you.

[6]   Finally, conclude by allowing these desires to fade from your consciousness as you offer this traditional Irish prayer collected by Douglas Hyde in *The Religious Songs of Connacht*:

> *Confirm me in your love divine,*
> *Smooth for my feet life's rugged way;*
> *My will with yours entwine,*
> *Lest evil lead my steps astray.*
> *Be with my still as guard and guide,*
> *Keep me in holy sanctity,*
> *Let my firm faith on you abide,*
> *From fraud and error hold me free. Amen.*

[7]   Afterward, take 10-15 minutes in a quiet space to reflect on the most significant moments from this time of prayer and record your reflections in your retreat journal.

In this contemplation of John 18:15-18,25-27, you will see and hear Peter deny Jesus after his arrest.

[1]   Begin by reading the biblical selection and reviewing your notes on it from your earlier preparations.

[2]   Then, focus on this specific time and place as you allow all other concerns to fall away. Then, when you are ready, consider the people and place in this moment of prayer.

• Allow an image of Peter to emerge in your imagination, noting his physical characteristics and mannerisms. Look at what he is wearing or carrying, observing his clothing and any objects he is holding. Ponder this mental image, allowing any other observations about Jesus to form in your mind.

• Then, observe the men and women around Peter. Note how many people are around Peter, making a mental note of their appearance and demeanor. Look at Jesus' disciples, observing where they are standing and how they behave toward Peter. Observe whether the people are sitting, standing, or walking. Take a moment to ponder this mental image, allowing other impressions of these people to form. Become familiar with the men and women you will encounter during your prayer as well as their behavior.

• Gradually, allow yourself to become aware of the location of this moment of prayer. Pay attention to its physical characteristics and the arrangement of the people in it. As you ponder this mental image, look around the place and notice more details about it – noting if it is still or boisterous, if it is crowded or not, etc. Become familiar with the location of your upcoming prayer.

• Take a moment to remain in this place with these men and women, then allow these images to fade from your consciousness.

[3]   After you become still, become aware of your desires during this moment of prayer. Remember your desire to experience the divine presence all around you and to trust in God's plan for you, asking that you may feel deep grief and confusion because it is for your sins that the Lord is going to his passion. Ask for grief with Christ and grief to be broken with Christ broken for tears and interior suffering on account of the great suffering the Christ endured for you. Recall your desire that, in this day or week of prayer, to join completely with Jesus during this difficult moment, experiencing his solitude and aloneness that his

choices may cause while praying for the strength to follow through with it.

As these desires fill your consciousness, let all other concerns fall aside as you focus on this specific time and place of prayer.

[4]   Again, when you are ready, allow the image of Peter to reemerge in your imagination.

• Watch as Peter approaches the house where Jesus has been taken after his arrest. Listen to the sounds of this moment. Feel the tension of the people around you and share in their concern.

• Ask God to help you enter this moment – either by joining these events or by listening quietly to them. Focus your attention on Peter, noting his physical appearance and his emotional demeanor.

• Then, watch and listen Peter as he denies knowing Jesus. You may want to quietly read the passage while remaining prayerfully aware of your mental image of Peter or you may choose to stay completely within the imagined realm of your prayer. Whichever you choose, know that God will offer you the words from the biblical passage that you need to hear – even if only in fragments.

– Look around as Peter is approached about knowing Jesus. Become aware of his fear and how the other people behave toward him and one another.

– Remember that Peter has been disappointed when his expectations of Jesus were not met. Remember that you have shared this experience.

• Afterward, allow this image to fade from your imagination as you become aware of the phrases and images from this moment which touched you most deeply. Recall the emotions and memories – including any sounds or smells – evoked during your prayer. Allow these seminal aspects of your meditation to linger on your mind and in your heart, noting any special feelings evoked by them.

[5]   When you are ready, become aware of Jesus' presence with you in this moment and have an open and informal conversation about this prayer period and how the passage from John's gospel expresses your own needs or desires – giving space for Jesus to respond or to highlight different aspects from the biblical account and your experiences during this contemplation. Then, gradually allow your thoughts to recede as you focus on God's broader presence in your life and in the world around you.

[6]   Finally, conclude by allowing these desires to fade from your consciousness as you offer this traditional Irish prayer collected by Douglas Hyde in *The Religious Songs of Connacht*:

> *Confirm me in your love divine,*
> *Smooth for my feet life's rugged way;*
> *My will with yours entwine,*
> *Lest evil lead my steps astray.*
> *Be with my still as guard and guide,*
> *Keep me in holy sanctity,*
> *Let my firm faith on you abide,*
> *From fraud and error hold me free. Amen.*

[7]   Afterward, take 10-15 minutes in a quiet space to reflect on the most significant moments from this time of prayer and record your reflections in your retreat journal.

In this meditation on John 3:16-21, you will see and hear Saint Columba teaches his disciples the importance of persevering in their faith.

[1]   Begin by reading the biblical selection and reviewing your notes on it from your earlier preparations.

[2]   Then, focus on this specific time and place as you allow all other concerns to fall away. Then, when you are ready, consider the people and place in this moment of prayer.

• Allow an image of Columba to emerge in your imagination, noting his physical characteristics and mannerisms. Look at what he is wearing or carrying, observing his clothing and any objects he is holding. Make a note of whether he is sitting, standing, or walking. Ponder this mental image, allowing any other observations about Columba to form in your mind.

• Then, observe the disciples around Saint Columba. Note how many disciples are with Columba, making a mental note of their appearance and demeanor. Observe whether they are sitting, standing, or walking. Take a moment to ponder this mental image, allowing other impressions of these people to form. Become familiar with the men and women you will encounter during your prayer as well as their behavior.

• Gradually, allow yourself to become aware of the location of this encounter with Saint Columba. Observe whether it is inside or outside, paying attention to its physical characteristics and the arrangement of the people in it. As you ponder this mental image, look around the place and notice more details about it – noting if it is in dim or bright light, if it is still and silent or filled with noise, if it has an unusual smell or not, etc. Become familiar with the location of your upcoming prayer.

• Take a moment to remain in this place with these people, then allow these images to fade from your consciousness.

[3]   After you become still, become aware of your desires during this moment of prayer. Remember your desire to experience the divine presence all around you and to trust in God's plan for you, asking that you may feel deep grief and confusion because it is for your sins that the Lord is going to his passion. Ask for grief with Christ and grief to be broken with Christ broken for tears and interior suffering on account of the great suffering the Christ endured for you. Recall your desire that,

in this day or week of prayer, to join completely with Jesus during this difficult moment, experiencing his solitude and aloneness that his choices may cause while praying for the strength to follow through with it.

As these desires fill your consciousness, let all other concerns fall aside as you focus on this specific time and place of prayer.

[4]   Again, when you are ready, allow the image of Saint Columba and his disciples to reemerge in your imagination.

• Watch as the group assembles around Columba. Listen to the sounds of this moment and become comfortable as you prepare to hear Columba speak. Feel the anticipation of the people around you and share in that enthusiasm.

• Ask God to help you enter this moment – either by joining these events or by listening quietly to them. Focus your attention on Saint Columba, noting his physical appearance and his emotional demeanor.

• Then, relying on your earlier prayers, watch and listen as Columba tells the story of Peter's denial of Jesus before discussing the biblical passage from Saint John. You may want to quietly read the passage while remaining prayerfully aware of your mental image of Columba or you may choose to stay completely within the imagined realm of your prayer. Whichever you choose, know that God will offer you the words from the biblical passage that you need to hear – even if only in fragments.

– Look around as Columba speaks and see the reactions of his disciples. Become aware of their feelings and how they behave toward Columba and one another.

– Remember that Columba is speaking to men and women struggling to remain faithful to God's desires and promises. Remember that he also is speaking to you.

• After Saint Columba finishes speaking, allow this image to fade from your imagination as you become aware of the phrases and images from this moment of prayer which touched you most deeply. Recall the emotions and memories – including any sounds or smells – evoked during your prayer. Allow these seminal aspects of your meditation to linger on your mind and in your heart, making a mental note of any special feelings evoked by them.

[5]   When you are ready, become aware of Jesus' presence with you in this moment and have an open and informal conversation about this prayer period and how the passage from John's gospel expresses your

own needs or desires – giving space for Jesus to respond or to highlight different aspects from the biblical account and your experiences during this contemplation. Then, gradually allow your thoughts to recede as you focus on God's broader presence in your life and in the world around you.

[6]   Finally, conclude by allowing these desires to fade from your consciousness as you offer this traditional Irish prayer collected by Douglas Hyde in *The Religious Songs of Connacht*:

> *Confirm me in your love divine,*
> *Smooth for my feet life's rugged way;*
> *My will with yours entwine,*
> *Lest evil lead my steps astray.*
> *Be with my still as guard and guide,*
> *Keep me in holy sanctity,*
> *Let my firm faith on you abide,*
> *From fraud and error hold me free. Amen.*

[7]   Afterward, take 10-15 minutes in a quiet space to reflect on the most significant moments from this time of prayer and record your reflections in your retreat journal.

3.6   An Application of the Senses

[1]   Become aware of your prayerful desires during this day or week. Bring to mind your desire to feel deep grief and confusion because it is for your sins that the Lord is going to his passion. Ask also that, in this day or week of prayer, you may go to the garden with Jesus and see his sadness as he is becoming completely alone.

[2]   When you are ready, in your imagination, call to mind the various prayers of the preceding day or days. Allow the images and words of these prayers to linger and then slowly fade from your consciousness.

     • Remember your imaginative contemplations of Mark 14:26-42. Consider the images and feelings evoked in you during your prayer, feeling God's presence in these memories and becoming aware of the specific sensations associated with each image.

     • Recall your imaginative contemplation of Mark 14:43-53, considering them in the same way as your earlier memories of Mark 14.

     • Review your imaginative contemplation of John 18:15-18, 25-27 in the same manner as the previous prayers.

     • Revisit your mediation on John 3:16-21 in the same manner as the previous prayers.

As these prayers enter your memory, make a mental note of which senses are most active. You may see an image or a color, hear a sound or a phrase, or smell a scent or a fragrance. You may even taste a flavor or feel a sensation on your skin.

[3]   Then, relax and allow these various memories and experiences to quietly enter and leave your consciousness without being controlled – whether they are clear or diffuse, whether they come quickly or slowly. Linger on the sensory images and memories being evoked in you – noticing any images or colors, any sounds or phrases, any scents or fragrances, any flavors or physical sensations associated with each prayer.

[4]   When you are ready, become completely still and clear your mind of all thoughts and concerns. Allow an image of a special personal space to form in your imagination, a place where you are completely comfortable and alone. Then, watch as God enters that place and forms a small image or object for you that expresses the thought or awareness that you most need to carry with you into your life.

Reverently pick up the object or image, a reflection of the most important gift you have been given during this time of prayer. Look at it carefully and become aware of the divine presence contained within it. Take a moment to register what it looks like and how it feels in your hand. Then, feel the joy and confidence that comes from touching the presence of God as you accept this gift, offering a short prayer of gratitude while you relax into the pleasure of this moment.

[5]   Then, conclude by allowing these images to fade from your consciousness as you offer this traditional Irish prayer collected by Douglas Hyde in *The Religious Songs of Connacht*:

> *Confirm me in your love divine,*
> *Smooth for my feet life's rugged way;*
> *My will with yours entwine,*
> *Lest evil lead my steps astray.*
> *Be with my still as guard and guide,*
> *Keep me in holy sanctity,*
> *Let my firm faith on you abide,*
> *From fraud and error hold me free. Amen.*

[6]   While your experiences are still fresh in your mind, record the most significant impressions or sensations from this time of prayer in your retreat journal.

[1]   Remember your desires during the preceding day or week of prayer. As you become aware of the divine presence all around you, ask that you may feel deep grief and confusion because it is for your sins that the Lord is going to his passion. Recall your desire to go to the garden with Jesus and see his sadness as he is becoming completely alone.

After bringing these thoughts and desires into your consciousness, ask God once again to fulfill these desires in your own life and in your interactions with others.

[2]   Then, take a moment to allow the words, thoughts, and feelings from your prayers during the last day or week to linger – on your mind and in your heart – before asking God to reveal the fulfillment of your deepest desires in these various memories.

• Think about the prayer sequence at the beginning of this day or week. Make a mental note of any words, insights or images that remain particularly significant or meaningful to you.

• Ponder the story, "Columba Nears Death". Note any words, insights, or images from it that remain particularly significant or meaningful to you.

• Remember your imaginative contemplations of Mark 14: 26–42.

– Consider the most powerful images, phrases, or feelings from your prayer. Ask yourself what gifts God gave to you through these moments, perhaps offering you new insights or perhaps affirming an important aspect of your faith. Ask yourself how God may be calling you to change through these moments, being as specific as possible.

– Examine your disposition as you prayed, noting whether prayer came easily or with resistance. Recall the easiest moments in your prayer and any moments of joy you may have experienced. Remember also if you encountered any difficulty opening yourself to God or if you felt any sadness as you prayed. Ask God to help you understand why these feelings surfaced.

– Bring to mind any moments when you added personal elements (e.g., familiar places or people from your life) or connected your prayers to other scriptures or spiritual writings. Ask yourself how these additions helped or hindered you as you prayed. Again, if you do not know why this happened, ask God to help you understand.

• Recall your imaginative contemplation of Mark 14:43-53. Then, review your prayer in the same way as your earlier reflection on Mark 14.

• Review your meditation on your imaginative contemplation of John 18: 15-18,25-27 in the same manner as the previous prayers.

• Revisit your meditation on John 3:16-21 in the same manner as the previous prayers.

• Reflect on the ebb and flow of sensory impressions and feelings that marked your application of the senses. Isolate the most memorable moments and sensory impressions from your prayer and reflect on how God used these moments to give you a particular gift, perhaps offering you new insights or changing you in some way.

[3]   Finally, ponder the times when images or feelings from the readings of this day or week surfaced outside these prayer periods. Consider those moments or events in which God's presence or guidance was especially strong as well as any moments when you were struggling. Think about the most memorable aspects of these experiences, asking God to explain their significance.

[4]   Take a moment to allow the words, thoughts, and feelings of these prayers to linger on your mind and in your heart. Finally, conclude by allowing these desires to fade from your consciousness as you offer this traditional Irish prayer collected by Douglas Hyde in *The Religious Songs of Connacht*:

> *O God, I believe in you; strengthen my belief.*
> *I trust in you; confirm my trust.*
> *I love you; double my love.*
> *I repent that I angered you,*
> *Increase my repentance.*
> *Fill you my heart with awe without despair;*
> *With hope, without over-confidence;*
> *With piety without infatuation;*
> *And with joy without excess.*
> *My God, consent to guide me by your wisdom;*
> *To constrain me by your right;*
> *To comfort me by your mercy;*
> *And to protect me by your power. Amen.*

[5]   After finishing these prayers, summarize your reflections on the gifts or graces you received during the prayers of this last day or week and record these thoughts in your retreat journal.

4. Jesus' Trial

a prayer on Jesus' Passion

Take a moment to quiet your spirit, becoming completely present to this time and place. Allow all other thoughts and concerns to fall away as you come into the presence of God. Then, when you are ready, begin.

My eyes should fall in grief, my tears should flow,
And from my deepest heart the groan of woe
  Should rise, when I remember all the pangs
  The Saviour suffered, and the mortal blow.

The savage throng the gentle Saviour brings
Before the scornful priest's false questionings;
  Delivered to the soldiers, lo, they dare
  Raise impious hands against the King of Kings.

A Hymn, sung or heard (optional)

Consider and quake, lest devils scorn you,
Repentance make, as now I warn you,
  For Christ's words be – they are words to cherish,
  "Who turns to Me shall never perish."

Alas for him who puts off repentance,
'Til the Seeker grim comes with awful sentence,
  Those who rode to-day without grief or trouble,
  To-morrow the clay upon them others shovel.

What then of your halls where guests are laughing,
What then of your balls where wines are quaffing,
  Horses in throngs, and drink in cellars,
  Men of songs and story-tellers!

Prayer should we seek, and for prayer go hunger,
For a single week in this world is longer
  Than a thousand years where the Tree of Life is,
  Where in God's garden no fear nor strife is.

No sinful mind can imagine, even,
The joys he shall find in his home in heaven,
  There music, and story, and mirth surround them,
  Waiting for glory with glory round them.

Read or recite Psalm 31.

Holy Lord,
Under my thoughts may I God-thoughts find.
Half of my sins escape my mind.
  For what I said, or did not say,
  Pardon me, O Lord, I pray.

Read Luke 23:1-12, aloud or quietly.

O Lord, Jesus the Christ,
If I were in Heaven my harp I would sound
With apostles and angels and saints all around,
  Praising and thanking the Son who is crowned,
  May the poor race of Eve for that heaven be bound!

Holy Lord,
Each sin I have sinned
From the day of my fall,
  May the One Son of Mary
  Forgive me them all!
May the child who was tortured,
God-man without stain,
  Guide me safe through the torments
  And shoutings of pain.

O Holy Lord,
  God with the Father and the Spirit,
For me is many a snare designed,
To fill my mind with doubts and fears;
  Far from the land of holy saints,
  I dwell within my vale of tears.
Let faith, let hope, let love –
Traits far above the cold world's way –
  With patience, humility, and awe,

Become my guides from day to day.

I acknowledge, the evil I have done.
From the day of my birth till the day of my death,
    Through the sight of my eyes,
Through the hearing of my ears,
    Through the sayings of my mouth,
Through the thoughts of my heart,
    Through the touch of my hands,
Through the course of my way,
    Through all I said and did not,
Through all I promised and fulfilled not,
    Through all the laws and holy commandments I broke.
I ask even now absolution of you,
    For fear I may have never asked it as was right,
    And that I might not live to ask it again,

O Holy Lord, my King in Heaven,
May you not let my soul stray from you,
May you keep me in a good state,
    May you turn me toward what is good to do,
    May you protect me from dangers, small and great.
May you fill my eyes with tears of repentance,
    So I may avoid the sinner's awful sentence.
May the Grace of the God for ever be with me,
    And whatever my needs, may the Triune God give me.

Select one of the following options for the Lord's Prayer.

Option A

O Jesus Christ,
Lord of heaven and earth,
Help me pray as you yourself taught:
    "Our Father in heaven,
    hallowed be your name.
    Your kingdom come.
    Your will be done,
    on earth as it is in heaven.
    Give us this day our daily bread.

And forgive us our debts,
as we also have forgiven our debtors.
And do not bring us to the time of trial,
but rescue us from the evil one."
(Matthew 6: 9-13)
From the foes of my land,
from the foes of my faith,
From the foes who would us dissever,
>O Lord, preserve me, in life and in death,
>With the Sign of the Cross for ever.
>*For the kingdom, the power, and the glory*
>*are yours now and for ever. Amen.*

Please proceed with "I beseech you, O Lord...," found after Option B.

Option B

O Jesus Christ,
Lord of heaven and earth,
Help me pray as you yourself taught:
>*Our Father in heaven,*
>*hallowed be your name,*
>*your kingdom come,*
>*your will be done,*
>*on earth as in heaven.*
>*Give us today our daily bread.*
>*Forgive us our sins*
>*as we forgive those who sin against us.*
>*Lead us not into temptation*
>*but deliver us from evil.*
From the foes of my land,
from the foes of my faith,
From the foes who would us dissever,
>O Lord, preserve me, in life and in death,
>With the Sign of the Cross for ever.
>*For the kingdom, the power, and the glory*
>*are yours now and for ever. Amen.*

I beseech you, O Lord.

God in Heaven, unsurpassed in power and might;
>Be behind me, Be on my left,
>Be before me, Be on my right!
Against each danger, you are my help;
In distress, upon you I call.
>In dark times, may you sustain me
>And lift me up again when I fall.
Lord over heaven and of earth,
You know my offenses.
>Yet, listening to my pleadings,
>You guide me away from sinful pretenses.
Lord of all creation and the many creatures,
You bestow on me many earthly treasures.
>Revealing love in each life and season,
>You share with me heavenly pleasures.
May you arouse me
In moments both of joy and of strife;
>Most holy Lord, bring me new life!

A Hymn, sung or heard (optional)

O Jesus Christ,
>Lord of heaven and earth,
>You are my riches, my store, my provision,
My star through the years
When troubles rend me,
>Through times of strife and tears,
>Sweet Jesus, defend me.

Jesus mine, your glorious passion
Be my stay forevermore,
>Be my strong defense in danger,
>And of love the blessed store;
you I trust in bliss and trial,
you I cherish and adore.

>Let the splendor of your features
>Rest upon me night and day;
Fill my soul with sweet affection
Driving evil thoughts away,

Keep my body free from danger,
Let no fraud my soul waylay.

End this time of prayer by taking some time to bring to mind the various ways God shields you from harm or guides you through the world's tumult. Then, when you are ready, conclude by saying:

O Holy Lord, King in Heaven,
I place myself at the edge of your grace,
     On the floor of your house myself I place,
And to banish the sin of my heart away,
     I lower my knee to you this day.
Through life's torrents of pain may you bring me whole,
    And, O Lord Jesus Christ, preserve also my soul. Amen.

Consideration of the Readings

After reciting or prayerfully reading the prayer sequence for this day or week:

• Read about Jesus' treatment after his arrest and the beginning of his trial in Luke 22:63-71. Again, note each person's appearance and actions during the episode as well as the key elements of the story and its setting, including the setting in your workbook. Then, record any aspects of this story that speak strongly to you.

• Read about Jesus' trial in Luke 23:1-12 and Luke 23:13-23, noting each person's appearance and actions during these episodes as well as the key elements of the story and its setting before recording any aspects of this story that speak strongly to you.

• Read Philippians 2:5-11. Again, pay careful attention to any phrases or images that seem particularly meaningful to you. Then, record these highlights in your workbook so you will remember them during this day or week of prayer.

Note: You also should consider any aspect of the prayer sequence from this day or week that seemed particularly significant to you.

Contemplation of Your Needs

When you are ready, allow any distractions to fade from your consciousness as you become aware of your desire to live in God's goodness. Feel yourself yearning to properly use the many gifts God has given you, to experience God's continuing care, and to be open to the immense love God shows for you, then:

• Read "Columba and the Mourning Nag" (found on page 302). Allow yourself to linger on any thoughts, phrases or images that seem particularly meaningful or significant to your earlier preparations or prayer.

• Pray for your desires in the coming day or week. Ask that the divine presence all around you may be revealed, so you may feel deep grief and confusion because it is for your sins that the Lord is going to his passion. Ask also that, in this day or week of prayer, you may witness the trial of Jesus and see his complete aloneness in this moment, recognizing and mourning the disappearance of the godly qualities Jesus has demonstrated in the past as they now become hidden behind the suffering of a man.

• Conclude by praying to feel the complete sorrow that this moment causes for you.

Then, record any significant thoughts, emotions, or reactions from these moments in your workbook.

After this, put your notes aside. Without straining your memory, consider in turn each of the readings for the coming day or week and allow them to take shape in your imagination. Prayerfully ponder how each reading affects you emotionally without overtly thinking about their content, asking God to illuminate the spiritual gifts offered in each reading – quieting your mind and creating a receptive space in yourself to see or hear the response.

Finally, conclude by allowing these desires to fade from your consciousness as you offer this traditional Irish prayer:

> *O God, I believe in you; strengthen my belief.*
> *I trust in you; confirm my trust.*
> *I love you; double my love.*
> *I repent that I angered you,*
> *Increase my repentance.*
> *Fill you my heart with awe without despair;*
> *With hope, without over-confidence;*
> *With piety without infatuation;*
> *And with joy without excess.*
> *My God, consent to guide me by your wisdom;*
> *To constrain me by your right;*
> *To comfort me by your mercy;*
> *And to protect me by your power. Amen.*

Allow these words to linger on your mind and in your heart for a few moments and then, while they are still fresh in your memory, write the most important thoughts, feelings, and desires from this preparatory time in your journal.

In this contemplation of Luke 22:63-71, you will see and hear Jesus' treatment after his arrest and Jesus being tried by the chief priests and scribes.

[1]   Begin by reading the biblical selection and reviewing your notes on it from your earlier preparations.

[2]   Focus on this specific time and place as you allow all other concerns to fall away. Then, when you are ready, consider the people and place of this encounter with Jesus.

• Allow an image of Jesus to emerge in your imagination, noting his physical characteristics and mannerisms. Look at what he is wearing or carrying. Make a note of whether he is sitting, standing, or walking. Ponder this mental image, allowing any other observations about Jesus to form in your mind.

• Note how many people are with Jesus, making a mental note of their appearance and demeanor. Look at the priests and scribes gathered around Jesus, observing where they are standing and how they behave toward Jesus. Look at the soldiers and other people at the trial, noting their attitude and behavior toward Jesus. Observe whether the people are sitting or standing. Take a moment to ponder this mental image, allowing other impressions of these people to form. Become familiar with the men and women you will encounter during your prayer as well as their behavior.

• Allow yourself to become aware of the location of this moment of prayer. Observe whether it is inside or outside, paying attention to its physical characteristics and the arrangement of the people in it. Look around the place and notice more details about it – if it in dim or bright light, if it is still and silent or filled with noise, etc. Become familiar with the location of your upcoming prayer.

• Take a moment to remain in this place with these people before allowing these images to fade from your consciousness.

[3]   Become aware of your desires during this moment of prayer. Remember your desire to experience the divine presence all around you and to trust in God's plan for you, asking that you may feel deep grief and confusion because it is for your sins that the Lord is going to his passion. Ask for grief with Christ and grief to be broken with Christ broken for tears and interior suffering on account of the great suffering the Christ endured for you. Recall your desire that, in this day or week

of prayer, to witness the trial of Jesus and see his complete aloneness in this moment, recognizing and mourning the disappearance of the godly qualities Jesus has demonstrated in the past as they now become hidden behind the suffering of a man.

As these desires fill your consciousness, let all other concerns fall aside as you focus on this time and place of prayer.

[4]   Allow the image of Jesus and the assembly of priests and scribes to reemerge in your imagination.

• Watch as the group assembles around Jesus. Listen to the sounds of this moment and feel the different emotions of the men and women around you – e.g., anger, hatred, vindication, worry, etc.

• Ask God to help you share in this moment – either by joining it or by listening quietly to it. Focus your attention on Jesus, noting his physical appearance and his demeanor.

• Then, watch and listen as Jesus' formal trial begins, remembering the abuse Jesus has already received. You may want to quietly read the passage while remaining prayerfully aware of your mental image of Jesus or you may choose to stay completely within the imagined realm of your prayer. Whichever you choose, know that God will offer you the words from the biblical passage that you need to hear – even if only in fragments.

– Look around during the trial and see the reactions of the priests, scribes, and the people in the crowd. Become aware of their feelings and how they behave toward Jesus and one another.

– Remember that Jesus is suffering for you.

• Afterward, allow this image to fade from your imagination as you become aware of the phrases and images from this moment which touched you most deeply. Recall the emotions and memories – including any sounds or smells – evoked during your prayer. Allow these seminal aspects of your meditation to linger on your mind and in your heart, noting any special feelings evoked by them.

[5]   When you are ready, become aware of Jesus' presence with you in this moment and have an open and informal conversation about this prayer period and how the passage from Luke's gospel expresses your own needs or desires – giving space for Jesus to respond or to highlight different aspects from the biblical account and your experiences during this contemplation. Then, gradually allow your thoughts to recede as you focus on God's broader presence in your life and in the world around you.

[6]   Conclude by allowing these desires to fade from your consciousness as you offer this traditional Irish prayer:

> *Confirm me in your love divine,*
> *Smooth for my feet life's rugged way;*
> *My will with yours entwine,*
> *Lest evil lead my steps astray.*
> *Be with my still as guard and guide,*
> *Keep me in holy sanctity,*
> *Let my firm faith on you abide,*
> *From fraud and error hold me free. Amen.*

[7]   Afterward, take 10-15 minutes in a quiet space to reflect on the most significant moments from this time of prayer and record your reflections in your retreat journal.

In this contemplation of Luke 23:1-12, you will see and hear Jesus being taken before Pilate and Herod for judgment.

[1]   Begin by reading the biblical selection and reviewing your notes on it from your earlier preparations.

[2]   Focus on this specific time and place as you allow all other concerns to fall away. Then, when you are ready, consider the people and place of this encounter with Jesus.

• Allow an image of Jesus to emerge in your imagination, noting his physical characteristics and mannerisms. Look at what he is wearing or carrying. Make a note of whether he is sitting, standing, or walking. Ponder this mental image, allowing any other observations about Jesus to form in your mind.

• Note how many people are with Jesus, making a mental note of their appearance and demeanor. Look at Pilate and Herod, observing where they are standing and how they behave toward Jesus. Look at the soldiers and other people around Jesus, noting their attitude and behavior toward Jesus. Observe whether the people are sitting or standing. Take a moment to ponder this mental image, allowing other impressions of these people to form. Become familiar with the men and women you will encounter during your prayer as well as their behavior.

• Allow yourself to become aware of the locations of this moment of prayer as Pilate and Herod question Jesus. Observe whether they inside or outside, paying attention to its physical characteristics and the arrangement of the people in it. Look around the place and notice more details about it – if it in dim or bright light, if it is still and silent or filled with noise, etc. Become familiar with the location of your upcoming prayer.

• Take a moment to remain in this place with these people before allowing these images to fade from your consciousness.

[3]   Become aware of your desires during this moment of prayer. Remember your desire to experience the divine presence all around you and to trust in God's plan for you, asking that you may feel deep grief and confusion because it is for your sins that the Lord is going to his passion. Ask for grief with Christ and grief to be broken with Christ broken for tears and interior suffering on account of the great suffering the Christ endured for you. Recall your desire that, in this day or week of prayer, to witness the trial of Jesus and see his complete aloneness

in this moment, recognizing and mourning the disappearance of the godly qualities Jesus has demonstrated in the past as they now become hidden behind the suffering of a man.

As these desires fill your consciousness, let all other concerns fall aside as you focus on this time and place of prayer.

[4]   Allow the image of Jesus and Pilate to reemerge in your imagination.

• Watch as Jesus comes before Pilate. Listen to the sounds of this moment and feel the different emotions of the people around you – e.g., anger, hatred, vindication, worry, etc.

• Ask God to help you share in this moment – either by joining it or by listening quietly to it. Focus your attention on Jesus, noting his physical appearance and his demeanor.

• Then, watch and listen as Pilate speaks to Jesus before sending him on to Herod. You may want to quietly read the passage while remaining prayerfully aware of your mental image of Jesus or you may choose to stay completely within the imagined realm of your prayer. Whichever you choose, know that God will offer you the words from the biblical passage that you need to hear – even if only in fragments.

– Look around as Jesus speaks and see the reactions of Pilate, Herod, and the other people around Jesus. Become aware of their feelings and how they behave toward Jesus and one another.

– Remember that Jesus is suffering for you.

• Afterward, allow this image to fade from your imagination as you become aware of the phrases and images from this moment which touched you most deeply. Recall the emotions and memories – including any sounds or smells – evoked during your prayer. Allow these seminal aspects of your meditation to linger on your mind and in your heart, noting any special feelings evoked by them.

[5]   When you are ready, become aware of Jesus' presence with you in this moment and have an open and informal conversation about this prayer period and how the passage from Luke's gospel expresses your own needs or desires – giving space for Jesus to respond or to highlight different aspects from the biblical account and your experiences during this contemplation. Then, gradually allow your thoughts to recede as you focus on God's broader presence in your life and in the world around you.

[6]   Conclude by allowing these desires to fade from your consciousness as you offer this traditional Irish prayer:

Confirm me in your love divine,

Smooth for my feet life's rugged way;
My will with yours entwine,
Lest evil lead my steps astray.
Be with my still as guard and guide,
Keep me in holy sanctity,
Let my firm faith on you abide,
From fraud and error hold me free. Amen.

[7]   Afterward, take 10-15 minutes in a quiet space to reflect on the most significant moments from this time of prayer and record your reflections in your retreat journal.

In this contemplation of Luke 23:13-23, you will see and hear Jesus being condemned to death.

[1]   Begin by reading the biblical selection and reviewing your notes on it from your earlier preparations.

[2]   Focus on this specific time and place as you allow all other concerns to fall away. Then, when you are ready, consider the people and place of this encounter with Jesus.

• Allow an image of Jesus to emerge in your imagination, noting his physical characteristics and mannerisms. Look at what he is wearing or carrying. Make a note of whether he is sitting, standing, or walking. Ponder this mental image, allowing any other observations about Jesus to form in your mind.

• Look at Pilate, observing any changes in his appearance or demeanor. Look at the priests and scribes, noting their attitude and behavior toward Jesus. Observe the various men and women in crowd (including any of Jesus' disciples), making a mental note of their appearance and demeanor. Look around to see if people are sitting or standing. Take a moment to ponder this mental image, allowing other impressions of these men and women to form. Become familiar with the men and women you will encounter during your prayer as well as their behavior.

• Allow yourself to become aware of the location of this moment of prayer. Observe its physical characteristics and the arrangement of the people in it. Look around the place and notice more details about it. Become familiar with the location of your upcoming prayer.

• Take a moment to remain in this place with these men and women before allowing these images to fade from your consciousness.

[3]   Become aware of your desires during this moment of prayer. Remember your desire to experience the divine presence all around you and to trust in God's plan for you, asking that you may feel deep grief and confusion because it is for your sins that the Lord is going to his passion. Ask for grief with Christ and grief to be broken with Christ broken for tears and interior suffering on account of the great suffering the Christ endured for you. Recall your desire that, in this day or week of prayer, to witness the trial of Jesus and see his complete aloneness in this moment, recognizing and mourning the disappearance of the

godly qualities Jesus has demonstrated in the past as they now become hidden behind the suffering of a man.

As these desires fill your consciousness, let all other concerns fall aside as you focus on this time and place of prayer.

[4]   Allow the image of Jesus to reemerge in your imagination.

• Watch as Jesus again comes before Pilate. Listen to the sounds of this moment and feel the different emotions of the men and women around you – e.g., anger, hatred, vindication, worry, etc.

• Ask God to help you share in this moment – either by joining it or by listening quietly to it. Focus your attention on Jesus, noting his physical appearance and his demeanor.

• Then, watch and listen as Pilate speaks to Jesus. You may want to quietly read the passage while remaining prayerfully aware of your mental image of Jesus or you may choose to stay completely within the imagined realm of your prayer. Whichever you choose, know that God will offer you the words from the biblical passage that you need to hear – even if only in fragments.

– Look around during the trial and see the reactions of Pilate, the priests, the scribes, and the people in the crowd. Become aware of their feelings and how they behave toward Jesus and one another.

– Remember that Jesus is suffering for you.

• Afterward, allow this image to fade from your imagination as you become aware of the phrases and images from this moment which touched you most deeply. Recall the emotions and memories – including any sounds or smells – evoked during your prayer. Allow these seminal aspects of your meditation to linger on your mind and in your heart, noting any special feelings evoked by them.

[5]   When you are ready, become aware of Jesus' presence with you in this moment and have an open and informal conversation about this prayer period and how the passage from Luke's gospel expresses your own needs or desires – giving space for Jesus to respond or to highlight different aspects from the biblical account and your experiences during this contemplation. Then, gradually allow your thoughts to recede as you focus on God's broader presence in your life and in the world around you.

[6]   Conclude by allowing these desires to fade from your consciousness as you offer this traditional Irish prayer:

Confirm me in your love divine,
Smooth for my feet life's rugged way;
My will with yours entwine,

Lest evil lead my steps astray.
Be with my still as guard and guide,
Keep me in holy sanctity,
Let my firm faith on you abide,
From fraud and error hold me free. Amen.

[7]   Afterward, take 10-15 minutes in a quiet space to reflect on the most significant moments from this time of prayer and record your reflections in your retreat journal.

In this meditation on Philippians 2:5-11, you will see and hear Saint Columba preach on the sacrificial nature of Jesus' crucifixion.

[1]   Begin by reading the biblical selection and reviewing your notes on it from your earlier preparations.

[2]   Focus on this specific time and place as you allow all other concerns to fall away. Then, when you are ready, consider the people and place of this encounter with Columba.

• Allow an image of Columba to emerge in your imagination, noting his physical characteristics and mannerisms. Look at what he is wearing or carrying. Make a note of whether he is sitting, standing, or walking. Ponder this mental image, allowing any other observations about Columba to form in your mind.

• Note how many people are with Columba, making a mental note of their appearance and demeanor. Look at Columba's disciples, observing where they are standing and how they behave toward Columba. Look at the crowd, noting their attitude and behavior toward Columba. Observe whether the people are sitting, standing, or walking. Take a moment to ponder this mental image, allowing other impressions of these men and women to form. Become familiar with the men and women you will encounter during your prayer as well as their behavior.

• Allow yourself to become aware of the location of this moment of prayer. Observe whether it is inside or outside, paying attention to its physical characteristics and the arrangement of the people in it. Look around the place and notice more details about it – if it in dim or bright light, if it is still and silent or filled with noise, if it has an unusual smell or not, etc. Become familiar with the location of your upcoming prayer.

• Take a moment to remain in this place with these men and women before allowing these images to fade from your consciousness.

[3]   Become aware of your desires during this moment of prayer. Remember your desire to experience the divine presence all around you and to trust in God's plan for you, asking that you may feel deep grief and confusion because it is for your sins that the Lord is going to his passion. Ask for grief with Christ and grief to be broken with Christ broken for tears and interior suffering on account of the great suffering the Christ endured for you. Recall your desire that, in this day or week

of prayer, to witness the trial of Jesus and see his complete aloneness in this moment, recognizing and mourning the disappearance of the godly qualities Jesus has demonstrated in the past as they now become hidden behind the suffering of a man.

As these desires fill your consciousness, let all other concerns fall aside as you focus on this time and place of prayer.

[4]   Allow the image of Saint Columba and the crowd to reemerge in your imagination.

• Watch as the group assembles around Columba, either from a distance or as a participant. Listen to the sounds of this moment and become comfortable as you prepare to hear Columba speak. Feel the anticipation of the men and women around you and share in that enthusiasm.

• Ask God to help you share in this moment – either by joining it or by listening quietly to it. Focus your attention on Saint Columba, noting his physical appearance and his demeanor.

• Then, watch and listen as Columba presents and explains the early Christian hymn from Paul's letter to the Philippians. You may want to quietly read the passage while remaining prayerfully aware of your mental image of Columba or you may choose to stay completely within the imagined realm of your prayer. Whichever you choose, know that God will offer you the words from the biblical passage that you need to hear – even if only in fragments.

– Again, look around as Columba speaks and see the reactions of his disciples and the men and women in the crowd. Become aware of their feelings and how they behave toward Columba and one another.

– Remember that Columba is speaking to men and women struggling with the contradictory nature of the cross. Remember that he is speaking to you.

• After Saint Columba finishes speaking, allow this image to fade from your imagination as you become aware of the phrases and images from this moment which touched you most deeply. Recall the emotions and memories – including any sounds or smells – evoked during your prayer. Allow these seminal aspects of your meditation to linger on your mind and in your heart, noting any special feelings evoked by them.

[5]   When you are ready, become aware of Jesus' presence with you in this moment and have an open and informal conversation about this prayer period and how the passage from Paul's epistle expresses your

own needs or desires – giving space for Jesus to respond or to highlight different aspects from the biblical account and your experiences during this contemplation. Then, gradually allow your thoughts to recede as you focus on God's broader presence in your life and in the world around you.

[6]   Conclude by allowing these desires to fade from your consciousness as you offer this traditional Irish prayer:

> *Confirm me in your love divine,*
> *Smooth for my feet life's rugged way;*
> *My will with yours entwine,*
> *Lest evil lead my steps astray.*
> *Be with my still as guard and guide,*
> *Keep me in holy sanctity,*
> *Let my firm faith on you abide,*
> *From fraud and error hold me free. Amen.*

[7]   Afterward, take 10-15 minutes in a quiet space to reflect on the most significant moments from this time of prayer and record your reflections in your retreat journal.

4.6   An Application of the Senses

[1]   Become aware of your prayerful desires during this day or week. Bring to mind your desire to feel deep grief and confusion because it is for your sins that the Lord is going to his passion. Ask also that, in this day or week of prayer, you may witness the trial of Jesus and see his complete aloneness in this moment, recognizing and mourning the disappearance of the godly qualities Jesus has demonstrated in the past as they now become hidden behind the suffering of a man.

[2]   When you are ready, call to mind the various prayers of the preceding day or days. Allow the images and words of these prayers to linger and then slowly fade from your consciousness.

• Remember your imaginative contemplation of Luke 22:63-71. Consider the images and feelings evoked in you during your prayer, feeling God's presence in these memories and becoming aware of the specific sensations associated with each image.

• Recall your imaginative contemplation of Luke 23:1-12, considering it in the same way as the memories of your meditation on Luke 22.

• Review your imaginative contemplation of Luke 23:13-23 in the same manner as the previous prayers.

• Revisit your mediation on Philippians 2:5-11 in the same manner as the previous prayers.

Make a mental note of which senses are most active. You may see an image or a color, hear a sound or a phrase, or smell a scent or a fragrance. You may even taste a flavor or feel a sensation on your skin.

[3]   Then, relax and allow these various memories and experiences to quietly enter and leave your consciousness without being controlled. Linger on the sensory images and memories being evoked in you – noticing any images or colors, any sounds or phrases, any scents or fragrances, any flavors or physical sensations associated with each prayer.

[4]   When you are ready, become completely still and clear your mind of all thoughts and concerns. Allow an image of a special personal space to form in your imagination. Then, watch as God enters that place and forms a small image or object for you that expresses the thought or awareness that you most need to carry with you into your life.

Reverently pick up the object or image, a reflection of the most important gift you have been given during this time of prayer. Look at it carefully and become aware of the divine presence contained within it. Take a moment to register what it looks like and how it feels in your hand. Then, feel the joy and confidence that comes from touching the presence of God as you accept this gift, offering a short prayer of gratitude while you relax into the pleasure of this moment.

[5]   Then, conclude by allowing these images to fade from your consciousness as you offer this traditional Irish prayer:

Confirm me in your love divine,
Smooth for my feet life's rugged way;
My will with yours entwine,
Lest evil lead my steps astray.
Be with my still as guard and guide,
Keep me in holy sanctity,
Let my firm faith on you abide,
From fraud and error hold me free. Amen.

[6]   While your experiences are still fresh in your mind, record the most significant impressions or sensations from this time of prayer in your retreat journal.

[1]   Remember your desires during the preceding day or week of prayer. As you become aware of the divine presence all around you, ask that you may feel deep grief and confusion because it is for your sins that the Lord is going to his passion. Recall your desire to witness the trial of Jesus and see his complete aloneness in this moment, recognizing and mourning the disappearance of the godly qualities Jesus has demonstrated in the past as they now become hidden behind the suffering of a man.

Ask God once again to fulfill these desires in your own life and in your interactions with others.

[2]   Then, take a moment to allow the words, thoughts, and feelings from your prayers during the last day or week to linger before asking God to reveal the fulfillment of your deepest desires in these various memories.

• Think about the prayer sequence at the beginning of this day or week. Make a mental note of any words, insights or images that remain particularly significant or meaningful to you.

• Ponder the story, "Columba and the Mourning Nag". Note any words, insights, or images from it that remain particularly significant or meaningful to you.

• Remember your imaginative contemplation of Luke 22:63-71.

– Consider the most powerful images, phrases, or feelings from your prayer. Ask yourself what gifts God gave to you through these moments, perhaps offering you new insights or perhaps affirming an important aspect of your faith. Ask yourself how God may be calling you to change through these moments, being as specific as possible.

– Examine your disposition as you prayed, noting whether prayer came easily or with resistance. Recall the easiest moments in your prayer and any moments of joy you may have experienced. Remember also if you encountered any difficulty opening yourself to God or if you felt any sadness as you prayed. Ask God to help you understand why these feelings surfaced.

– Bring to mind any moments when you added personal elements (e.g., familiar places or people from your life) or connected your prayers to other scriptures or spiritual writings. Ask yourself how these additions helped or hindered you as you prayed. Again, if you do not know why this happened, ask God to help you understand.

• Recall your imaginative contemplation of Luke 23:1-12. Then, review your prayer in the same way as your earlier reflection on Luke 22.

• Review your imaginative contemplations of Luke 23:13-23 in the same manner as the previous prayers.

• Revisit your meditation on Philippians 2:5-11 in the same manner as the previous prayers.

• Reflect on the ebb and flow of sensory impressions and feelings that marked your application of the senses. Isolate the most memorable moments and sensory impressions from your prayer and reflect on how God used these moments to give you a particular gift.

[3]   Finally, ponder the times when images or feelings from the readings of this day or week surfaced outside these prayer periods. Consider those moments or events in which God's presence or guidance was especially strong as well as any moments when you were struggling. Think about the most memorable aspects of these experiences, asking God to explain their significance.

[4]   Take a moment to allow the words, thoughts, and feelings of these prayers to linger on your mind and in your heart. Finally, conclude by allowing these desires to fade from your consciousness as you offer this traditional Irish prayer:

> *O God, I believe in you; strengthen my belief.*
> *I trust in you; confirm my trust.*
> *I love you; double my love.*
> *I repent that I angered you,*
> *Increase my repentance.*
> *Fill you my heart with awe without despair;*
> *With hope, without over-confidence;*
> *With piety without infatuation;*
> *And with joy without excess.*
> *My God, consent to guide me by your wisdom;*
> *To constrain me by your right;*
> *To comfort me by your mercy;*
> *And to protect me by your power. Amen.*

[5]   After finishing these prayers, summarize your reflections on the gifts or graces you received during the prayers of this last day or week and record these thoughts in your retreat journal.

5. Jesus' Death

5.1a   You Gave Your Life Upon The Tree

a penitent's prayer on Jesus' death upon the cross

***Take a moment to quiet your spirit, becoming completely
present to this time and place. Allow all other thoughts and concerns
to fall away as you come into the presence of God. Then, when you
are ready, begin.***

You gave your life upon the tree,
Dear Jesus, my Saviour you be;
        Who denies your true divinity
        Denies also your gift to humanity.

All godless errors, proud or vain,
The false belief and murmuring strain
        Insult your love, your law profane,
        And, my Redeemer, your hope disdain.

A Hymn, sung or heard (optional)

Think of the cross of Christ each day,
Think how he suffered for all to view,
        Think of the boon his passion gave,
        Think of the grave that gapes for you.

Think of the Son of God, how He
Died on the tree our souls to save,
        Think of the nails that pierced Him through,
        Think of Him, too, in lowly grave.

Think of the spear the soldier bore,
Think how it tore His holy side,
        Think of the bitter gall for drink,
        Think of it, think for us He died.

Think upon Christ who gave His blood
Poured in a food our souls to win,
        Think of tho mingled tide that gushed
        Forth at the thrust to wash our sin.

Think of repentance timely made,
Think like a shade our time flits, too,
      Think upon Death with poisoned dart
      Piercing the heart and body through.

Read or recite Psalm 22.

Holy Lord,
Under my thoughts may I God-thoughts find.
Half of my sins escape my mind.
      For what I said, or did not say,
      Pardon me, O Lord, I pray.

Read John 19:31-37, aloud or quietly.

O Lord, Jesus the Christ,
If I were in Heaven my harp I would sound
With apostles and angels and saints all around,
      Praising and thanking the Son who is crowned,
      May the poor race of Eve for that heaven be bound!

I pray unto the Son, that He
Toward me be minded still,
      His will is to redeem all,
      I pray that He be of my will.

I pray unto the Father most high,
With the Holy Ghost, for safety.
      They, together as three in one,
      My life and salvation do guarantee.

O Holy Lord,
      God with the Father and the Spirit,
For me is many a snare designed,
To fill my mind with doubts and fears;
      Far from the land of holy saints,
      I dwell within my vale of tears.
Let faith, let hope, let love –
Traits far above the cold world's way –
      With patience, humility, and awe,

Become my guides from day to day.

I acknowledge, the evil I have done.
From the day of my birth till the day of my death,
      Through the sight of my eyes,
Through the hearing of my ears,
      Through the sayings of my mouth,
Through the thoughts of my heart,
      Through the touch of my hands,
Through the course of my way,
      Through all I said and did not,
Through all I promised and fulfilled not,
      Through all the laws and holy commandments I broke.
I ask even now absolution of you,
      For fear I may have never asked it as was right,
      And that I might not live to ask it again,

O Holy Lord, my King in Heaven,
May you not let my soul stray from you,
May you keep me in a good state,
      May you turn me toward what is good to do,
      May you protect me from dangers, small and great.
May you fill my eyes with tears of repentance,
      So I may avoid the sinner's awful sentence.
May the Grace of the God for ever be with me,
      And whatever my needs, may the Triune God give me.

Select one of the following options for the Lord's Prayer.

Option A

O Jesus Christ,
Lord of heaven and earth,
Help me pray as you yourself taught:
      "Our Father in heaven,
      hallowed be your name.
      Your kingdom come.
      Your will be done,
      on earth as it is in heaven.
      Give us this day our daily bread.

And forgive us our debts,
as we also have forgiven our debtors.
And do not bring us to the time of trial,
but rescue us from the evil one."
(Matthew 6: 9-13)
From the foes of my land,
from the foes of my faith,
From the foes who would us dissever,
O Lord, preserve me, in life and in death,
With the Sign of the Cross for ever.
For the kingdom, the power, and the glory
are yours now and for ever. Amen.

Please proceed with "I beseech you, O Lord...," found after Option B.

Option B

O Jesus Christ,
Lord of heaven and earth,
Help me pray as you yourself taught:
Our Father in heaven,
hallowed be your name,
your kingdom come,
your will be done,
on earth as in heaven.
Give us today our daily bread.
Forgive us our sins
as we forgive those who sin against us.
Lead us not into temptation
but deliver us from evil.
From the foes of my land,
from the foes of my faith,
From the foes who would us dissever,
O Lord, preserve me, in life and in death,
With the Sign of the Cross for ever.
For the kingdom, the power, and the glory
are yours now and for ever. Amen.

I beseech you, O Lord.

God in Heaven, unsurpassed in power and might;
      Be behind me, Be on my left,
      Be before me, Be on my right!
Against each danger, you are my help;
In distress, upon you I call.
      In dark times, may you sustain me
      And lift me up again when I fall.
Lord over heaven and of earth,
You know my offenses.
      Yet, listening to my pleadings,
      You guide me away from sinful pretenses.
Lord of all creation and the many creatures,
You bestow on me many earthly treasures.
      Revealing love in each life and season,
      You share with me heavenly pleasures.
May you arouse me
In moments both of joy and of strife;
      Most holy Lord, bring me new life!

A Hymn, sung or heard (optional)

O Jesus Christ,
      Lord of heaven and earth,
      You are my riches, my store, my provision,
My star through the years
When troubles rend me,
      Through times of strife and tears,
      Sweet Jesus, defend me.

And so he came unto Calvary
And died nailed upon the shameful tree,
      He died burdened by all human woe,
      And yielded his pure life, to make men free.

Yea, for my miseries the cruel pain
He bore; to bring new life his life was slain;
      So let his glory ring through earth and heaven,
      Our living God and King of endless reign.

End this time of prayer by taking some time to bring to mind the various ways God shields you from harm or guides you through the world's tumult. Then, when you are ready, conclude by saying:

O Holy Lord, King in Heaven,
I place myself at the edge of your grace,
    On the floor of your house myself I place,
And to banish the sin of my heart away,
    I lower my knee to you this day.
Through life's torrents of pain may you bring me whole,
    And, O Lord Jesus Christ, preserve also my soul. Amen.

Consideration of the Readings

After reciting or prayerfully reading the prayer sequence for this day or week:
• Read about Jesus' crucifixion in John 19:13-30. Make a mental note of Jesus' appearance and actions during the episode, the people listening to him, and the key elements of Jesus' message. Then, consider any aspects of this story that speak strongly to you before recording these observations in your workbook.
• Read about the dead Jesus on the cross in John 19:31-37. Then, consider any aspects of this moment that speak strongly to you before recording these observations in your workbook.
• Read about Jesus' burial in John 19:38-42, noting each person's appearance and actions during the episode as well as the key elements of the story and its setting. Then, record any aspects of this story that speak strongly to you.

Note: You also should consider any aspect of the prayer sequence from this day or week that seemed particularly significant to you.

Contemplation of Your Needs

When you are ready, allow any distractions to fade from your consciousness as you become aware of your desire to live in God's goodness. Feel yourself yearning to properly use the many gifts God has given you, to experience God's continuing care, and to be open to the immense love God shows for you, then:
• Read "The Miraculous Cowl of Aed Slane" (found on page 303). Allow yourself to linger on any thoughts, phrases or images that seem particularly meaningful or significant to your earlier preparations or prayer.
• Pray for your desires in the coming day or week. Ask that the divine presence all around you may be revealed, so you may feel deep grief and confusion because it is for your sins that the Lord is going to his passion. Ask also that, in this day or week of prayer, you may watch as Jesus is abused and crucified – witnessing the pain and agony of his

126

death, the anger of the jeering crowd, and the sorrow of those who mourn his death.

• Conclude by praying that you may feel remorse for that part of you that rejects Jesus as well as sorrow for that part of you that is now in the mourning.

Then, record any significant thoughts, emotions, or reactions from these moments in your workbook.

After this, put your notes aside. Without straining your memory, consider in turn each of the readings for the coming day or week and allow them to take shape in your imagination. Prayerfully ponder how each reading affects you emotionally without overtly thinking about their content, asking God to illuminate the spiritual gifts offered in each reading – quieting your mind and creating a receptive space in yourself to see or hear the response.

Finally, conclude by allowing these desires to fade from your consciousness as you offer this traditional Irish prayer:

> *O God, I believe in you; strengthen my belief.*
> *I trust in you; confirm my trust.*
> *I love you; double my love.*
> *I repent that I angered you,*
> *Increase my repentance.*
> *Fill you my heart with awe without despair;*
> *With hope, without over-confidence;*
> *With piety without infatuation;*
> *And with joy without excess.*
> *My God, consent to guide me by your wisdom;*
> *To constrain me by your right;*
> *To comfort me by your mercy;*
> *And to protect me by your power. Amen.*

Allow these words to linger on your mind and in your heart for a few moments and then, while they are still fresh in your memory, write the most important thoughts, feelings, and desires from this preparatory time in your journal.

In this contemplation of John 19:13-30, you will see and hear Jesus being crucified and dying.

Note: This contemplation (and subsequent ones during this day or week of prayer) use an adaptation of a special colloquy with Jesus on the cross introduced by Ignatius in his Spiritual Exercises, *so you may want to read this colloquy as Ignatius presented it (see page 296). This review might offer you different perspectives on various aspects of this exercise, illuminate your reflections, and open you to a broader awareness of God's activity during your prayer. However, you should feel free to ignore this suggestion if it distracts you from your prayers.*

[1]   Begin by reading the biblical selection and reviewing your notes on it.

[2]   Then, focus on this specific time and place as you allow all other concerns to fall away before considering the people and place of this moment of prayer.

    • Allow an image of the suffering Jesus to emerge in your imagination. Ponder this mental image, allowing any other observations about Jesus to take shape in your mind.

    • Look at Pilate, observing where he is standing and how he behaves toward Jesus. Look at the crowd (including the priests, scribes, and Jesus' disciples), noting their attitude and behavior toward Jesus. Take a moment to ponder this mental image, allowing other impressions of these people to form. Become familiar with the men and women you will encounter during your prayer as well as their behavior.

    • Allow yourself to become aware of the location of this moment of prayer, paying attention to its physical characteristics and the arrangement of the people in it. Look around the place and notice more details about it. Become familiar with the location of your upcoming prayer.

    • Take a moment to remain in this place with these people before allowing these images to fade from your consciousness.

[3]   Become aware of your desires during this moment of prayer. Remember your desire to experience the divine presence all around you and to trust in God's plan for you, asking that you may feel deep grief and confusion because it is for your sins that the Lord is going to his passion. Ask for grief with Christ and grief to be broken with Christ

broken for tears and interior suffering on account of the great suffering the Christ endured for you.

Recall your desire that, in this day or week of prayer, to watch as Jesus is abused and crucified – witnessing the pain and agony of his death, the anger of the jeering crowd, and the sorrow of those who mourn his death. Finally, ask that you may feel remorse for that part of you that rejects Jesus as well as sorrow for that part of you that is now in the mourning.

As these desires fill your consciousness, let all other concerns fall aside as you focus on this time and place of prayer.

[4]   Allow the image of Jesus, Pilate and the crowd to reemerge in your imagination.

• Watch as Pilate condemns Jesus before sending him to be crucified. Listen to the sounds of this moment and feel the different emotions of the people around you – e.g., anger, hatred, vindication, worry, etc.

• Ask God to help you share in this moment – either by joining it or by listening quietly to it. Focus your attention on Jesus, noting his changing physical appearance and his demeanor.

• Then, watch and listen as Jesus is condemned and crucified. You may want to quietly read the passage while remaining prayerfully aware of your mental image of Jesus or you may choose to stay completely within the imagined realm of your prayer. Whichever you choose, know that God will offer you the words from the biblical passage that you need to hear – even if only in fragments.

– Look around as Pilate orders Jesus' death and the soldiers crucify him. See the reactions of the crowd (including Jesus' mother and disciples), becoming aware of their many different feelings and how they behave toward Jesus and one another.

– Remember that Jesus is suffering for you.

[5]   When you are ready, become aware of yourself standing below Jesus on the cross. Looking up from the base of the cross at the dying Jesus, become aware of the phrases and images from this moment which touched you most deeply. Recall the emotions and memories – including any sounds or smells – evoked during your prayer. Allow these seminal aspects of your meditation to linger on your mind and in your heart before speaking to Jesus about your sorrow for the many times you failed him in your thoughts, words, and actions.

Feel the depth of your grief for Jesus suffering on the cross because of your many sins and ask, "What have I done for Christ? What am I now doing for Christ? What more ought I do for Christ?" Allow Jesus and the Spirit to guide your thoughts and desires as you address each question in turn, highlighting different aspects of your experiences during this consideration. Then, gradually allow your thoughts to recede as you focus on God's forgiving presence in your life and in the world around you.

Dwell in this moment in silence before allowing this image to fade from your consciousness.

[6]   Then, conclude by allowing these desires to fade from your consciousness as you offer this traditional Irish prayer:

> *Confirm me in your love divine,*
> *Smooth for my feet life's rugged way;*
> *My will with yours entwine,*
> *Lest evil lead my steps astray.*
> *Be with my still as guard and guide,*
> *Keep me in holy sanctity,*
> *Let my firm faith on you abide,*
> *From fraud and error hold me free. Amen.*

[7]   Afterward, take 10-15 minutes in a quiet space to reflect on the most significant moments from this time of prayer and record your reflections in your journal.

In this contemplation of John 19:31-37, you will see Jesus dead on the cross.

[1]   Begin by reading the biblical selection and reviewing your notes on it from your earlier preparations.

[2]   Then, focus on this specific time and place as you allow all other concerns to fall away before considering the people and place of this encounter with the crucified Jesus.

• Allow an image of Jesus to emerge in your imagination, dead on the cross. Ponder this mental image, allowing any other observations about Jesus to form in your mind.

• Look at the crowd around the cross (including any of the priests and scribes as well as any of Jesus' disciples), noting their attitude and behavior toward Jesus. Take a moment to ponder this mental image, allowing other impressions of these people to form. Become familiar with the men and women you will encounter during your prayer as well as their behavior.

• Allow yourself to become aware of the location of this moment of prayer, paying attention to its physical characteristics and the arrangement of the people in it. Look around the place and notice more details about it – if it is overcast or clear, if it is still and silent or filled with noise, if it has an unusual smell or not, etc. Become familiar with the location of your upcoming prayer.

• Take a moment to remain in this place with these people before allowing these images to fade from your consciousness.

[3]   Become aware of your desires during this moment of prayer. Remember your desire to experience the divine presence all around you and to trust in God's plan for you, asking that you may feel deep grief and confusion because it is for your sins that the Lord is going to his passion. Ask for grief with Christ and grief to be broken with Christ broken for tears and interior suffering on account of the great suffering the Christ endured for you.

Recall your desire that, in this day or week of prayer, to watch as Jesus is abused and crucified – witnessing the pain and agony of his death, the anger of the jeering crowd, and the sorrow of those who mourn his death. Finally, ask that you may feel remorse for that part of you that rejects Jesus as well as sorrow for that part of you that is now in the mourning.

As these desires fill your consciousness, let all other concerns fall aside as you focus on this time and place of prayer.

[4]   Allow the image of Jesus on the cross, surrounded by a crowd, to reemerge in your imagination.

• Look at hanging Jesus dead on the cross and at the crowd. Listen to the sounds of this moment and feel the different emotions of the men and women around you – e.g., anger, hatred, vindication, sorrow, etc.

• Ask God to help you share in this moment – either by joining it or by listening quietly to it. Focus your attention on Jesus, dead and lifeless.

• Then, watch and listen as the soldier approach the dead Jesus. You may want to quietly read the passage while remaining prayerfully aware of your mental image of Jesus or you may choose to stay completely within the imagined realm of your prayer. Whichever you choose, know that God will offer you the words from the biblical passage that you need to hear – even if only in fragments.

– See the reactions of crowd as they look at Jesus on the cross, becoming aware of their many different feelings and how they behave toward Jesus and one another.

– Remember that Jesus died for you.

[5]   When you are ready, become aware of yourself standing below Jesus on the cross. Looking up from the base of the cross at the dead Jesus, become aware of the phrases and images from this moment which touched you most deeply. Recall the emotions and memories – including any sounds or smells – evoked during your prayer. Allow these seminal aspects of your meditation to linger on your mind and in your heart before speaking to Jesus about your sorrow for the many times you failed him in your thoughts, words, and actions.

Feel the depth of your grief for Jesus hanging dead on the cross because of your many sins and ask, "What have I done for Christ? What am I now doing for Christ? What more ought I do for Christ?" Allow Jesus and the Spirit to guide your thoughts and desires as you address each question in turn, highlighting different aspects of your experiences during this consideration. Then, gradually allow your thoughts to recede as you focus on God's forgiving presence in your life and in the world around you.

Dwell in this moment in silence before allowing this image to fade from your consciousness.

[6]   Then, conclude by allowing these desires to fade from your consciousness as you offer this traditional Irish prayer:

> *Confirm me in your love divine,*
> *Smooth for my feet life's rugged way;*
> *My will with yours entwine,*
> *Lest evil lead my steps astray.*
> *Be with my still as guard and guide,*
> *Keep me in holy sanctity,*
> *Let my firm faith on you abide,*
> *From fraud and error hold me free. Amen.*

[7]   Afterward, take 10-15 minutes in a quiet space to reflect on the most significant moments from this time of prayer and record your reflections in your journal.

In this contemplation of John 19:38-42, you will see and hear Joseph of Arimathea and Nicodemus place Jesus in his tomb.

[1]   Begin by reading the biblical selection and reviewing your notes on it from your earlier preparations.

[2]   Then, focus on this specific time and place as you allow all other concerns to fall away before considering the people and place of this moment of prayer.

• Allow an image of Joseph of Arimathea and Nicodemus to emerge in your imagination, noting their physical characteristics and mannerisms. Look at what they are wearing or carrying. Make a note of whether he is sitting, standing, or walking. Ponder this mental image, allowing any other observations about Jesus to form in your mind.

• Look at Pilate, observing any changes in his appearance or demeanor as Joseph and Nicodemus request the body of Jesus. Look at the soldiers who Pilate commands to assist in the burial of Jesus, noting appearance and demeanor. Observe any men or women accompanying Joseph of Arimathea and Nicodemus, making a mental note of their appearance and demeanor. Take a moment to ponder this mental image, allowing other impressions of these people to form. Become familiar with the men and women you will encounter during your prayer as well as their behavior.

• Allow yourself to become aware of the location of this moment of prayer. Observe whether it is inside or outside, paying attention to its physical characteristics and the arrangement of the people in it. Look around the place and notice more details about it – if it in dim or bright light, if it is still and silent or filled with noise, etc. Become familiar with the location of your upcoming prayer.

• Take a moment to remain in this place with these people before allowing these images to fade from your consciousness.

[3]   Become aware of your desires during this moment of prayer. Remember your desire to experience the divine presence all around you and to trust in God's plan for you, asking that you may feel deep grief and confusion because it is for your sins that the Lord is going to his passion. Ask for grief with Christ and grief to be broken with Christ broken for tears and interior suffering on account of the great suffering the Christ endured for you.

Recall your desire that, in this day or week of prayer, to watch as Jesus is abused and crucified – witnessing the pain and agony of his death, the anger of the jeering crowd, and the sorrow of those who mourn his death. Finally, ask that you may feel remorse for that part of you that rejects Jesus as well as sorrow for that part of you that is now in the mourning.

As these desires fill your consciousness, let all other concerns fall aside as you focus on this time and place of prayer.

[4]   Allow the image of Joseph of Arimathea to reemerge in your imagination.

• Watch as the Joseph approaches Pilate. Listen to the sounds of this moment and feel the different emotions of the people around you.

• Ask God to help you share in this moment – either by joining it or by listening quietly to it.

• Then, watch and listen as Pilate speaks with Joseph of Arimathea before giving him Jesus' body for burial. You may want to quietly read the passage while remaining prayerfully aware of your mental image of Jesus or you may choose to stay completely within the imagined realm of your prayer. Whichever you choose, know that God will offer you the words from the biblical passage that you need to hear – even if only in fragments.

– Become aware of how of Pilate, Joseph of Arimathea and Nicodemus behave toward one another.

– Remember that Jesus died for you.

{5}   Looking down upon Jesus in his tomb, become aware of the phrases and images from this moment which touched you most deeply. Recall the emotions and memories – including any sounds or smells – evoked during your prayer. Allow these seminal aspects of your meditation to linger on your mind and in your heart before speaking to Jesus about your sorrow for the many times you failed him in your thoughts, words, and actions.

Feel the depth of your grief for Jesus' suffering on the cross because of your many sins and ask, "What have I done for Christ? What am I now doing for Christ? What more ought I do for Christ?" Allow Jesus and the Spirit to guide your thoughts and desires as you address each question in turn, highlighting different aspects of your experiences during this consideration. Then, gradually allow your thoughts to recede as you focus on God's forgiving presence in your life and in the world around you.

Dwell in this moment in silence before allowing this image to fade from your consciousness.

[6] Then, conclude by allowing these desires to fade from your consciousness as you offer this traditional Irish prayer:

Confirm me in your love divine,
Smooth for my feet life's rugged way;
My will with yours entwine,
Lest evil lead my steps astray.
Be with my still as guard and guide,
Keep me in holy sanctity,
Let my firm faith on you abide,
From fraud and error hold me free. Amen.

[7] Afterward, take 10-15 minutes in a quiet space to reflect on the most significant moments from this time of prayer and record your reflections in your journal.

In this consideration, you will review your sins in the manner presented in *The Spiritual Exercises of Saint Ignatius*.

[1]   Begin by focusing on this specific time and place as you allow all other concerns to fall away.

[2]   As you become still, become aware of your desires during this moment of prayer. Remember your desire to experience the divine presence all around you and to trust in God's plan for you, asking that you may feel deep grief and confusion because it is for your sins that the Lord is going to his passion. Ask for grief with Christ and grief to be broken with Christ broken for tears and interior suffering on account of the great suffering the Christ endured for you. Recall your desire that, in this day or week of prayer, to watch as Jesus is abused and crucified – witnessing the pain and agony of his death, the anger of the jeering crowd, and the sorrow of those who mourn his death. Finally, ask that you may feel remorse for that part of you that rejects Jesus as well as sorrow for that part of you that is now in the mourning.

As these desires fill your consciousness, let all other concerns fall aside as you focus on this specific time and place of prayer.

Note: At this point, you may want to read the text of this exercise as Ignatius presented it in his Spiritual Exercises *(see page 296). Since the points of the following review correspond to #56-60 in this exercise, you may find the different perspectives of this review and the review presented by Ignatius will help illuminate your reflections and open you to a broader awareness of your sins. However, you should feel free to ignore this suggestion if it becomes distracting or leads you away from prayerful reflection.*

[3]   Then, review your life and the many sins you have committed.

• In your memory, review the span of your life, the places you have lived and the many people with whom you have interacted. Going year-by-year or period-by-period (e.g., childhood, adolescence, early adulthood, etc.), consider the events of your life. Consider the various people you have met in your life and your interactions with them. Consider the various occupations and activities during your life. Then ask: How and when did you sin during these times, places, and activities with these people?

• Ponder the varying degrees of sinfulness you expressed during the events of your life and in your interactions with others. Consider the moments when you deliberately sinned and harmed either yourself or others. Consider also the moments when you harmed yourself or others unintentionally. Then ask: Have you expressed sorrow for these sins and sought to redress them?

• Reflect on how your sins have separated you from God and all of those who have lived righteous lives. Reflect on the ways that your sins – both large and small, intentional and unintentional, conscious and unconscious – have festered and corrupted your choices in life and your relationships with others (including God). Then ask: How have you endured this state of life that emerged from placing your desires above those of God and others, despite know the effects of these choices?

• Consider how God's attributes and behaviors contrast so completely from your sinful nature and choices. Reflect on the goodness and power that God displays in sustaining the world around you and in nurturing virtuous behaviors (e.g., kindness, justice, etc.) in the world while your actions undermine God's efforts and desires. Then ask: What makes God so loving and merciful toward you when you consistently choose to sin and place your desires above those of God and others?

• Express your dismay that God has continued to support and sustain you when your choices and actions deserve condemnation. Consider the many ways that God's creation makes your life possible despite your disdainful and sinful behavior toward it. Ponder how you are treated despite your contemptuous behavior toward God's actions on your behalf. Then ask: Why have you not been consigned to Hell for your numerous sinful choices and actions?

[4]   When you are ready, become aware of yourself standing below Jesus on the cross. Looking up from the base of the cross at the dying Jesus, watch his final moments as dies. Become aware of the phrases and images from this moment which touched you most deeply. Recall the emotions and memories evoked during your earlier prayer.

Feel the depth of your grief for Jesus' suffering on the cross because of your many sins and ask, "What have I done for Christ? What am I now doing for Christ? What more ought I do for Christ?" Allow Jesus and the Spirit to guide your thoughts and desires as you address each question in turn, highlighting different aspects of your experiences during this consideration.

Then, gradually allow your thoughts to recede as you focus on God's forgiving presence in your life and in the world around you.

[5]   Then, conclude by allowing these desires to fade from your consciousness as you offer this traditional Irish prayer:

> Confirm me in your love divine,
> Smooth for my feet life's rugged way;
> My will with yours entwine,
> Lest evil lead my steps astray.
> Be with my still as guard and guide,
> Keep me in holy sanctity,
> Let my firm faith on you abide,
> From fraud and error hold me free. Amen.

[6]   Afterward, take 10-15 minutes in a quiet space to reflect on the most significant moments from this time of prayer and record your reflections in your journal.

[1]   Become aware of your prayerful desires during this day or week. Bring to mind your desire to feel deep grief and confusion because it is for your sins that the Lord is going to his passion. Ask also that, in this day or week of prayer, you may watch as Jesus is abused and crucified – witnessing the pain and agony of his death, the anger of the jeering crowd, and the sorrow of those who mourn his death.

[2]   When you are ready, call to mind the various prayers of the preceding day or days. Allow the images and words of these prayers to linger and then slowly fade from your consciousness.

• Remember your imaginative contemplation of John 19:13-30. Consider the images and feelings evoked in you during your prayer, feeling God's presence in these memories and becoming aware of the specific sensations associated with each image.

• Recall your imaginative contemplations of John 19:31-37, considering them in the same way as the memories of your meditation on your earlier prayers.

• Review your imaginative contemplation of John 19:38-42 in the same manner as the previous prayers.

• Revisit the consideration of your personal sins from *The Spiritual Exercises of Saint Ignatius* in the same manner as the previous prayers.

Make a mental note of which senses are most active. You may see an image or a color, hear a sound or a phrase, or smell a scent or a fragrance. You may even taste a flavor or feel a sensation on your skin.

[3]   Then, relax and allow these various memories and experiences to quietly enter and leave your consciousness without being controlled. Linger on the sensory images and memories being evoked in you – noticing any images or colors, any sounds or phrases, any scents or fragrances, any flavors or physical sensations associated with each prayer.

[4]   When you are ready, become completely still and clear your mind of all thoughts and concerns. Allow an image of a special personal space to form in your imagination. Then, watch as God enters that place and forms a small image or object for you that expresses the thought or awareness that you most need to carry with you into your life.

Reverently pick up the object or image, a reflection of the most important gift you have been given during this time of prayer. Look at it carefully and become aware of the divine presence contained within it. Take a moment to register what it looks like and how it feels in your hand. Then, feel the joy and confidence that comes from touching the presence of God as you accept this gift, offering a short prayer of gratitude while you relax into the pleasure of this moment.

[5]   Then, conclude by allowing these images to fade from your consciousness as you offer this traditional Irish prayer:

> Confirm me in your love divine,
> Smooth for my feet life's rugged way;
> My will with yours entwine,
> Lest evil lead my steps astray.
> Be with my still as guard and guide,
> Keep me in holy sanctity,
> Let my firm faith on you abide,
> From fraud and error hold me free. Amen.

[6]   While your experiences are still fresh in your mind, record the most significant impressions or sensations from this time of prayer in your retreat journal.

[1]   Remember your desires during the preceding day or week of prayer. As you become aware of the divine presence all around you, ask that you may feel deep grief and confusion because it is for your sins that the Lord is going to his passion. Recall your desire to watch as Jesus is abused and crucified – witnessing the pain and agony of his death, the anger of the jeering crowd, and the sorrow of those who mourn his death.

Ask God once again to fulfill these desires in your own life and in your interactions with others.

[2]   Then, take a moment to allow the words, thoughts, and feelings from your prayers during the last day or week to linger before asking God to reveal the fulfillment of your deepest desires in these various memories.

• Think about the prayer sequence at the beginning of this day or week. Make a mental note of any words, insights or images that remain particularly significant or meaningful to you.

• Ponder the story, "The Miraculous Cowl of Aed Slane". Note any words, insights, or images from it that remain particularly significant or meaningful to you.

• Remember your imaginative contemplation of John 19:13-30.

– Consider the most powerful images, phrases, or feelings from your prayer. Ask yourself what gifts God gave to you through these moments, perhaps offering you new insights or perhaps affirming an important aspect of your faith. Ask yourself how God may be calling you to change through these moments, being as specific as possible.

– Examine your disposition as you prayed, noting whether prayer came easily or with resistance. Recall the easiest moments in your prayer and any moments of joy you may have experienced. Remember also if you encountered any difficulty opening yourself to God or if you felt any sadness as you prayed. Ask God to help you understand why these feelings surfaced.

– Bring to mind any moments when you added personal elements (e.g., familiar places or people from your life) or connected your prayers to other scriptures or spiritual writings. Ask yourself how these additions helped or hindered you as you prayed. Again, if you do not know why this happened, ask God to help you understand.

• Recall your imaginative contemplations of John 19:31-37. Then, review your prayer in the same way as your memories of your earlier prayer.

• Review your imaginative contemplation of John 19:38-42 in the same manner as the previous prayers.

• Revisit the consideration of your personal sins from *The Spiritual Exercises of Saint Ignatius* in the same manner as the previous prayers.

• Reflect on the ebb and flow of sensory impressions and feelings that marked your application of the senses. Isolate the most memorable moments and sensory impressions from your prayer and reflect on how God used these moments to give you a particular gift.

[3]   Finally, ponder the times when images or feelings from the readings of this day or week surfaced outside these prayer periods. Consider those moments or events in which God's presence or guidance was especially strong as well as any moments when you were struggling. Think about the most memorable aspects of these experiences, asking God to explain their significance.

[4]   Take a moment to allow the words, thoughts, and feelings of these prayers to linger on your mind and in your heart. Finally, conclude by allowing these desires to fade from your consciousness as you offer this traditional Irish prayer:

> *O God, I believe in you; strengthen my belief.*
> *I trust in you; confirm my trust.*
> *I love you; double my love.*
> *I repent that I angered you,*
> *Increase my repentance.*
> *Fill you my heart with awe without despair;*
> *With hope, without over-confidence;*
> *With piety without infatuation;*
> *And with joy without excess.*
> *My God, consent to guide me by your wisdom;*
> *To constrain me by your right;*
> *To comfort me by your mercy;*
> *And to protect me by your power. Amen.*

[5]   After finishing these prayers, summarize your reflections on the gifts or graces you received during the prayers of this last day or week and record these thoughts in your retreat journal.

6. The Empty Tomb

6.1a   The Sad Disciples Sat In Gloom

a prayer of joy and surprise for Jesus' Resurrection

Take a moment to quiet your spirit, becoming completely present to this time and place. Allow all other thoughts and concerns to fall away as you come into the presence of God. Then, when you are ready, begin.

The sad disciples sat in gloom,
For in the grave the Crucified
    Was laid to rest; they mourned his doom,
    And shuddered o'er the death he died.

An angel to the women gave
The truth of truths: "God is not dead;
    The Lord is risen from the grave,
    And bids his flock be comforted."

A Hymn, sung or heard (optional)

You my Redeemer are, O Christ,
My heart's desire, my fervent love;
    Creator of the world, you came
    To wear our flesh, from heaven above.

'Twas love that brought you to our aid,
To bear the burden of our woe,
    To bow the head in shameful death,
    And life, immortal life, bestow.

Asunder burst the bands of hell,
The captives hailed your glorious day;
    And by your mighty triumph crowned,
    you are at God's right hand today.

O may your mercy still abound,
That, by the goodness of your grace,
    We daily o'er our sin may rise,
    And see the beauty of your face.

Spring of our joy, be you, O Christ;
Hereafter shall be our great reward;
      And while the endless ages run,
      Our praises shall we duly record.

Read or recite Psalm 2.

Holy Lord,
Under my thoughts may I God-thoughts find.
Half of my sins escape my mind.
      For what I said, or did not say,
      Pardon me, O Lord, I pray.

Read John 20: 1-18, aloud or quietly.

O Lord, Jesus the Christ,
If I were in Heaven my harp I would sound
With apostles and angels and saints all around,
      Praising and thanking the Son who is crowned,
      May the poor race of Eve for that heaven be bound!

Holy Lord,
Born of a virgin void of stain,
your birth, your death, your broken tomb,
      Cleansing and lifting man again
      Redeemed the soul from mortal doom.

Shepherd, whose love with grief condoles,
Your baptism comes, a heavenly rain,
      Bathing with grace our waking souls,
      And washing out each deadly stain.

O Holy Lord,
      God with the Father and the Spirit,
For me is many a snare designed,
To fill my mind with doubts and fears;
      Far from the land of holy saints,
      I dwell within my vale of tears.
Let faith, let hope, let love –
Traits far above the cold world's way –

With patience, humility, and awe,
Become my guides from day to day.

I acknowledge, the evil I have done.
From the day of my birth till the day of my death,
    Through the sight of my eyes,
Through the hearing of my ears,
    Through the sayings of my mouth,
Through the thoughts of my heart,
    Through the touch of my hands,
Through the course of my way,
    Through all I said and did not,
Through all I promised and fulfilled not,
    Through all the laws and holy commandments I broke.
I ask even now absolution of you,
    For fear I may have never asked it as was right,
    And that I might not live to ask it again,

O Holy Lord, my King in Heaven,
May you not let my soul stray from you,
May you keep me in a good state,
    May you turn me toward what is good to do,
    May you protect me from dangers, small and great.
May you fill my eyes with tears of repentance,
    So I may avoid the sinner's awful sentence.
May the Grace of the God for ever be with me,
    And whatever my needs, may the Triune God give me.

Select one of the following options for the Lord's Prayer.

Option A

O Jesus Christ,
Lord of heaven and earth,
Help me pray as you yourself taught:
    "Our Father in heaven,
    hallowed be your name.
    Your kingdom come.
    Your will be done,
    on earth as it is in heaven.

Give us this day our daily bread.
And forgive us our debts,
as we also have forgiven our debtors.
And do not bring us to the time of trial,
but rescue us from the evil one."
(Matthew 6: 9-13)
From the foes of my land,
from the foes of my faith,
From the foes who would us dissever,
    O Lord, preserve me, in life and in death,
    With the Sign of the Cross for ever.
    For the kingdom, the power, and the glory
    are yours now and for ever. Amen.

Please proceed with "I beseech you, O Lord...," found after Option B.

Option B

O Jesus Christ,
Lord of heaven and earth,
Help me pray as you yourself taught:
    Our Father in heaven,
    hallowed be your name,
    your kingdom come,
    your will be done,
    on earth as in heaven.
    Give us today our daily bread.
    Forgive us our sins
    as we forgive those who sin against us.
    Lead us not into temptation
    but deliver us from evil.
From the foes of my land,
from the foes of my faith,
From the foes who would us dissever,
    O Lord, preserve me, in life and in death,
    With the Sign of the Cross for ever.
    For the kingdom, the power, and the glory
    are yours now and for ever. Amen.

I beseech you, O Lord.
God in Heaven, unsurpassed in power and might;
    Be behind me, Be on my left,
    Be before me, Be on my right!
Against each danger, you are my help;
In distress, upon you I call.
    In dark times, may you sustain me
    And lift me up again when I fall.
Lord over heaven and of earth,
You know my offenses.
    Yet, listening to my pleadings,
    You guide me away from sinful pretenses.
Lord of all creation and the many creatures,
You bestow on me many earthly treasures.
    Revealing love in each life and season,
    You share with me heavenly pleasures.
May you arouse me
In moments both of joy and of strife;
    Most holy Lord, bring me new life!

A Hymn, sung or heard (optional)

O Jesus Christ,
    Lord of heaven and earth,
    You are my riches, my store, my provision,
My star through the years
When troubles rend me,
    Through times of strife and tears,
    Sweet Jesus, defend me.

Be with us, Jesus, evermore,
Our paschal joy forever be;
    Renew our lives, our hopes restore,
    From sin and sorrow set us free.

For Christ, the King of love and might,
Has conquered death and broke the tomb;
    He leads forth to heavenly light
    The souls that long have pined in gloom.

End this time of prayer by taking some time to bring to mind the various ways God shields you from harm or guides you through the world's tumult. Then, when you are ready, conclude by saying:

O Holy Lord, King in Heaven,
I place myself at the edge of your grace,
    On the floor of your house myself I place,
And to banish the sin of my heart away,
    I lower my knee to you this day.
Through life's torrents of pain may you bring me whole,
    And, O Lord Jesus Christ, preserve also my soul. Amen.

Consideration of the Readings

After reciting or prayerfully reading the prayer sequence for this day or week:

• Read #230-234 in "The Contemplation to Attain Love" from *The Spiritual Exercises of Saint Ignatius* (found on page 298). Allow yourself to linger on any thoughts or phrases that seem particularly meaningful to you or especially relevant to your life. Then, record these highlights in your workbook.

• Read about the risen Jesus' first appearances in Mark 16:1-8 and John 20:1-18. Make a mental note of each person's appearance and actions during these episodes as well as the key elements of the story and its setting. Again, consider any aspects of this story that speak strongly to you before recording these observations in your workbook.

• Read 2 Corinthians 5:1-9. Again, pay careful attention to any phrases or images that seem particularly meaningful to you. Then, record these highlights in your workbook.

<u>Note:</u> *You also should consider any aspect of the prayer sequence from this day or week that seemed particularly significant to you.*

Contemplation of Your Needs

When you are ready, allow any distractions to fade from your consciousness as you become aware of your desire to live in God's goodness. Feel yourself yearning to properly use the many gifts God has given you, to experience God's continuing care, and to be open to the immense love God shows for you, then:

• Read "Columba and the Miracle of the Barley" (found on page 303). Allow yourself to linger on any thoughts, phrases or images that seem particularly meaningful or significant to your earlier preparations or prayer.

• Pray for your desires in the coming day or week. Ask that the divine presence all around you may be revealed, so you may feel gladness fully and rejoice intensely over the great glory and joy of Christ our Risen Lord. Ask also that you may witness the disciples as they go to the tomb and find that Jesus is not there – sharing their sense of confusion, anger, and sorrow as they do not know what to do before feeling their joy as they realize that Jesus has risen.

• Conclude by asking to feel the joy of God's many gifts to you as you consider the first point of The Contemplation to Attain Love – including the power that comes to the risen Jesus – so you may offer yourself in service and love to the triune God.

Then, record any significant thoughts, emotions, or reactions from these moments in your workbook.

After this, put your notes aside. Without straining your memory, consider in turn each of the readings for the coming day or week and allow them to take shape in your imagination. Prayerfully ponder how each reading affects you emotionally without overtly thinking about their content, asking God to illuminate the spiritual gifts offered in each reading – quieting your mind and creating a receptive space in yourself to see or hear the response.

Finally, conclude by allowing these desires to fade from your consciousness as you offer this traditional Irish prayer:

O God, I believe in you; strengthen my belief.
I trust in you; confirm my trust.
I love you; double my love.
I repent that I angered you,
Increase my repentance.
Fill you my heart with awe without despair;
With hope, without over-confidence;
With piety without infatuation;
And with joy without excess.
My God, consent to guide me by your wisdom;
To constrain me by your right;
To comfort me by your mercy;
And to protect me by your power. Amen.

Allow these words to linger on your mind and in your heart for a few moments and then, while they are still fresh in your memory, write the most important thoughts, feelings, and desires from this preparatory time in your journal.

In this meditation on the first point in "The Contemplation to Attain Love" presented in *The Spiritual Exercises of Saint Ignatius*, you will ponder the generosity of the Divine Majesty and the many gifts you have received from God before reflecting on how you should respond to this beneficence.

[1]   Begin by reading the preliminary considerations and first point of "The Contemplation to Attain Love" (#230-233 and #234) in *The Spiritual Exercises of Saint Ignatius* (found on page 298) and reviewing your notes on it.

[2]   Then, focus on this specific time and place as you allow all other concerns to fall away. As you become still, become aware of your desires during this moment of prayer. Remember your desire to experience the divine presence all around you and to trust in God's plan for you, asking that you may feel gladness fully and rejoice intensely over the great glory and joy of Christ our Risen Lord.

Recall your desire that, in this day or week of prayer, to witness the disciples as they go to the tomb and find that Jesus is not there – sharing their sense of confusion, anger and sorrow as they do not know what to do before feeling their joy as they realize that Jesus has risen. Finally, ask to feel the joy of God's many gifts to you as you consider the first point of The Contemplation to Attain Love – including the power that comes to the risen Jesus – so you may offer yourself in service and love to the triune God.

As these desires fill your consciousness, let all other concerns fall aside as you focus on this specific time and place of prayer.

[3]   Then, slowly and deliberately, re-read the "The Contemplation to Attain Love".

• As you read, take time to stop and ponder each statement within it as you read. When you pause, allow images shaped by the words and thoughts of the passages to form in your imagination. See and hear the way each statement expresses a need or desire in your life.

• Take more time with words that seem particularly significant or meaning to you. Become aware of the sections from the "The Contemplation to Attain Love" which you accept easily and any of those which cause you difficulty. Clarify these thoughts and feeling as much as possible while remaining focused on each specific statement within this meditation.

• After finishing the reading, allow the various words and images of your prayer to flow freely in your consciousness without being controlled. Become aware of those aspects of the "The Contemplation to Attain Love" that arouse holy desires in you, toward God and toward others (including nonhuman creatures). Become aware of those aspects of the reading that make you feel shame for those times you fall short of these holy aspirations.

• When you are ready, become aware of God's presence – experienced in your imagination either as a single entity or as the Holy Trinity – presence with you in this moment and have an open and informal conversation about your experience of the "The Contemplation to Attain Love". Speak about how it expresses your own desires and fears, giving space for the God to explain the love that motivates the divine actions presented in this meditation.

• Then, gradually allow your thoughts to recede as you focus on God's broader presence in your life and in the world around you.

[4] Conclude by offering this prayer presented by Saint Ignatius in his *Spiritual Exercises*:

> *Receive, Lord, my whole liberty.*
> *Accept my memory, understanding, and whole will.*
> *Whatsoever I have, or possess, you have given me:*
> *this all I restore to you, and to your will altogether*
> *deliver up to be governed.*
> *Give me only the love of you,*
> *with your grace, and I am rich enough,*
> *and desire nothing else beyond. Amen.*

[5] Afterward, take 10-15 minutes in a quiet space to reflect on the most significant moments from this time of prayer and record your reflections in your journal.

In this contemplation of Mark 16:1-8, you will see and hear the confusion among Jesus' disciples caused by his resurrection.

[1]   Begin by reading the biblical selection and reviewing your notes on it.

[2]   Then, focus on this specific time and place as you allow all other concerns to fall away before considering the people and place of this moment of prayer.

   • Allow an image of the people at Jesus' tomb to emerge in your imagination, noting their physical characteristics and mannerisms. Look at Mary Magdalene, Mary (the mother of James) and Salome. Notice their different demeanors and how they behave toward each other. See the young man sitting in the tomb, looking at what he is wearing or holding. Ponder this mental image, allowing any other observations about this event to form in your mind.

   • Gradually, become aware of the location of this moment of prayer. Observe the tomb, paying attention to its physical characteristics and the arrangement of the people around it. Is the interior of the tomb dark or well-lit from outside? Notice the location of the tomb's stone. Become familiar with the location of your upcoming prayer.

   • Take a moment to remain in this place with these people before allowing these images to fade from your consciousness.

[3]   Become aware of your desires during this moment of prayer. Remember your desire to experience the divine presence all around you and to trust in God's plan for you, asking that you may feel gladness fully and rejoice intensely over the great glory and joy of Christ our Risen Lord.

   Recall your desire that, in this day or week of prayer, to witness the disciples as they go to the tomb and find that Jesus is not there – sharing their sense of confusion, anger and sorrow as they do not know what to do before feeling their joy as they realize that Jesus has risen.

   As these desires fill your consciousness, let all other concerns fall aside as you focus on this time and place of prayer.

[4]   Allow the image of the empty tomb to reemerge in your imagination.

• Watch as the women approach the tomb. Listen to the sounds of this moment and become comfortable as you prepare to hear Jesus speak. Feel the women's sorrow and share in their sadness.

• Ask God to help you share in this moment – either by joining it or by listening quietly to it.

• Then, watch and listen as the women approach and enter the tomb. You may want to quietly read the passage while remaining prayerfully aware of your mental image of Jesus or you may choose to stay completely within the imagined realm of your prayer. Whichever you choose, know that God will offer you the words from the biblical passage that you need to hear – even if only in fragments.

– Notice the different dispositions of the women as they enter the tomb and meet the strange young man as well as how they behave toward the young man and one another.

– Become are of your own feelings of confusion and joy as you pray at the empty tomb.

• Afterward, allow these images to fade from your imagination as you become aware of the phrases and images from this moment which touched you most deeply. Recall the emotions and memories – including any sounds or smells – evoked during your prayer. Allow these seminal aspects of your meditation to linger on your mind and in your heart, noting any special feelings evoked by them.

5] When you are ready, become aware of the risen Jesus' presence with you in this moment and have an open and informal conversation about this prayer period and how the passage from Mark's gospel expresses your own needs or desires – giving space for Jesus to respond or to highlight different aspects from the biblical account and your experiences during this contemplation. Then, gradually allow your thoughts to recede as you focus on the risen Jesus' continuing presence in your life and in the world around you.

[6] Then, conclude by allowing these desires to fade from your consciousness as you offer this traditional Irish prayer:

> Confirm me in your love divine,
> Smooth for my feet life's rugged way;
> My will with yours entwine,
> Lest evil lead my steps astray.
> Be with my still as guard and guide,
> Keep me in holy sanctity,
> Let my firm faith on you abide,
> From fraud and error hold me free. Amen.

[7]   Afterward, take 10-15 minutes in a quiet space to reflect on the most significant moments from this time of prayer and record your reflections in your journal.

6.4   A Contemplation of John 20:1-18

In this contemplation of John 20:1-18, you will see and hear the risen Jesus appear to Mary Magdalene.

[1]   Begin by reading the biblical selection and reviewing your notes on it.

[2]   Then, focus on this specific time and place as you allow all other concerns to fall away before considering the people and place of this moment of prayer.

• Allow an image of the risen Jesus to emerge in your imagination, noting any changes in his physical characteristics and mannerisms. Look at what he is wearing or carrying. Ponder this mental image, allowing any other observations about Jesus to form in your mind.

• Then observe the men and women at Jesus' tomb, noting their physical characteristics and mannerisms. Look at Mary Magdalene, Simon Peter and the unnamed disciple. Notice their different demeanor and how they behave toward each other. Ponder this mental image, allowing any other observations about Jesus to form in your imagination.

• Gradually, become aware of the location of this moment of prayer. Observe the tomb, paying attention to its physical characteristics and the arrangement of the people around it. Take a moment to notice more details about it. Become familiar with the location of your upcoming prayer.

• Take a moment to remain in this place with these men and women before allowing these images to fade from your consciousness.

[3]   Become aware of your desires during this moment of prayer. Remember your desire to experience the divine presence all around you and to trust in God's plan for you, asking that you may feel gladness fully and rejoice intensely over the great glory and joy of Christ our Risen Lord. Recall your desire that, in this day or week of prayer, to witness the disciples as they go to the tomb and find that Jesus is not there – sharing their sense of confusion, anger and sorrow as they do not know what to do before feeling their joy as they realize that Jesus has risen.

As these desires fill your consciousness, let all other concerns fall aside as you focus on this time and place of prayer.

[4]   Allow the image of Mary Magdalene at the tomb to reemerge in your imagination.

• Watch as the Mary approaches and enters the tomb before running to Peter and then meeting the risen Jesus. Listen to the sounds of this moment, feeling Mary's sorrow and sharing in her sadness.

• Ask God to help you share in this moment – either by joining it or by listening quietly to it.

• Then, watch and listen as Mary Magdalene approaches and enters the tomb before running find Simon Peter. You may want to quietly read the passage while remaining prayerfully aware of your mental image of Jesus or you may choose to stay completely within the imagined realm of your prayer. Whichever you choose, know that God will offer you the words from the biblical passage that you need to hear – even if only in fragments.

– Notice the different dispositions Mary Magdalene, Simon Peter, and the other disciple as they approach the tomb as well as the different emotions evoked in each of them at the tomb.

– Become are of your own feelings of confusion and joy as you pray at the empty tomb.

• See and hear Mary as Simon Peter and the other disciple leave. Watch her as she approaches the empty tomb and sees the angels. Listen as she speaks with them before turning around to encounter the risen Jesus. Observe their conversation and notice the behavior of Mary and Jesus as they speak – trying to share in Mary's emotions during this moment.

• Afterward, allow these images to fade from your imagination as you become aware of the phrases and images from this moment which touched you most deeply. Recall the emotions and memories – including any sounds or smells – evoked during your prayer. Allow these seminal aspects of your meditation to linger on your mind and in your heart, noting any special feelings evoked by them.

5]   When you are ready, become aware of the risen Jesus' presence with you in this moment and have an open and informal conversation about this prayer period and how the passage from John's gospel expresses your own needs or desires – giving space for Jesus to respond or to highlight different aspects from the biblical account and your experiences during this contemplation. Then, gradually allow your thoughts to recede as you focus on the risen Jesus' continuing presence in your life and in the world around you.

[6]   Then, conclude by allowing these desires to fade from your consciousness as you offer this traditional Irish prayer:

> *Confirm me in your love divine,*
> *Smooth for my feet life's rugged way;*
> *My will with yours entwine,*
> *Lest evil lead my steps astray.*
> *Be with my still as guard and guide,*
> *Keep me in holy sanctity,*
> *Let my firm faith on you abide,*
> *From fraud and error hold me free. Amen.*

[7]   Afterward, take 10-15 minutes in a quiet space to reflect on the most significant moments from this time of prayer and record your reflections in your journal.

In this meditation on 2 Corinthians 5:1-9, you will see and hear Columba preaching on the necessity of trusting God's promises in a Christian life.

[1]   Begin by reading the biblical selection and reviewing your notes on it.

[2]   Then, focus on this specific time and place as you allow all other concerns to fall away before considering the people and place of this moment of prayer.

• Allow an image of Columba to emerge in your imagination, noting his physical characteristics and mannerisms. Look at what he is wearing or carrying. Make a note of whether he is sitting, standing, or walking. Ponder this mental image, allowing any other observations about Columba to form in your mind.

• Note how many men and women are with Columba, making a mental note of their appearance and demeanor. Look at Columba's disciples, observing where they are standing and how they behave toward Columba. Look at the crowd, noting their attitude and behavior toward Columba. Observe whether the people are sitting, standing, or walking. Take a moment to ponder this mental image, allowing other impressions of these men and women to form. Become familiar with the men and women you will encounter during your prayer as well as their behavior.

• Allow yourself to become aware of the location of this moment of prayer. Observe whether it is inside or outside, paying attention to its physical characteristics and the arrangement of the people in it. Look around the place and notice more details about it. Become familiar with the location of your upcoming prayer.

• Take a moment to remain in this place with these men and women before allowing these images to fade from your consciousness.

[3]   Become aware of your desires during this moment of prayer. Remember your desire to experience the divine presence all around you and to trust in God's plan for you, asking that you may feel gladness fully and rejoice intensely over the great glory and joy of Christ our Risen Lord. Recall your desire that, in this day or week of prayer, to witness the disciples as they go to the tomb and find that Jesus is not there – sharing their sense of confusion, anger and sorrow as they do

162

not know what to do before feeling their joy as they realize that Jesus has risen.

As these desires fill your consciousness, let all other concerns fall aside as you focus on this time and place of prayer.

[4]   Allow the image of Saint Columba and the crowd to reemerge in your imagination.

• Watch as the group assembles around Columba, either from a distance or as a participant. Listen to the sounds of this moment and become comfortable as you prepare to hear Columba speak. Feel the anticipation of the people around you and share in that enthusiasm.

• Ask God to help you share in this experience – either by joining these events or by listening quietly to them. Focus your attention on Saint Columba, noting his physical appearance and his demeanor.

• Then, watch and listen as Columba presents the passage from Paul's second letter to the Corinthians. You may want to quietly read the passage while remaining prayerfully aware of your mental image of Columba or you may choose to stay completely within the imagined realm of your prayer. Whichever you choose, know that God will offer you the words from the biblical passage that you need to hear – even if only in fragments.

– Look around as Columba speaks and see the reactions both of his disciples and of the people in the crowd. Become aware of their feelings and how they behave toward Columba and one another.

– Remember that Columba is speaking to men and women struggling with the sometimes-confusing nature of Christian life. Remember that he is speaking to you.

• After Saint Columba finishes speaking, allow this image to fade from your imagination as you become aware of the phrases and images from this moment which touched you most deeply. Recall the emotions and memories – including any sounds or smells – evoked during your prayer. Allow these seminal aspects of your meditation to linger on your mind and in your heart, noting any special feelings evoked by them.

5]   When you are ready, become aware of the risen Jesus' presence with you in this moment and have an open and informal conversation about this prayer period and how the passage from Paul's epistle expresses your own needs or desires – giving space for Jesus to respond or to highlight different aspects from the biblical account and your experiences during this contemplation. Then, gradually allow your thoughts to recede as you focus on the risen Jesus' continuing presence in your life and in the world around you.

[6]   Then, conclude by allowing these desires to fade from your consciousness as you offer this traditional Irish prayer:

> *Confirm me in your love divine,*
> *Smooth for my feet life's rugged way;*
> *My will with yours entwine,*
> *Lest evil lead my steps astray.*
> *Be with my still as guard and guide,*
> *Keep me in holy sanctity,*
> *Let my firm faith on you abide,*
> *From fraud and error hold me free. Amen.*

[7]   Afterward, take 10-15 minutes in a quiet space to reflect on the most significant moments from this time of prayer and record your reflections in your journal.

[1]   Become aware of your prayerful desires during this day or week. Bring to mind your desire to feel gladness fully and rejoice intensely over the great glory and joy of Christ our Risen Lord. Ask also that you may witness the women as they go to the tomb and find that Jesus is not there – sharing their sense of confusion, anger, and sorrow as they do not know what to do before feeling their joy as they recognize the risen Jesus and run to tell others.

[2]   When you are ready, call to mind the various prayers of the preceding day or days. Allow the images and words of these prayers to linger and then slowly fade from your consciousness.

• Remember your contemplation of the first part of The Contemplation to Attain Love from *The Spiritual Exercises of Saint Ignatius* before reviewing it in the same manner as your earlier prayers.

• Recall your imaginative contemplation of Mark 16:1-8. Consider the images and feelings evoked in you during your prayer, feeling God's presence in these memories and becoming aware of the specific sensations associated with each image.

• Review your imaginative contemplation of John 20:1-18 in the same manner as the previous prayers.

• Revisit your meditation on 2 Corinthians 5:1-9 in the same manner as the previous prayers.

Make a mental note of which senses are most active. You may see an image or a color, hear a sound or a phrase, or smell a scent or a fragrance. You may even taste a flavor or feel a sensation on your skin.

[3]   Then, relax and allow these various memories and experiences to quietly enter and leave your consciousness without being controlled. Linger on the sensory images and memories being evoked in you – noticing any images or colors, any sounds or phrases, any scents or fragrances, any flavors or physical sensations associated with each prayer.

[4]   When you are ready, become completely still and clear your mind of all thoughts and concerns. Allow an image of a special personal space to form in your imagination. Then, watch as God enters that place and forms a small image or object for you that expresses the thought or awareness that you most need to carry with you into your life.

Reverently pick up the object or image, a reflection of the most important gift you have been given during this time of prayer. Look at it carefully and become aware of the divine presence contained within it. Take a moment to register what it looks like and how it feels in your hand. Then, feel the joy and confidence that comes from touching the presence of God as you accept this gift, offering a short prayer of gratitude while you relax into the pleasure of this moment.

[5]   Then, conclude by allowing these images to fade from your consciousness as you offer this traditional Irish prayer:

> *Confirm me in your love divine,*
> *Smooth for my feet life's rugged way;*
> *My will with yours entwine,*
> *Lest evil lead my steps astray.*
> *Be with my still as guard and guide,*
> *Keep me in holy sanctity,*
> *Let my firm faith on you abide,*
> *From fraud and error hold me tree. Amen.*

[6]   While your experiences are still fresh in your mind, record the most significant impressions or sensations from this time of prayer in your journal.

[1]   Remember your desires during the preceding day or week of prayer. As you become aware of the divine presence all around you, ask that you may feel gladness fully and rejoice intensely over the great glory and joy of Christ our Risen Lord. Recall your desire to witness the women as they go to the tomb and find that Jesus is not there – sharing their sense of confusion, anger, and sorrow as they do not know what to do before feeling their joy as they recognize the risen Jesus and run to tell others.

Ask God once again to fulfill these desires in your own life and in your interactions with others.

[2]   Then, take a moment to allow the words, thoughts, and feelings from your prayers during the last day or week to linger before asking God to reveal the fulfillment of your deepest desires in these various memories.

• Think about the prayer sequence at the beginning of this day or week. Make a mental note of any words, insights or images that remain particularly significant or meaningful to you.

• Ponder the story, "Columba and the Miracle of the Barley". Note any words, insights, or images from it that remain particularly significant or meaningful to you.

• Remember your contemplation of the first part of "The Contemplation to Attain Love" from The Spiritual Exercises of Saint Ignatius before reviewing it in the same manner as your earlier prayers.

• Recall your imaginative contemplation of Mark 16:1-8.

– Consider the most powerful images, phrases, or feelings from your prayer. Ask yourself what gifts God gave to you through these moments, perhaps offering you new insights or perhaps affirming an important aspect of your faith. Ask yourself how God may be calling you to change through these moments, being as specific as possible.

– Examine your disposition as you prayed, noting whether prayer came easily or with resistance. Recall the easiest moments in your prayer and any moments of joy you may have experienced. Remember also if you encountered any difficulty opening yourself to God or if you felt any sadness as you prayed. Ask God to help you understand why these feelings surfaced.

– Bring to mind any moments when you added personal elements (e.g., familiar places or people from your life) or connected your prayers to other scriptures or spiritual writings. Ask yourself how these additions helped or hindered you as you prayed. Again, if you do not know why this happened, ask God to help you understand.

• Review your imaginative contemplation of John 20:1-18 in the same manner as the previous prayers.

• Revisit your meditation on 2 Corinthians 5:1-9 in the same manner as the previous prayers.

• Reflect on the ebb and flow of sensory impressions and feelings that marked your application of the senses. Isolate the most memorable moments and sensory impressions from your prayer and reflect on how God used these moments to give you a particular gift.

[3]   Finally, ponder the times when images or feelings from the readings of this day or week surfaced outside these prayer periods. Consider those moments or events in which God's presence or guidance was especially strong as well as any moments when you were struggling. Think about the most memorable aspects of these experiences, asking God to explain their significance.

[4]   Take a moment to allow the words, thoughts, and feelings of these prayers to linger on your mind and in your heart. Finally, conclude by allowing these desires to fade from your consciousness as you offer this traditional Irish prayer:

> *O God, I believe in you; strengthen my belief.*
> *I trust in you; confirm my trust.*
> *I love you; double my love.*
> *I repent that I angered you,*
> *Increase my repentance.*
> *Fill you my heart with awe without despair;*
> *With hope, without over-confidence;*
> *With piety without infatuation;*
> *And with joy without excess.*
> *My God, consent to guide me by your wisdom;*
> *To constrain me by your right;*
> *To comfort me by your mercy;*
> *And to protect me by your power. Amen.*

[5]   After finishing these prayers, summarize your reflections on the gifts or graces you received during the prayers of this last day or week and record these thoughts in your journal.

7. The Early Appearances of the Risen Jesus

7.1a   Most Clement Jesus, Tender King

a prayer of praise for Jesus' redemption of humanity

Take a moment to quiet your spirit, becoming completely present to this time and place. Allow all other thoughts and concerns to fall away as you come into the presence of God. Then, when you are ready, begin.

Most clement Jesus, tender King,
Possess our souls that, all aglow,
> The tongue may fitly say and sing
> The love that unto you I owe.

Be with me evermore, O Lord,
And let your resurrection be
> My paschal joy; from crimes abhorred,
> In loving mercy make me free.

A Hymn, sung or heard (optional)

By death on the cross was the race restored,
For vain was our endeavour;
> Henceforward blessed, O blessed Lord,
> Be the Sign of the Cross for ever.

Rent were the rocks, tho sun did fade,
The darkening world did quiver,
> When on the tree our Saviour made
> The Sign of the Cross for ever.

Therefore I mourn for him whose heart
Shall neither shrink nor shiver,
> Whose tears of sorrow refuse to start
> At the Sign of the Cross for ever.

Swiftly we pass to the unknown land,
Down like an ebbing river,
> But the devils themselves cannot withstand
> The Sign of the Cross for ever.

When the hour shall come that shall make us dust,
When the soul and the body sever,
>Fearful the fear if we may not trust
>On the Sign of the Cross for ever.

Read or recite Psalm 62.

Holy Lord,
Under my thoughts may I God-thoughts find.
Half of my sins escape my mind.
>For what I said, or did not say,
>Pardon me, O Lord, I pray.

Read Luke 24: 13-35, aloud or quietly.

O Lord, Jesus the Christ,
If I were in Heaven my harp I would sound
With apostles and angels and saints all around,
>Praising and thanking the Son who is crowned,
>May the poor race of Eve for that heaven be bound!

O Christ, the King of love and might,
You have conquered death and broke the tomb;
>You lead me forth to heavenly light –
>My soul that long has pined in gloom.

Your holy grave, a guard defended
And at the door they placed a stone,
>The guarded tomb the you <u>rended</u>,
>And death and doom are overthrown.

O Holy Lord,
>God with the Father and the Spirit,
For me is many a snare designed,
To fill my mind with doubts and fears;
>Far from the land of holy saints,
>I dwell within my vale of tears.
Let faith, let hope, let love –
Traits far above the cold world's way –
>With patience, humility, and awe,

171

Become my guides from day to day.

I acknowledge, the evil I have done.
From the day of my birth till the day of my death,
    Through the sight of my eyes,
Through the hearing of my ears,
    Through the sayings of my mouth,
Through the thoughts of my heart,
    Through the touch of my hands,
Through the course of my way,
    Through all I said and did not,
Through all I promised and fulfilled not,
    Through all the laws and holy commandments I broke.
I ask even now absolution of you,
    For fear I may have never asked it as was right,
    And that I might not live to ask it again,

O Holy Lord, my King in Heaven,
May you not let my soul stray from you,
May you keep me in a good state,
    May you turn me toward what is good to do,
    May you protect me from dangers, small and great.
May you fill my eyes with tears of repentance,
    So I may avoid the sinner's awful sentence.
May the Grace of the God for ever be with me,
    And whatever my needs, may the Triune God give me.

Select one of the following options for the Lord's Prayer.

Option A

O Jesus Christ,
Lord of heaven and earth,
Help me pray as you yourself taught:
    "Our Father in heaven,
    hallowed be your name.
    Your kingdom come.
    Your will be done,
    on earth as it is in heaven.
    Give us this day our daily bread.

And forgive us our debts,
as we also have forgiven our debtors.
And do not bring us to the time of trial,
but rescue us from the evil one."
(Matthew 6: 9-13)
From the foes of my land,
from the foes of my faith,
From the foes who would us dissever,
 O Lord, preserve me, in life and in death,
 With the Sign of the Cross for ever.
 For the kingdom, the power, and the glory
 are yours now and for ever. Amen.

Please proceed with "I beseech you, O Lord...," found after Option B.

Option B

O Jesus Christ,
Lord of heaven and earth,
Help me pray as you yourself taught:
 Our Father in heaven,
 hallowed be your name,
 your kingdom come,
 your will be done,
 on earth as in heaven.
 Give us today our daily bread.
 Forgive us our sins
 as we forgive those who sin against us.
 Lead us not into temptation
 but deliver us from evil.
From the foes of my land,
from the foes of my faith,
From the foes who would us dissever,
 O Lord, preserve me, in life and in death,
 With the Sign of the Cross for ever.
 For the kingdom, the power, and the glory
 are yours now and for ever. Amen.

I beseech you, O Lord.

God in Heaven, unsurpassed in power and might;
      Be behind me, Be on my left,
      Be before me, Be on my right!
Against each danger, you are my help;
In distress, upon you I call.
      In dark times, may you sustain me
      And lift me up again when I fall.
Lord over heaven and of earth,
You know my offenses.
      Yet, listening to my pleadings,
      You guide me away from sinful pretenses.
Lord of all creation and the many creatures,
You bestow on me many earthly treasures.
      Revealing love in each life and season,
      You share with me heavenly pleasures.
May you arouse me
In moments both of joy and of strife;
      Most holy Lord, bring me new life!

A Hymn, sung or heard (optional)

O Jesus Christ,
      Lord of heaven and earth,
      You are my riches, my store, my provision,
My star through the years
When troubles rend me,
      Through times of strife and tears,
      Sweet Jesus, defend me.

By the cruel mob surrounded
Scourged, and crowned with thorns and wounded,
Faint with agonizing pain;
      Bowed beneath your cross, forsaken,
      Jeered and scorned, I see you taken
      To the mount where you are slain.

Gentle Jesus, my Salvation!
You have wrought sweet reparation
To the world for pain and loss;
      Made yourself our bulwark, shielding

Man from misery by yielding
Thy pure life upon the cross.

End this time of prayer by taking some time to bring to mind the various ways God shields you from harm or guides you through the world's tumult. Then, when you are ready, conclude by saying:

O Holy Lord, King in Heaven,
I place myself at the edge of your grace,
    On the floor of your house myself I place,
And to banish the sin of my heart away,
    I lower my knee to you this day.
Through life's torrents of pain may you bring me whole,
    And, O Lord Jesus Christ, preserve also my soul. Amen.

Consideration of the Readings

After reciting or prayerfully reading the prayer sequence for this day or week:

• Read #230-233 and #235 in "The Contemplation to Attain Love" from *The Spiritual Exercises of Saint Ignatius* (found on page 298), allowing yourself to linger on any thoughts or phrases that seem particularly meaningful to you or especially relevant to your life. Then, record these highlights in your workbook.

• Read about the risen Jesus' appearance at Emmaus in Luke 24:13 35, noting each person's appearance and actions during the episode as well as the key elements of the story and its setting. Then, record any aspects of this story that speak strongly to you.

• Read about the risen Jesus' appearances to his disciples in John 20:19-29, noting Jesus' appearance and actions during these episodes, the people listening to him, and the key elements of Jesus' message. Then, consider any aspects of this story that speak strongly to you before recording these observations in your workbook.

• Read Hebrews 11:1-3. Again, pay careful attention to any phrases or images that seem particularly meaningful to you. Then, record these highlights in your workbook.

Note: You also should consider any aspect of the prayer sequence from this day or week that seemed particularly significant to you.

Contemplation of Your Needs

When you are ready, allow any distractions to fade from your consciousness as you become aware of your desire to live in God's goodness. Feel yourself yearning to properly use the many gifts God has given you, to experience God's continuing care, and to be open to the immense love God shows for you, then:

• Read "Columba Arrives at Hy (Iona)" (found on page 303). Allow yourself to linger on any thoughts, phrases or images that seem particularly meaningful or significant to your earlier preparations or prayer.

• Pray for your desires in the coming day or week. Ask that the divine presence all around you may be revealed, so you may feel gladness fully and rejoice intensely over the great glory and joy of Christ our Risen Lord. Ask also that you may share completely in the experience of the various disciples who encounter the risen Jesus after the resurrection.

• Conclude by praying for a deeply felt awareness of God's love as you consider the second point of The Contemplation to Attain Love, giving thanks for the actions of God in this new world of love and offering yourself in service and love.

Then, record any significant thoughts, emotions, or reactions from these moments in your workbook.

After this, put your notes aside. Without straining your memory, consider in turn each of the readings for the coming day or week and allow them to take shape in your imagination. Prayerfully ponder how each reading affects you emotionally without overtly thinking about their content, asking God to illuminate the spiritual gifts offered in each reading.

Finally, conclude by offering this prayer:

O God, I believe in you; strengthen my belief.
I trust in you; confirm my trust.
I love you; double my love.
I repent that I angered you,
Increase my repentance.
Fill you my heart with awe without despair;
With hope, without over-confidence;
With piety without infatuation;
And with joy without excess.
My God, consent to guide me by your wisdom;
To constrain me by your right;
To comfort me by your mercy;
And to protect me by your power. Amen.

Allow these words to linger on your mind and in your heart for a few moments and then write the most important thoughts, feelings, and desires in your journal.

In this meditation on the second point in "The Contemplation to Attain Love" presented in *The Spiritual Exercises of Saint Ignatius*, you will ponder the ways in which the Divine Majesty resides in and sustains all creation, including you, before reflecting on how you should respond to this beneficence.

[1]   Begin by reading the preliminary considerations and first point of "The Contemplation to Attain Love" (#230-233 and #235) in *The Spiritual Exercises of Saint Ignatius* (found on page 298) and reviewing your notes on it.

[2]   Then, focus on this specific time and place as you allow all other concerns to fall away. As you become still, become aware of your desires during this moment of prayer. Remember your desire to experience the divine presence all around you and to trust in God's plan for you, asking that you may feel gladness fully and rejoice intensely over the great glory and joy of Christ our Risen Lord.

Recall your desire that, in this day or week of prayer, to share completely in the experience of the various disciples who encounter the risen Jesus after the resurrection. Finally, ask for a deeply felt awareness of God's love as you consider the second point of The Contemplation to Attain Love, giving thanks for the actions of God in this new world of love and offering yourself in service and love.

As these desires fill your consciousness, let all other concerns fall aside as you focus on this specific time and place of prayer.

[3]   Then, slowly and deliberately, re-read the "The Contemplation to Attain Love".

• As you read, take time to stop and ponder each statement within it as you read. When you pause, allow images shaped by the words and thoughts of the passages to form in your imagination. See and hear the way each statement expresses a need or desire in your life.

• Take more time with words that seem particularly significant or meaning to you. Become aware of the sections from the "The Contemplation to Attain Love" which you accept easily and any of those which cause you difficulty. Clarify these thoughts and feeling as much as possible while remaining focused on each specific statement within this meditation.

• After finishing the reading, allow the various words and images of your prayer to flow freely in your consciousness without being controlled. Become aware of those aspects of the "The Contemplation to Attain Love" that arouse holy desires in you, toward God and toward others (including nonhuman creatures). Become aware of those aspects of the reading that make you feel shame for those times you fall short of these holy aspirations.

• When you are ready, become aware of God's presence – again, experienced in your imagination either as a single entity or as the Holy Trinity – with you in this moment and have an open and informal conversation about your experience of the "The Contemplation to Attain Love". Speak about how it expresses your own desires and fears, giving space for the God to explain the love that motivates the divine actions presented in this meditation.

• Then, gradually allow your thoughts to recede as you focus on God's broader presence in your life and in the world around you.

[4]   Conclude by offering this prayer presented by Saint Ignatius in his *Spiritual Exercises*:

Receive, Lord, my whole liberty.
Accept my memory, understanding, and whole will.
Whatsoever I have, or possess, you have given me:
this all I restore to you, and to your will altogether
deliver up to be governed.
Give me only the love of you,
with your grace, and I am rich enough,
and desire nothing else beyond. Amen.

[5]   Afterward, take 10-15 minutes in a quiet space to reflect on the most significant moments from your prayer and record your reflections in your journal.

In this contemplation of Luke 24:13-35, you will see and hear the risen Jesus Christ appear to two disciples at Emmaus.

[1] Begin by reading the biblical selection and reviewing your notes on it.

[2] Then, focus on this specific time and place as you allow all other concerns to fall away before considering the people and place of this moment of prayer.

• Allow an image of Jesus to emerge in your imagination, noting any changes in his physical characteristics and demeanor. Look at what he is wearing or carrying, observing his clothing and any objects he is holding. Make a note of whether he is sitting, standing, or walking. Ponder this mental image, allowing any other observations about Jesus to form in your mind.

• Then, observe the two traveling disciples, observing what they are doing and how they behave toward Jesus. Notice the various men and women at the tavern in Emmaus, making a mental note about their different appearances and mannerisms. Take a moment to ponder this mental image, allowing other impressions of these people to form. Become familiar with the men and women you will encounter during your prayer as well as their behavior.

• Gradually, become aware of the location of this moment of prayer. Pay attention to its physical characteristics and the arrangement of the people in it. As you ponder this mental image, look around the place and notice more details about it. Become familiar with the location of your upcoming prayer.

• Take a moment to remain in this place with these men and women, then allow these images to fade from your consciousness.

[3] After you become still, become aware of your desires during this moment of prayer. Remember your desire to experience the divine presence all around you and to trust in God's plan for you, asking that you may feel gladness fully and rejoice intensely over the great glory and joy of Christ our Risen Lord. Recall your desire that, in this day or week of prayer, to share completely in the experience of the various disciples who encounter the risen Jesus after the resurrection.

As these desires fill your consciousness, let all other concerns fall aside as you focus on this specific time and place of prayer.

[4]   Again, when you are ready, allow the image of Jesus and his disciples to reemerge in your imagination.

• Watch as the risen Jesus approaches the two disciples on the road. Listen to the sounds of this moment. Feel the sadness of the two disciples and share in their sorrow.

• Ask God to help you share in their experience – either by joining them or by listening quietly to them. Focus your attention on Jesus, noting his physical appearance and his emotional demeanor.

• Then, watch and listen as Jesus approaches to the disciples and see their response as he joins them and begins speaking. You may want to quietly read the passage while remaining prayerfully aware of your mental image of Jesus or you may choose to stay completely within the imagined realm of your prayer. Whichever you choose, know that God will offer you the words from the biblical passage that you need to hear – even if only in fragments.

– Look around as Jesus speaks, see the reactions of both disciples and their eagerness to hear more from this stranger. Become aware of their feelings and how they behave toward Jesus and one another, both before and after Jesus reveals himself to them.

– Remember that Jesus also is speaking to you.

• Afterward, allow this image to fade from your imagination as you become aware of the phrases and images from this moment which touched you most deeply. Recall the emotions and memories evoked during your prayer. Allow these seminal aspects of your meditation to linger on your mind and in your heart, noting any special feelings evoked by them.

[5]   When you are ready, become aware of the risen Jesus' presence with you in this moment and have an open and informal conversation about this prayer period and how the passage from Luke's gospel expresses your own needs or desires – giving space for Jesus to respond or to highlight different aspects from the biblical account and your experiences during this contemplation. Then, gradually allow your thoughts to recede as you focus on the risen Jesus' continuing presence in your life and in the world around you.

[6]   Then, conclude by offering this prayer:

> Confirm me in your love divine,
> Smooth for my feet life's rugged way;
> My will with yours entwine,
> Lest evil lead my steps astray.
> Be with my still as guard and guide,

Keep me in holy sanctity,
Let my firm faith on you abide,
From fraud and error hold me free. Amen.

[7]   Afterward, take 10-15 minutes in a quiet space to reflect on the most significant moments from your prayer and record your reflections in your journal.

In this contemplation of John 20:19-29, you will see and hear the risen Jesus Christ appear to his disciples in the locked room.

[1]   Begin by reading the biblical selection and reviewing your notes on it.

[2]   Then, focus on this specific time and place as you allow all other concerns to fall away before considering the people and place of this moment of prayer.

• Allow an image of Jesus to emerge in your imagination. Look at what he is wearing or carrying, observing his clothing and any objects he is holding. Make a note of whether he is sitting, standing, or walking. Ponder this mental image, allowing any other observations about Jesus to form in your mind.

• Then, observe the various men and women gathered in the locked house, observing what they are doing and how they behave toward Jesus. Look at Thomas, making a mental note about his different appearances and mannerisms. Take a moment to ponder this mental image, allowing other impressions of these men and women to form. Become familiar with the men and women you will encounter during your prayer as well as their behavior.

• Gradually, become aware of the location of this moment of prayer. Pay attention to its physical characteristics and the arrangement of the people in it. As you ponder this mental image, look around the place and notice more details about it. Become familiar with the location of your upcoming prayer.

• Take a moment to remain in this place with these men and women, then allow these images to fade from your consciousness.

[3]   After you become still, become aware of your desires during this moment of prayer. Remember your desire to experience the divine presence all around you and to trust in God's plan for you, asking that you may feel gladness fully and rejoice intensely over the great glory and joy of Christ our Risen Lord. Recall your desire that, in this day or week of prayer, to share completely in the experience of the various disciples who encounter the risen Jesus after the resurrection.

As these desires fill your consciousness, let all other concerns fall aside as you focus on this specific time and place of prayer.

[4]   Again, when you are ready, allow the image of Jesus and his disciples to reemerge in your imagination.

• Watch as the risen Jesus enters. Listen to the sounds of this moment. Feel the many different emotions evoked among the disciples by Jesus' appearance and share in these feelings.

• Ask God to help you enter this moment – either by joining these events or by listening quietly to them. Focus your attention on Jesus, noting his physical appearance and his emotional demeanor.

• Then, watch and listen as Jesus approaches to the disciples and begins speaking. You may want to quietly read the passage while remaining prayerfully aware of your mental image of Jesus or you may choose to stay completely within the imagined realm of your prayer. Whichever you choose, know that God will offer you the words from the biblical passage that you need to hear – even if only in fragments.

– Become aware of the reactions of the disciples and notice how their behavior changes after Jesus reveals himself to them.

– Observe Thomas' stubbornness before Jesus' second visit – and the other disciples' reaction to his intransigence –and how his attitude changes when he meets the risen Jesus.

– Remember that the risen Jesus continues to reveal himself to you.

• Afterward, allow this image to fade from your imagination as you become aware of the phrases and images from this moment which touched you most deeply. Recall the emotions and memories evoked during your prayer. Allow these seminal aspects of your meditation to linger on your mind and in your heart, noting any special feelings evoked by them.

[5]	When you are ready, become aware of the risen Jesus' presence with you in this moment and have an open and informal conversation about this prayer period and how the passage from John's gospel expresses your own needs or desires – giving space for Jesus to respond or to highlight different aspects from the biblical account and your experiences during this contemplation. Then, gradually allow your thoughts to recede as you focus on the risen Jesus' continuing presence in your life and in the world around you.

[6]	Then, conclude by offering this prayer:

Confirm me in your love divine,
Smooth for my feet life's rugged way;
My will with yours entwine,
Lest evil lead my steps astray.
Be with my still as guard and guide,
Keep me in holy sanctity,

184

Let my firm faith on you abide,
From fraud and error hold me free. Amen.

[7]   Afterward, take 10-15 minutes in a quiet space to reflect on the most significant moments from your prayer and record your reflections in your journal.

In this mediation on Hebrews 11:1-3, you will see and hear Columba preach on the nature of faith while discussing the risen Jesus' appearance to Thomas.

[1]   Begin by reading the biblical selection and reviewing your notes on it.

[2]   Then, focus on this specific time and place as you allow all other concerns to fall away before considering the people and place of this moment of prayer.

• Allow an image of Columba to emerge in your imagination, noting his physical characteristics and mannerisms. Look at what he is wearing or carrying. Make a note of whether he is sitting, standing, or walking. Ponder this mental image, allowing any other observations about Columba to form in your mind.

• Note how many men and women are with Columba, making a mental note of their appearance and demeanor. Look at Columba's disciples, observing where they are standing and how they behave toward Columba. Look at the crowd, noting their attitude and behavior toward Columba. Observe whether the people are sitting, standing, or walking. Take a moment to ponder this mental image, allowing other impressions of these people to form. Become familiar with the men and women you will encounter during your prayer as well as their behavior.

• Allow yourself to become aware of the location of this moment of prayer. Observe whether it is inside or outside, paying attention to its physical characteristics and the arrangement of the people in it. Look around the place and notice more details about it – if it in dim or bright light, if it is still and silent or filled with noise, if it has an unusual smell or not, etc. Become familiar with the location of your upcoming prayer.

• Take a moment to remain in this place with these men and women before allowing these images to fade from your consciousness.

[3]   After you become still, become aware of your desires during this moment of prayer. Remember your desire to experience the divine presence all around you and to trust in God's plan for you, asking that you may feel gladness fully and rejoice intensely over the great glory and joy of Christ our Risen Lord. Recall your desire that, in this day or week of prayer, to share completely in the experience of the various disciples who encounter the risen Jesus after the resurrection.

As these desires fill your consciousness, let all other concerns fall aside as you focus on this time and place of prayer.

[4]   Allow the image of Saint Columba and the crowd to reemerge in your imagination.

• Watch as the group assembles around Columba, either from a distance or as a participant. Listen to the sounds of this moment and become comfortable as you prepare to hear Columba speak. Feel the anticipation of the people around you and share in that enthusiasm.

• Ask God to help you share in this moment – either by joining it or by listening quietly to it. Focus your attention on Saint Columba, noting his physical appearance and his demeanor.

• Then, relying on your earlier prayers, watch and listen as Columba tells the story of before discussing the passage from Paul's letter to the Hebrews. You may want to quietly read the passage while remaining prayerfully aware of your mental image of Columba or you may choose to stay completely within the imagined realm of your prayer. Whichever you choose, know that God will offer you the words from the biblical passage that you need to hear – even if only in fragments.

– Look around as Columba speaks and see the reactions both of his disciples and of the people in the crowd. Become aware of their feelings and how they behave toward Columba and one another.

– Remember that Columba is speaking to men and women struggling with their faith. Remember that he is speaking to you.

• After Saint Columba finishes speaking, allow this image to fade from your imagination as you become aware of the phrases and images from this moment which touched you most deeply. Recall the emotions and memories – including any sounds or smells – evoked during your prayer. Allow these seminal aspects of your meditation to linger on your mind and in your heart, noting any special feelings evoked by them.

[5]   When you are ready, become aware of the risen Jesus' presence with you in this moment and have an open and informal conversation about this prayer period and how the passage from the epistle to the Hebrews expresses your own needs or desires – giving space for Jesus to respond or to highlight different aspects from the biblical account and your experiences during this contemplation. Then, gradually allow your thoughts to recede as you focus on the risen Jesus' continuing presence in your life and in the world around you.

[6]   Then, conclude by offering this prayer:

Confirm me in your love divine,
Smooth for my feet life's rugged way;
My will with yours entwine,
Lest evil lead my steps astray.
Be with my still as guard and guide,
Keep me in holy sanctity,
Let my firm faith on you abide,
From fraud and error hold me free. Amen.

[7]   Afterward, take 10-15 minutes in a quiet space to reflect on the most significant moments from this time of prayer and record your reflections in your journal.

7.6   An Application of the Senses

[1]   Become aware of your prayerful desires during this day or week. Bring to mind your desire to feel gladness fully and rejoice intensely over the great glory and joy of Christ our Risen Lord. Ask also that you may share completely in the experience of the various disciples who encounter the risen Jesus after the resurrection.

[2]   Call to mind the various prayers of the preceding day or days. Allow the images and words of these prayers to linger and then slowly fade from your consciousness.

• Remember your contemplation of the second part of The Contemplation to Attain Love from *The Spiritual Exercises of Saint Ignatius* before reviewing it in the same manner as your earlier prayers.

• Recall your imaginative contemplation of Luke 24:13-35. Consider the images and feelings evoked in you during your prayer, feeling God's presence in these memories and becoming aware of the specific sensations associated with each image.

• Review your imaginative contemplation of John 20:19-29, considering it in the same way as your earlier memories of Luke 24.

• Revisit your meditation on Hebrews 11:1-3 in the same manner as the previous prayers.

Make a mental note of which senses are most active. You may see an image or a color, hear a sound or a phrase, or smell a scent or a fragrance. You may even taste a flavor or feel a sensation on your skin.

[3]   Then, relax and allow these various memories and experiences to quietly enter and leave your consciousness. Linger on the sensory images and memories being evoked in you – noticing any images or colors, any sounds or phrases, any scents or fragrances, any flavors or physical sensations associated with each prayer.

[4]   When you are ready, become completely still and clear your mind of all thoughts and concerns. Allow an image of a special personal space to form in your imagination. Then, watch as God enters that place and forms a small image or object for you that expresses the thought or awareness that you most need to carry with you into your life.

Reverently pick up the object or image, a reflection of the most important gift you have been given during this time of prayer. Look at it carefully and become aware of the divine presence contained within it. Register what it looks like and how it feels in your hand. Then, feel the joy and confidence that comes from touching the presence of God as you accept this gift, offering a short prayer of gratitude while you relax into the pleasure of this moment.

[5]   Then, conclude by offering this prayer:

> *Confirm me in your love divine,*
> *Smooth for my feet life's rugged way;*
> *My will with yours entwine,*
> *Lest evil lead my steps astray.*
> *Be with my still as guard and guide,*
> *Keep me in holy sanctity,*
> *Let my firm faith on you abide,*
> *From fraud and error hold me free. Amen.*

[6]   While your experiences are still fresh in your mind, record the most significant impressions or sensations from this time of prayer in your journal.

[1]   Remember your desires during the preceding day or week of prayer. Become aware of the divine presence all around you, offering you inner knowledge of Jesus Christ who became human for you so you may better love and follow him. Recall your desire to share completely in the experience of the various disciples who encounter the risen Jesus after the resurrection.

Ask God once again to fulfill these desires in your own life and in your interactions with others.

[2]   Then, take a moment to allow the words, thoughts, and feelings from your prayers during the last day or week to linger before asking God to reveal the fulfillment of your deepest desires in these various memories.

• Think about the prayer sequence at the beginning of this day or week. Make a mental note of any words, insights or images that remain particularly significant or meaningful to you.

• Ponder the story, "Columba Arrives at Hy (Iona)". Note any words, insights, or images from it that remain particularly significant or meaningful to you.

• Remember your contemplation of the second part of "The Contemplation to Attain Love" from *The Spiritual Exercises of Saint Ignatius* before reviewing it in the same manner as your earlier prayers.

• Recall your imaginative contemplation of Luke 24:13-35.

– Consider the most powerful images, phrases, or feelings from your prayer. Ask yourself what gifts God gave to you through these moments, perhaps offering you new insights or perhaps affirming an important aspect of your faith. Ask yourself how God may be calling you to change through these moments, being as specific as possible.

– Examine your disposition as you prayed. Recall the easiest moments in your prayer and any moments of joy you may have experienced. Remember also if you encountered any difficulty opening yourself to God or if you felt any sadness as you prayed. Ask God to help you understand why these feelings surfaced.

– Bring to mind any moments when you added personal elements (e.g., familiar places or people from your life) or connected your prayers to other scriptures or spiritual writings. Ask yourself how these additions helped or hindered you as you prayed. Again, if you do not know why this happened, ask God to help you understand.

• Review your imaginative contemplation of John 20:19-29. Then, review your prayer in the same way as your earlier reflection on Luke 24.

• Revisit your meditation on Hebrews 11:1-3 in the same manner as the previous prayers.

• Reflect on the ebb and flow of sensory impressions and feelings that marked your application of the senses. Isolate the most memorable moments and sensory impressions from your prayer and reflect on how God used these moments to give you a particular gift.

[3]   Finally, ponder the times when images or feelings from the readings of this day or week surfaced outside these prayer periods. Think about the most memorable aspects of these experiences, asking God to explain their significance.

[4]   Take a moment to allow the words, thoughts, and feelings of these prayers to linger on your mind and in your heart. Finally, conclude by offering this prayer:

O God, I believe in you; strengthen my belief.
I trust in you; confirm my trust.
I love you; double my love.
I repent that I angered you,
Increase my repentance.
Fill you my heart with awe without despair;
With hope, without over-confidence;
With piety without infatuation;
And with joy without excess.
My God, consent to guide me by your wisdom;
To constrain me by your right;
To comfort me by your mercy;
And to protect me by your power. Amen.

[5]   After finishing these prayers, summarize your reflections on the gifts or graces you received during the prayers of this last day or week and record these thoughts in your journal.

8. The Later Appearances of the Risen Jesus

8.1a Eternal Builder Of The Skies

a petition for the Risen Jesus' continuing presence

Take a moment to quiet your spirit, becoming completely present to this time and place. Allow all other thoughts and concerns to fall away as you come into the presence of God. Then, when you are ready, begin.

Eternal builder of the skies,
Dread ruler of the night and day.
　　With glories you have blessed my eyes.
　　To drive the stain of pride away.

To those that seem in gloom forlorn
you are a light; your scattered fold
　　Now hear the herald of the morn,
　　The splendour of its rays behold.

A Hymn, sung or heard (optional)

Christ, the light that shines eternal,
Light that gilds the rolling spheres,
　　Dawn upon our night, and keep us
　　Pure as light when day appears.

Let no tricks of Satan snare us,
Let no enemy oppress;
　　Wakeful aye with garments spotless,
　　May we walk life's wilderness.

Keep our hearts in your safe-keeping,
Be your flock your special care;
　　In your fold in mercy tend them,
　　Guard their footsteps everywhere.

Impart a noble life, and may
Our spirit's warmth be heightened.
　　Bid night depart, and with your love,
　　O may our lives be brightened.

And our souls shall sing triumphant
When our eyes shall see your light,
       And with you in heavenly pleasures,
       O great Triune God, we delight.

Read or recite Psalm 30.

Holy Lord,
Under my thoughts may I God-thoughts find.
Half of my sins escape my mind.
       For what I said, or did not say,
       Pardon me, O Lord, I pray.

Read John 21: 1-14, aloud or quietly.

O Lord, Jesus the Christ,
If I were in Heaven my harp I would sound
With apostles and angels and saints all around,
       Praising and thanking the Son who is crowned,
       May the poor race of Eve for that heaven be bound!

Holy Lord,
May you restrain from words of sin;
For bitter strife give calm within;
       Veil from my eyes the garish light,
       That lures the soul to darkest night.

Pure may my inmost heart remain
From evil thoughts and fancies vain;
       And may I curb my flesh control,
       That drags to earth the aspiring soul.

O Holy Lord,
       God with the Father and the Spirit,
For me is many a snare designed,
To fill my mind with doubts and fears;
       Far from the land of holy saints,
       I dwell within my vale of tears.
Let faith, let hope, let love –
Traits far above the cold world's way –

With patience, humility, and awe,
Become my guides from day to day.

I acknowledge, the evil I have done.
From the day of my birth till the day of my death,
    Through the sight of my eyes,
Through the hearing of my ears,
    Through the sayings of my mouth,
Through the thoughts of my heart,
    Through the touch of my hands,
Through the course of my way,
    Through all I said and did not,
Through all I promised and fulfilled not,
    Through all the laws and holy commandments I broke.
I ask even now absolution of you,
    For fear I may have never asked it as was right,
    And that I might not live to ask it again,

O Holy Lord, my King in Heaven,
May you not let my soul stray from you,
May you keep me in a good state,
    May you turn me toward what is good to do,
    May you protect me from dangers, small and great.
May you fill my eyes with tears of repentance,
    So I may avoid the sinner's awful sentence.
May the Grace of the God for ever be with me,
    And whatever my needs, may the Triune God give me.

Select one of the following options for the Lord's Prayer.

Option A

O Jesus Christ,
Lord of heaven and earth,
Help me pray as you yourself taught:
    "Our Father in heaven,
    hallowed be your name.
    Your kingdom come.
    Your will be done,
    on earth as it is in heaven.

Give us this day our daily bread.
And forgive us our debts,
as we also have forgiven our debtors.
And do not bring us to the time of trial,
but rescue us from the evil one."
(Matthew 6: 9-13)
From the foes of my land,
from the foes of my faith,
From the foes who would us dissever,
    O Lord, preserve me, in life and in death,
    With the Sign of the Cross for ever.
    For the kingdom, the power, and the glory
    are yours now and for ever. Amen.

Please proceed with "I beseech you, O Lord...," found after Option B.

Option B

O Jesus Christ,
Lord of heaven and earth,
Help me pray as you yourself taught:
    Our Father in heaven,
    hallowed be your name,
    your kingdom come,
    your will be done,
    on earth as in heaven.
    Give us today our daily bread.
    Forgive us our sins
    as we forgive those who sin against us.
    Lead us not into temptation
    but deliver us from evil.
From the foes of my land,
from the foes of my faith,
From the foes who would us dissever,
    O Lord, preserve me, in life and in death,
    With the Sign of the Cross for ever.
    For the kingdom, the power, and the glory
    are yours now and for ever. Amen.

I beseech you, O Lord.
God in Heaven, unsurpassed in power and might;
      Be behind me, Be on my left,
      Be before me, Be on my right!
Against each danger, you are my help;
In distress, upon you I call.
      In dark times, may you sustain me
      And lift me up again when I fall.
Lord over heaven and of earth,
You know my offenses.
      Yet, listening to my pleadings,
      You guide me away from sinful pretenses.
Lord of all creation and the many creatures,
You bestow on me many earthly treasures.
      Revealing love in each life and season,
      You share with me heavenly pleasures.
May you arouse me
In moments both of joy and of strife;
      Most holy Lord, bring me new life!

A Hymn, sung or heard (optional)

O Jesus Christ,
      Lord of heaven and earth,
      You are my riches, my store, my provision,
My star through the years
When troubles rend me,
      Through times of strife and tears,
      Sweet Jesus, defend me.

Behold the golden light appears,
The blinding shadows pass away,
      That filled our souls with shuddering fears,
      And led our feeble feet astray.

Your gaze, O Lord, is on my way,
You walk a guardian by my side,
      You see my every act each day
      From earliest dawn to eventide.

End this time of prayer by taking some time to bring to mind the various ways God shields you from harm or guides you through the world's tumult. Then, when you are ready, conclude by saying:

O Holy Lord, King in Heaven,
I place myself at the edge of your grace,
     On the floor of your house myself I place,
And to banish the sin of my heart away,
     I lower my knee to you this day.
Through life's torrents of pain may you bring me whole,
    And, O Lord Jesus Christ, preserve also my soul. Amen.

Consideration of the Readings

After reciting or prayerfully reading the prayer sequence for this day or week:

• Read #230-233 and #236 in "The Contemplation to Attain Love" from *The Spiritual Exercises of Saint Ignatius* (found on page 298), allowing yourself to linger on any thoughts or phrases that seem particularly meaningful to you or especially relevant to your life. Then, record these highlights in your workbook.

• Read about the risen Jesus' other appearances in John 21:1-14 and Matthew 28:16-20, noting Jesus' appearance and actions during these episodes, the people listening to him, and the key elements of Jesus' message. Then, consider any aspects of this story that speak strongly to you before recording these observations in your workbook.

• Read Romans 8:1-17, paying careful attention to any phrases or images that seem particularly meaningful to you. Then, record these highlights in your workbook.

Note: You also should consider any aspect of the prayer sequence from this day or week that seemed particularly significant to you.

Contemplation of Your Needs

When you are ready, allow any distractions to fade from your consciousness as you become aware of your desire to live in God's goodness. Feel yourself yearning to properly use the many gifts God has given you, to experience God's continuing care, and to be open to the immense love God shows for you, then:

• Read "Columba Raises Two People from the Dead" (found on page 304). Allow yourself to linger on any thoughts, phrases or images that seem particularly meaningful or significant to your earlier preparations or prayer.

• Pray for your desires in the coming day or week. Ask that the divine presence all around you may be revealed, so you may feel gladness fully and rejoice intensely over the great glory and joy of Christ our Risen Lord. Ask also that you may have a deep "felt knowledge" of the meaning of the resurrection in the world around you and in your own as you experience the fullness of joy that should come to you with the resurrection of Jesus.

    • Conclude by praying for a deeply felt awareness of God's love as you consider the third point of The Contemplation to Attain Love, giving thanks for the labors of divine love that came to fruition in the resurrection of Jesus and offering yourself in loving service to God. Then, record any significant thoughts, emotions, or reactions from these moments in your workbook.

    After this, put your notes aside. Without straining your memory, consider in turn each of the readings for the coming day or week and allow them to take shape in your imagination. Prayerfully ponder how each reading affects you emotionally without overtly thinking about their content, asking God to illuminate the spiritual gifts offered in each reading.

    Finally, conclude by offering this prayer:
O God, I believe in you; strengthen my belief.
I trust in you; confirm my trust.
I love you; double my love.
I repent that I angered you,
Increase my repentance.
Fill you my heart with awe without despair;
With hope, without over-confidence;
With piety without infatuation;
And with joy without excess.
My God, consent to guide me by your wisdom;
To constrain me by your right;
To comfort me by your mercy;
And to protect me by your power. Amen.
Allow these words to linger on your mind and in your heart for a few moments and then write the most important thoughts, feelings, and desires in your journal.

In this meditation on the third point in "The Contemplation to Attain Love" presented in *The Spiritual Exercises of Saint Ignatius*, you will ponder the ways in which the Divine Majesty labors in all of creation – and in every creature – before reflecting on how you should respond to this beneficence.

[1]   Begin by reading the preliminary considerations and first point of "The Contemplation to Attain Love" (#230-233 and #236) in *The Spiritual Exercises of Saint Ignatius* (found on page 298) and reviewing your notes on it.

[2]   Then, focus on this specific time and place as you allow all other concerns to fall away. As you become still, become aware of your desires during this moment of prayer. Remember your desire to experience the divine presence all around you and to trust in God's plan for you, asking that you may feel gladness fully and rejoice intensely over the great glory and joy of Christ our Risen Lord.

Recall your desire that, in this day or week of prayer, to have a deep "felt knowledge" of the meaning of the resurrection in the world around you and in your own as you experience the fullness of joy that should come to you with the resurrection of Jesus. Finally, ask for a deeply felt awareness of God's love as you consider the third point of The Contemplation to Attain Love, giving thanks for the labors of divine love that came to fruition in the resurrection of Jesus and offering yourself in loving service to God.

As these desires fill your consciousness, let all other concerns fall aside as you focus on this specific time and place of prayer.

[3]   Then, slowly and deliberately, re-read the "The Contemplation to Attain Love".

• As you read, take time to stop and ponder each statement within it as you read. When you pause, allow images shaped by the words and thoughts of the passages to form in your imagination. See and hear the way each statement expresses a need or desire in your life.

• Take more time with words that seem particularly significant or meaning to you. Become aware of the sections from the "The Contemplation to Attain Love" which you accept easily and any of those which cause you difficulty. Clarify these thoughts and feeling as much as possible while remaining focused on each specific statement within this meditation.

• After finishing the reading, allow the various words and images of your prayer to flow freely in your consciousness without being controlled. Become aware of those aspects of the "The Contemplation to Attain Love" that arouse holy desires in you, toward God and toward others (including nonhuman creatures). Become aware of those aspects of the reading that make you feel shame for those times you fall short of these holy aspirations.

• When you are ready, become aware of God's presence – again, experienced either as a single entity or as the Holy Trinity – with you in this moment and have an open and informal conversation about your experience of the "The Contemplation to Attain Love". Speak about how it expresses your own desires and fears, giving space for the God to explain the love that motivates the divine actions presented in this meditation.

• Then, gradually allow your thoughts to recede as you focus on God's broader presence in your life and in the world around you.

[4]   Conclude by offering this prayer presented by Saint Ignatius in his *Spiritual Exercises*:

> *Receive, Lord, my whole liberty.*
> *Accept my memory, understanding, and whole will.*
> *Whatsoever I have, or possess, you have given me:*
> *this all I restore to you, and to your will altogether*
> *deliver up to be governed.*
> *Give me only the love of you,*
> *with your grace, and I am rich enough,*
> *and desire nothing else beyond. Amen.*

[5]   Afterward, take 10-15 minutes in a quiet space to reflect on the most significant moments from your prayer and record your reflections in your journal.

In this contemplation of John 21:1-14, you will see and hear the risen Jesus Christ appear to his disciples on the shores of Lake Tiberias.

[1]   Begin by reading the biblical selection and reviewing your notes on it.

[2]   Then, focus on this specific time and place as you allow all other concerns to fall away before considering the people and place of this moment of prayer.

• Allow an image of Jesus to emerge in your imagination. Look at what he is wearing or carrying, observing his clothing and any objects he is holding. Ponder this mental image, allowing any other observations about Jesus to form in your mind.

• Then, observe the various men and women gathered on the shore of Lake Tiberias, observing what they are doing and how they behave toward Jesus. Look at Simon Peter, making a mental note about his different appearances and mannerisms. Take a moment to ponder this mental image, allowing other impressions of these men and women to form. Become familiar with the men and women you will encounter during your prayer as well as their behavior.

• Gradually, become aware of the location of this moment of prayer. Pay attention to its physical characteristics and the arrangement of the people in it. As you ponder this mental image, look around the place and notice more details about it. Become familiar with the location of your upcoming prayer.

• Take a moment to remain in this place with these men and women, then allow these images to fade from your consciousness.

[3]   After you become still, become aware of your desires during this moment of prayer. Remember your desire to experience the divine presence all around you and to trust in God's plan for you, asking that you may feel gladness fully and rejoice intensely over the great glory and joy of Christ our Risen Lord. Recall your desire that, in this day or week of prayer, to have a deep "felt knowledge" of the meaning of the resurrection in the world around you and in your own as you experience the fullness of joy that should come to you with the resurrection of Jesus.

As these desires fill your consciousness, let all other concerns fall aside as you focus on this specific time and place of prayer.

[4]   Again, when you are ready, allow the image of Jesus and his disciples to reemerge in your imagination.

• Watch as the disciples are gathered on the shore. Listen to the sounds of this moment. Feel the many different emotions among the disciples and share in these feelings.

• Ask God to help you share in their experience – either by joining them or by listening quietly to them.

• Then, watch and listen as Simon Peter decides to go fishing before meeting the risen Jesus. You may want to quietly read the passage while remaining prayerfully aware of your mental image of Jesus or you may choose to stay completely within the imagined realm of your prayer. Whichever you choose, know that God will offer you the words from the biblical passage that you need to hear – even if only in fragments.

– Become aware of how the disciples' behavior changes after Jesus reveals himself to them.

– Remember that the risen Jesus continues to reveal himself to you.

• Afterward, allow this image to fade from your imagination as you become aware of the phrases and images from this moment which touched you most deeply. Recall the emotions and memories evoked during your prayer. Allow these seminal aspects of your meditation to linger on your mind and in your heart, noting any special feelings evoked by them.

[5]   When you are ready, become aware of the risen Jesus' presence with you in this moment and have an open and informal conversation about this prayer period and how the passage from John's gospel expresses your own needs or desires – giving space for Jesus to respond or to highlight different aspects from the biblical account and your experiences during this contemplation. Then, gradually allow your thoughts to recede as you focus on the risen Jesus' continuing presence in your life and in the world around you.

[6]   Conclude by offering this prayer:

> Confirm me in your love divine,
> Smooth for my feet life's rugged way;
> My will with yours entwine,
> Lest evil lead my steps astray.
> Be with my still as guard and guide,
> Keep me in holy sanctity,
> Let my firm faith on you abide,

From fraud and error hold me free. Amen.

[7]   Afterward, take 10-15 minutes in a quiet space to reflect on the most significant moments from your prayer and record your reflections in your journal.

In this contemplation of Matthew 28:16-20, you will see and hear the risen Jesus Christ commission his disciples to continue his redemptive mission.

[1]   Begin by reading the biblical selection and reviewing your notes on it.

[2]   Then, focus on this specific time and place as you allow all other concerns to fall away before considering the people and place of this moment of prayer.

  • Allow an image of Jesus to emerge in your imagination. Look at what he is wearing or carrying, observing his clothing and any objects he is holding. Ponder this mental image, allowing any other observations about Jesus to form in your mind.

  • Then, observe the various men and women gathered on the mountainside, observing what they are doing and how they behave toward Jesus. Take a moment to ponder this mental image, allowing other impressions of these men and women to form. Become familiar with the men and women you will encounter during your prayer as well as their behavior.

  • Gradually, become aware of the location of this moment of prayer. Pay attention to its physical characteristics and the arrangement of the people in it. As you ponder this mental image, look around the place and notice more details about it. Become familiar with the location of your upcoming prayer.

  • Take a moment to remain in this place with these men and women, then allow these images to fade from your consciousness.

[3]   After you become still, become aware of your desires during this moment of prayer. Remember your desire to experience the divine presence all around you and to trust in God's plan for you, asking that you may feel gladness fully and rejoice intensely over the great glory and joy of Christ our Risen Lord. Recall your desire that, in this day or week of prayer, to have a deep "felt knowledge" of the meaning of the resurrection in the world around you and in your own as you experience the fullness of joy that should come to you with the resurrection of Jesus.

  As these desires fill your consciousness, let all other concerns fall aside as you focus on this specific time and place of prayer.

[4]   Again, when you are ready, allow the image of Jesus and his disciples to reemerge in your imagination.

    • Watch as the risen Jesus and his disciples speak on the mountainside. Listen to the sounds of this moment. Feel the many different emotions among the disciples and share in these feelings.

    • Ask God to help you share in their experience – either by joining them or by listening quietly to them.

    • Then, watch and listen as Jesus speaks to the disciples and sends them out to continue his mission. You may want to quietly read the passage while remaining prayerfully aware of your mental image of Jesus or you may choose to stay completely within the imagined realm of your prayer. Whichever you choose, know that God will offer you the words from the biblical passage that you need to hear – even if only in fragments.

    – Become aware of how the disciples' behavior changes after Jesus reveals his desires for them.

    – Remember that the risen Jesus desires you to continue his mission.

    • Afterward, allow this image to fade from your imagination as you become aware of the phrases and images from this moment which touched you most deeply. Recall the emotions and memories evoked during your prayer. Allow these seminal aspects of your meditation to linger on your mind and in your heart, noting any special feelings evoked by them.

[5]   When you are ready, become aware of the risen Jesus' presence with you in this moment and have an open and informal conversation about this prayer period and how the passage from Matthew's gospel expresses your own needs or desires – giving space for Jesus to respond or to highlight different aspects from the biblical account and your experiences during this contemplation. Then, gradually allow your thoughts to recede as you focus on the risen Jesus' continuing presence in your life and in the world around you.

[6]   Conclude by offering this prayer:

> *Confirm me in your love divine,*
> *Smooth for my feet life's rugged way;*
> *My will with yours entwine,*
> *Lest evil lead my steps astray.*
> *Be with my still as guard and guide,*
> *Keep me in holy sanctity,*
> *Let my firm faith on you abide,*

From fraud and error hold me free. Amen.

[7]   Afterward, take 10-15 minutes in a quiet space to reflect on the most significant moments from your prayer and record your reflections in your journal.

In this meditation on Romans 8:1-17, you will see and hear Columba preaches to a crowd about the new life they receive through the resurrection of Jesus Christ.

[1]   Begin by reading the biblical selection and reviewing your notes on it.

[2]   Then, focus on this specific time and place as you allow all other concerns to fall away before considering the people and place of this moment of prayer.

• Allow an image of Columba to emerge in your imagination, noting his physical characteristics and mannerisms. Look at what he is wearing or carrying. Make a note of whether he is sitting, standing, or walking. Ponder this mental image, allowing any other observations about Columba to form in your mind.

• Note how many men and women are with Columba, making a mental note of their appearance and demeanor. Look at Columba's disciples, observing where they are standing and how they behave toward Columba. Look at the crowd, noting their attitude and behavior toward Columba. Observe whether the people are sitting, standing, or walking. Take a moment to ponder this mental image, allowing other impressions of these people to form. Become familiar with the men and women you will encounter during your prayer as well as their behavior.

• Allow yourself to become aware of the location of this moment of prayer. Observe whether it is inside or outside, paying attention to its physical characteristics and the arrangement of the people in it. Look around the place and notice more details about it – if it in dim or bright light, if it is still and silent or filled with noise, if it has an unusual smell or not, etc. Become familiar with the location of your upcoming prayer.

• Take a moment to remain in this place with these men and women before allowing these images to fade from your consciousness.

[3]   After you become still, become aware of your desires during this moment of prayer. Remember your desire to experience the divine presence all around you and to trust in God's plan for you, asking that you may feel gladness fully and rejoice intensely over the great glory and joy of Christ our Risen Lord. Recall your desire that, in this day or week of prayer, to have a deep "felt knowledge" of the meaning of the resurrection in the world around you and in your own as you

experience the fullness of joy that should come to you with the resurrection of Jesus.

As these desires fill your consciousness, let all other concerns fall aside as you focus on this time and place of prayer.

[4]   Allow the image of Saint Columba and the crowd to reemerge in your imagination.

• Watch as the group assembles around Columba, either from a distance or as a participant. Listen to the sounds of this moment and become comfortable as you prepare to hear Columba speak. Feel the anticipation of the people around you and share in that enthusiasm.

• Ask God to help you share in this moment – either by joining it or by listening quietly to it. Focus your attention on Saint Columba, noting his physical appearance and his demeanor.

• Then, watch and listen as Columba presents the passage from Paul's second letter to the Romans. You may want to quietly read the passage while remaining prayerfully aware of your mental image of Columba or you may choose to stay completely within the imagined realm of your prayer. Whichever you choose, know that God will offer you the words from the biblical passage that you need to hear – even if only in fragments.

– Look around as Columba speaks and see the reactions both of his disciples and of the people in the crowd. Become aware of their feelings and how they behave toward Columba and one another.

– Remember that Columba is speaking to men and women struggling with the sometimes-confusing nature of Christian life. Remember that he is speaking to you.

• After Saint Columba finishes speaking, allow this image to fade from your imagination as you become aware of the phrases and images from this moment which touched you most deeply. Recall the emotions and memories – including any sounds or smells – evoked during your prayer. Allow these seminal aspects of your meditation to linger on your mind and in your heart, noting any special feelings evoked by them.

[5]   When you are ready, become aware of the risen Jesus' presence with you in this moment and have an open and informal conversation about this prayer period and how the passage from Paul's epistle expresses your own needs or desires – giving space for Jesus to respond or to highlight different aspects from the biblical account and your experiences during this contemplation. Then, gradually allow your

thoughts to recede as you focus on the risen Jesus' continuing presence in your life and in the world around you.

[6]   Then, offer this traditional Irish prayer:

> *Confirm me in your love divine,*
> *Smooth for my feet life's rugged way;*
> *My will with yours entwine,*
> *Lest evil lead my steps astray.*
> *Be with my still as guard and guide,*
> *Keep me in holy sanctity,*
> *Let my firm faith on you abide,*
> *From fraud and error hold me free. Amen.*

[7]   Afterward, take 10-15 minutes in a quiet space to reflect on the most significant moments from this time of prayer and record your reflections in your journal.

[1]   Become aware of your prayerful desires during this day or week. Bring to mind your desire to feel gladness fully and rejoice intensely over the great glory and joy of Christ our Risen Lord. Ask also that you may have deep "felt knowledge" of the meaning of the resurrection in the world around you and in your own as you experience the fullness of joy that should come to you with the resurrection of Jesus.

[2]   Call to mind the various prayers of the preceding day or days. Allow the images and words of these prayers to linger and then slowly fade from your consciousness.

• Remember your contemplation of the third part of The Contemplation to Attain Love from *The Spiritual Exercises of Saint Ignatius* before reviewing it in the same manner as your earlier prayers.

• Recall your imaginative contemplation of John 21:1-14. Consider the images and feelings evoked in you during your prayer, feeling God's presence in these memories and becoming aware of the specific sensations associated with each image.

• Review your imaginative contemplation of Matthew 28:16-20, considering it in the same way as your memories of John 21.

• Revisit your meditation on Romans 8:1-17 in the same manner as the previous prayers.

Make a mental note of which senses are most active. You may see an image or a color, hear a sound or a phrase, or smell a scent or a fragrance. You may even taste a flavor or feel a sensation on your skin.

[3]   Then, relax and allow these various memories and experiences to quietly enter and leave your consciousness. Linger on the sensory images and memories being evoked in you – noticing any images or colors, any sounds or phrases, any scents or fragrances, any flavors or physical sensations associated with each prayer.

[4]   When you are ready, become completely still and clear your mind of all thoughts and concerns. Allow an image of a special personal space to form in your imagination. Then, watch as God enters that place and forms a small image or object for you that expresses the thought or awareness that you most need to carry with you into your life.

Reverently pick up the object or image, a reflection of the most important gift you have been given during this time of prayer. Look at it carefully and become aware of the divine presence contained within it. Register what it looks like and how it feels in your hand. Then, feel the joy and confidence that comes from touching the presence of God as you accept this gift, offering a short prayer of gratitude while you relax into the pleasure of this moment.

[5]   Then, conclude by offering this prayer:

Confirm me in your love divine,
Smooth for my feet life's rugged way;
My will with yours entwine,
Lest evil lead my steps astray.
Be with my still as guard and guide,
Keep me in holy sanctity,
Let my firm faith on you abide,
From fraud and error hold me free. Amen.

[6]   While your experiences are still fresh in your mind, record the most significant impressions or sensations from this time of prayer in your journal.

[1]   Remember your desires during the preceding day or week of prayer. Become aware of the divine presence all around you, offering you inner knowledge of Jesus Christ who became human for you so you may better love and follow him. Recall your desire to have a deep "felt knowledge" of the meaning of the resurrection in the world around you and in your own as you experience the fullness of joy that should come to you with the resurrection of Jesus.

Ask God once again to fulfill these desires in your own life and in your interactions with others.

[2]   Then, take a moment to allow the words, thoughts, and feelings from your prayers during the last day or week to linger before asking God to reveal the fulfillment of your deepest desires in these various memories.

• Think about the prayer sequence at the beginning of this day or week. Make a mental note of any words, insights or images that remain particularly significant or meaningful to you.

• Ponder the story, "Columba Raises Two People from the Dead". Note any words, insights, or images from it that remain particularly significant or meaningful to you.

• Revisit your contemplation of the third part of "The Contemplation to Attain Love" from The Spiritual Exercises of Saint Ignatius before reviewing it in the same manner as your earlier prayers.

• Recall your imaginative contemplation of John 21:1-14.

– Consider the most powerful images, phrases, or feelings from your prayer. Ask yourself what gifts God gave to you through these moments, perhaps offering you new insights or perhaps affirming an important aspect of your faith. Ask yourself how God may be calling you to change through these moments, being as specific as possible.

– Examine your disposition as you prayed. Recall the easiest moments in your prayer and any moments of joy you may have experienced. Remember also if you encountered any difficulty opening yourself to God or if you felt any sadness as you prayed. Ask God to help you understand why these feelings surfaced.

– Bring to mind any moments when you added personal elements (e.g., familiar places or people from your life) or connected your prayers to other scriptures or spiritual writings. Ask yourself how these additions helped or hindered you as you prayed. Again, if you do not know why this happened, ask God to help you understand.

- Review your imaginative contemplation of Matthew 28:16-20, considering it in the same way as your memories of John 21.
- Revisit your meditation on Romans 8:1-17 in the same manner as the previous prayers.
- Reflect on the ebb and flow of sensory impressions and feelings that marked your application of the senses. Isolate the most memorable moments and sensory impressions from your prayer and reflect on how God used these moments to give you a particular gift.

[3]   Finally, ponder the times when images or feelings from the readings of this day or week surfaced outside these prayer periods. Think about the most memorable aspects of these experiences, asking God to explain their significance.

[4]   Take a moment to allow the words, thoughts, and feelings of these prayers to linger on your mind and in your heart. Finally, conclude by offering this prayer:

O God, I believe in you; strengthen my belief.
I trust in you; confirm my trust.
I love you; double my love.
I repent that I angered you,
Increase my repentance.
Fill you my heart with awe without despair;
With hope, without over-confidence;
With piety without infatuation;
And with joy without excess.
My God, consent to guide me by your wisdom;
To constrain me by your right;
To comfort me by your mercy;
And to protect me by your power. Amen.

[5]   After finishing these prayers, summarize your reflections on the gifts or graces you received during the prayers of this last day or week and record these thoughts in your journal.

9. The Continuing Call to Discipleship and Witness

9.1a   O You Who Seek God To Find

a petition to live as a redeemed child of God

Take a moment to quiet your spirit, becoming completely present to this moment. Allow all other thoughts and concerns to fall away as you come into the presence of God. Then, when you are ready, begin.

O you who seek God to find,
Uplift your eyes on high;
      For lo!, to every humble mind
      His glory fills the sky.

God's mighty wonders there behold,
In boundless fields of light,
      Sublime, eternal, and as old
      As heaven and ancient night.

A Hymn, sung or heard (optional)

Be present, Holy Trinity,
One glory are you, one Deity;
      Where'er creation's bounds extend,
      You are beginning without end.

The hosts of heaven your praise proclaim,
Adoring, tell your matchless fame;
      Earth's threefold fabric joins the song,
      To bless you through the ages long.

And we, your humble servants, now
To you in courteous adoration bow;
      Our suppliant vows and prayers unite
      With hymns that fill the realms of light.

One Light, we to you our homage pay,
We worship you, O triple ray;
      You First and Last, we speak your fame,
      And every spirit lauds your name.

To the eternal loving Father, prayers we raise;
To You, the only begotten Son, we offer praise;
      And with love of the Spirit, our hearts are ablaze,
      O great Triune God, yet also One, always!

Read or recite Psalm 16.

Holy Triune God,
      Father, Son and Spirit
Under my thoughts may I God-thoughts find.
Half of my sins escape my mind.
      For what I said, or did not say,
      Pardon me, O Lord, I pray.

Read Acts 1: 3-9, aloud or quietly.

O Holy God,
      Father, Son and Spirit
If I were in Heaven my harp I would sound
With apostles and angels and saints all around,
      Praising and thanking the Son *who is* crowned,
      May the poor race of Eve for that heaven be bound!

Holy Triune God,
Pure may my inmost heart remain
From evil thoughts and fancies vain;
      And may the curb my flesh control,
      That drags to earth the aspiring soul.

So, when the last stray beams of light
Shall fade before the return of night,
      Kept in the path my feet have trod,
      I shall give glory to our God.

O Holy God,
      Father, Son and Spirit
For me is many a snare designed,
To fill my mind with doubts and fears;
      Far from the land of holy saints,
      I dwell within my vale of tears.

Let faith, let hope, let love –
Traits far above the cold world's way –
    With patience, humility, and awe,
    Become my guides from day to day.

I acknowledge, the evil I have done.
From the day of my birth till the day of my death,
    Through the sight of my eyes,
Through the hearing of my ears,
    Through the sayings of my mouth,
Through the thoughts of my heart,
    Through the touch of my hands,
Through the course of my way,
    Through all I said and did not,
Through all I promised and fulfilled not,
    Through all the laws and holy commandments I broke.
I ask even now absolution of you,
In the sweet name of Jesus Christ,
    For fear I may have never asked it as was right,
    And that I might not live to ask it again,

O Divine Majesty,
    Father, Son and Spirit
May you not let my soul stray from you,
May you keep me in a good state,
    May you turn me toward what is good to do,
    May you protect me from dangers, small and great.
May you fill my eyes with tears of repentance,
    So I may avoid the sinner's awful sentence.
May the Grace of the God for ever be with me,
    And whatever my needs, may the Triune God give me.

Select one of the following options for the Lord's Prayer.

Option A

O God,
Father, Son and Spirit,
help me pray as Jesus himself taught:
    "Our Father in heaven,

hallowed be your name.
Your kingdom come.
Your will be done,
on earth as it is in heaven.
Give us this day our daily bread.
And forgive us our debts,
as we also have forgiven our debtors.
And do not bring us to the time of trial,
but rescue us from the evil one."
(Matthew 6: 9-13)

From the foes of my land,
from the foes of my faith,
From the foes who would us dissever,
 O Trinity preserve me, in life, in death,
 With the Sign of the Cross for ever.
 For the kingdom, the power, and the glory
 are yours now and for ever. Amen.

**Please proceed with "I beseech the wonderful and blessed Trinity…,"
found after Option B.**

Option B

O God,
Father, Son and Spirit,
help me pray as Jesus himself taught:
 Our Father in heaven,
 hallowed be your name,
 your kingdom come,
 your will be done,
 on earth as in heaven.
 Give us today our daily bread.
 Forgive us our sins
 as we forgive those who sin against us.
 Lead us not into temptation
 but deliver us from evil.

From the foes of my land,
from the foes of my faith,
From the foes who would us dissever,
 O Trinity preserve me, in life, in death,

With the Sign of the Cross for ever.
For the kingdom, the power, and the glory
are yours now and for ever. Amen.

I beseech the wonderful and blessed Trinity,
God in Heaven, unsurpassed in power and might;
  Be behind me, Be on my left,
  Be before me, Be on my right!
Against each danger, God is my help;
In distress, upon the Divine Majesty I call.
  In dark times, may my God sustain me –
  And lift me up again when I fall.
Lord over heaven and of earth,
The Triune God knows my offenses.
  Yet, listening to my pleadings,
  Guides me away from sinful pretenses.
Lord of all creation and the many creatures,
My God bestows on me many earthly treasures.
  Revealing love in each life and season,
  My God shares with me heavenly pleasures.
May the Holy Trinity arouse me
In moments both of joy and of strife;
  God the Father, with Mary's mighty Son,
  And the noble Spirit, bring me new life!

A Hymn, sung or heard (optional)

O Divine Majesty,
Three in one Godhead, without division.
  You are my riches, my store, my provision,
My star through the years
When troubles rend me,
  Through times of strife and tears,
  O God, you defend me.

The light is yours, O Trinity, through all my years.
Your glory shines forth in the open day;
  I come to you with songs and tears;
  Lift up and guide my soul, I pray.

Cleanse me from stain of sinful pride,
And warm me in your living light;
  You are my heavenly lamp, my guide;
  Shine in your sweetness, clear and bright.

  End this time of prayer by taking some time to bring to mind the various ways God shields you from harm or guides you through the world's tumult. Then, when you are ready, conclude by saying:

O Holy Triune God,
Father, Son and Spirit,
I place myself at the edge of your grace,
  On the floor of your house myself I place,
And to banish the sin of my heart away,
  I lower my knee to you this day.
Through life's torrents of pain may you bring me whole,
  And, O Blessed Trinity, preserve also my soul. Amen.

Consideration of the Readings

After reciting or prayerfully reading the prayer sequence for this day or week:
• Read #230-233 and #237 in "The Contemplation to Attain Love" from *The Spiritual Exercises of Saint Ignatius* (found on page 298), allowing yourself to linger on any thoughts or phrases that seem particularly meaningful to you or especially relevant to your life. Then, record these highlights in your workbook.
• Read about Jesus' ascension in Acts 1:3-9, making a mental note of each person's appearance and actions during the episode as well as the key elements of the story and its setting. Again, consider any aspects of this story that speak strongly to you before recording these observations in your workbook.
• Read about the conversion of Saul in Acts 9:1-22, noting Saul's appearance and actions during the episode as well as the key elements of the story and its setting, including the setting. Then, record in your workbook any aspects of this story that speak strongly to you.
• Read Philippians 3:12-21 and "Helper of All Workers" (found on page 305), paying careful attention to any phrases or images that seem particularly meaningful to you. Then, record these highlights in your workbook.

Note: You also should consider any aspect of the prayer sequence from this day or week that seemed particularly significant to you.

Contemplation of Your Needs

When you are ready, allow any distractions to fade from your consciousness as you become aware of your desire to live in God's goodness. Feel yourself yearning to properly use the many gifts God has given you, to experience God's continuing care, and to be open to the immense love God shows for you, then:
• Read "Columba's Mother Has a Vision" (found on page 304). Allow yourself to linger on any thoughts, phrases or images that seem

particularly meaningful or significant to your earlier preparations or prayer.

• Pray for your desires in the coming day or week. Ask that the divine presence all around you may be revealed, so you may feel gladness fully and rejoice intensely over the great glory and joy of Christ our Risen Lord. Ask also that you may understand how you might fully participate in the ongoing redemption of God's creation.

• Conclude by praying to recognize through the fourth point of The Contemplation to Attain Love that you are not alone and that you arc receiving the gifts you need to fulfill your purpose in God's plan of creation. Again, offer yourself in service and in love.

Then, record any significant thoughts, emotions, or reactions from these moments in your workbook.

After this, put your notes aside. Without straining your memory, consider in turn each of the readings for the coming day or week and allow them to take shape in your imagination. Prayerfully ponder how each reading affects you emotionally without overtly thinking about their content, asking God to illuminate the spiritual gifts offered in each reading.

Finally, conclude by offering this prayer:
O God, I believe in you; strengthen my belief.
I trust in you; confirm my trust.
I love you; double my love.
I repent that I angered you,
Increase my repentance.
Fill you my heart with awe without despair;
With hope, without over-confidence;
With piety without infatuation;
And with joy without excess.
My God, consent to guide me by your wisdom;
To constrain me by your right;
To comfort me by your mercy;
And to protect me by your power. Amen.

Allow these words to linger on your mind and in your heart for a few moments and then write the most important thoughts, feelings, and desires in your journal.

In this meditation on the fourth and final point in "The Contemplation to Attain Love" presented in *The Spiritual Exercises of Saint Ignatius*, you will ponder the ways in which all aspects of goodness and order in creation descend as gifts from God before reflecting on how you should respond to this beneficence.

[1]   Begin by reading the preliminary considerations and first point of "The Contemplation to Attain Love" (#230-233 and #237) in *The Spiritual Exercises of Saint Ignatius* (found on page 298) and reviewing your notes on it.

[2]   Then, focus on this specific time and place as you allow all other concerns to fall away. As you become still, become aware of your desires during this moment of prayer. Remember your desire to experience the divine presence all around you and to trust in God's plan for you, asking that you may feel gladness fully and rejoice intensely over the great glory and joy of Christ our Risen Lord.

Recall your desire that, in this day or week of prayer, to understand how you might fully participate in the ongoing redemption of God's creation. Finally, ask to recognize through the fourth point of The Contemplation to Attain Love that you are not alone and that you are receiving the gifts you need to fulfill your purpose in God's plan of creation.

As these desires fill your consciousness, let all other concerns fall aside as you focus on this specific time and place of prayer.

[3]   Then, slowly and deliberately, re-read the "The Contemplation to Attain Love".

• As you read, take time to stop and ponder each statement within it as you read. When you pause, allow images shaped by the words and thoughts of the passages to form in your imagination. See and hear the way each statement expresses a need or desire in your life.

• Take more time with words that seem particularly significant or meaning to you. Become aware of the sections from the "The Contemplation to Attain Love" which you accept easily and any of those which cause you difficulty. Clarify these thoughts and feeling as much as possible while remaining focused on each specific statement within this meditation.

• After finishing the reading, allow the various words and images of your prayer to flow freely in your consciousness without being controlled. Become aware of those aspects of the "The Contemplation to Attain Love" that arouse holy desires in you, toward God and toward others (including nonhuman creatures). Become aware of those aspects of the reading that make you feel shame for those times you fall short of these holy aspirations.

• When you are ready, become aware of God's presence – either as a single entity or as the Holy Trinity – with you in this moment and have an open and informal conversation about your experience of the "The Contemplation to Attain Love". Speak about how it expresses your own desires and fears, giving space for the God to explain the love that motivates the divine actions presented in this meditation.

• Then, gradually allow your thoughts to recede as you focus on God's broader presence in your life and in the world around you.

[4]   Conclude by offering this prayer presented by Saint Ignatius in his *Spiritual Exercises*:

> *Receive, Lord, my whole liberty.*
> *Accept my memory, understanding, and whole will.*
> *Whatsoever I have, or possess, you have given me:*
> *this all I restore to you, and to your will altogether*
> *deliver up to be governed.*
> *Give me only the love of you,*
> *with your grace, and I am rich enough,*
> *and desire nothing else beyond. Amen.*

[5]   Afterward, take 10-15 minutes in a quiet space to reflect on the most significant moments from your prayer and record your reflections in your journal.

In this contemplation of Acts 1:3-9, you will see and hear the risen Jesus Christ ascend into heaven.

[1]   Begin by reading the biblical selection and reviewing your notes on it.

[2]   Then, focus on this specific time and place as you allow all other concerns to fall away before considering the people and place of this moment of prayer.

   • Allow an image of Jesus to emerge in your imagination. Look at what he is wearing or carrying, observing his clothing and any objects he is holding. Ponder this mental image, allowing any other observations about Jesus to form in your mind.

   • Then, observe the various men and women gathered around Jesus, noticing what they are doing and how they behave toward Jesus. Take a moment to ponder this mental image, allowing other impressions of these people to form. Become familiar with the men and women you will encounter during your prayer as well as their behavior.

   • Gradually, become aware of the location of this moment of prayer. Pay attention to its physical characteristics and the arrangement of the people in it. As you ponder this mental image, look around the place and notice more details about it. Become familiar with the location of your upcoming prayer.

   • Take a moment to remain in this place with these people, then allow these images to fade from your consciousness.

[3]   After you become still, become aware of your desires during this moment of prayer. Remember your desire to experience the divine presence all around you and to trust in God's plan for you, asking that you may feel gladness fully and rejoice intensely over the great glory and joy of Christ our Risen Lord. Recall your desire that, in this day or week of prayer, to understand how you might fully participate in the ongoing redemption of God's creation.

   As these desires fill your consciousness, let all other concerns fall aside as you focus on this specific time and place of prayer.

[4]   Again, when you are ready, allow the image of Jesus and his disciples to reemerge in your imagination.

   • Watch as the risen Jesus approaches his disciples. Listen to the sounds of this moment. Feel the many different emotions among the disciples and share in these feelings.

• Ask God to help you share in their experience – either by joining them or by listening quietly to them.

• Then, watch and listen as Jesus speaks to the disciples before ascending into heaven. You may want to quietly read the passage while remaining prayerfully aware of your mental image of Jesus or you may choose to stay completely within the imagined realm of your prayer. Whichever you choose, know that God will offer you the words from the biblical passage that you need to hear – even if only in fragments.

– Become aware of the mission Jesus gave to his disciples before his ascension and the joy the disciples experienced when they were told Jesus would return.

– Become aware that Jesus has given you a mission as well as a witness to the living presence of Jesus in the world.

• Afterward, allow this image to fade from your imagination as you become aware of the phrases and images from this moment which touched you most deeply. Recall the emotions and memories evoked during your prayer. Allow these seminal aspects of your meditation to linger on your mind and in your heart, noting any special feelings evoked by them.

[5]   Become aware of the risen Jesus' presence with you in this moment and have open and informal conversation about this prayer period and how the passage from the Acts of the Apostles expresses your own needs or desires – giving space for Jesus to respond or to highlight different aspects from the biblical account and your experiences during your prayer. Then, gradually allow your thoughts to recede as you focus on the risen Jesus' continuing presence in your life and in the world around you.

[6]   Conclude by offering this prayer:

> Confirm me in your love divine,
> Smooth for my feet life's rugged way;
> My will with yours entwine,
> Lest evil lead my steps astray.
> Be with my still as guard and guide,
> Keep me in holy sanctity,
> Let my firm faith on you abide,
> From fraud and error hold me free. Amen.

[7]   Afterward, take 10-15 minutes in a quiet space to reflect on the most significant moments from your prayer and record your reflections in your journal.

In this contemplation of Acts 9:1-22, you will see and hear the conversion of Saul.

[1]   Begin by reading the biblical selection and reviewing your notes on it.

[2]   Then, focus on this specific time and place as you allow all other concerns to fall away before considering the people and place of this moment of prayer.

  • Allow an image of Saul to emerge in your imagination, noting his appearance and demeanor. Look at what he is wearing or carrying, observing his clothing and any objects he is holding. Ponder this mental image, allowing any other observations about Jesus to form in your mind.

  • Then, observe Ananias and notice his appearance and demeanor. Look at what he is wearing or carrying, observing his clothing and any objects he is holding. Ponder this mental image, allowing any other observations about Jesus to form in your imagination.

  • Gradually, become aware of the location of this moment of prayer. Pay attention to its physical characteristics and the arrangement of the people in it. As you ponder this mental image, look around the place and notice more details about it. Become familiar with the location of your upcoming prayer.

  • Take a moment to remain in this place with these people, then allow these images to fade from your consciousness.

[3]   After you become still, become aware of your desires during this moment of prayer. Remember your desire to experience the divine presence all around you and to trust in God's plan for you, asking that you may feel gladness fully and rejoice intensely over the great glory and joy of Christ our Risen Lord. Recall your desire that, in this day or week of prayer, to understand how you might fully participate in the ongoing redemption of God's creation.

  As these desires fill your consciousness, let all other concerns fall aside as you focus on this specific time and place of prayer.

[4]   Again, when you are ready, allow the image of Paul to reemerge in your imagination.

  • Watch as Saul travels toward Damascus. Listen to the sounds of this moment.

• Ask God to help you share in this moment – either by joining in it or by listening quietly to it.

• Then, watch and listen as Saul experiences the presence of the risen Jesus and becomes blind before being told to seek out Ananias. You may want to quietly read the passage while remaining prayerfully aware of your mental image of Saul or you may choose to stay completely within the imagined realm of your prayer. Whichever you choose, know that God will offer you the words from the biblical passage that you need to hear – even if only in fragments.

– See the faith and courage of Ananias as he overcomes his fear and obeys the Lord's instructions to help Saul.

– Observe the transformation of Saul after his conversion as he proclaims the gospel he once persecuted.

– Remember that Jesus asks you to demonstrate your own faith and courage as a witness to his presence in the world.

• Afterward, allow this image to fade from your imagination as you become aware of the phrases and images from this moment which touched you most deeply. Recall the emotions and memories evoked during your prayer. Allow these seminal aspects of your meditation to linger on your mind and in your heart, noting any special feelings evoked by them.

[5]   When you are ready, become aware of the risen Jesus' presence with you in this moment and have an open and informal conversation about this prayer period and how the passage from the Acts of the Apostles expresses your own needs or desires – giving space for Jesus to respond or to highlight different aspects from the biblical account and your experiences during this contemplation. Then, gradually allow your thoughts to recede as you focus on the risen Jesus' continuing presence in your life and in the world around you.

[6]   Conclude by offering this prayer:

> Confirm me in your love divine,
> Smooth for my feet life's rugged way;
> My will with yours entwine,
> Lest evil lead my steps astray.
> Be with my still as guard and guide,
> Keep me in holy sanctity,
> Let my firm faith on you abide,
> From fraud and error hold me free. Amen.

[7]   Afterward, take 10-15 minutes in a quiet space to reflect on the most significant moments from your prayer and record your reflections in your journal.

In this meditation on Philippians 3:12-21 you will see and hear Columba preach on the need to remain diligent in living the new life given through the resurrection of Jesus Christ.

[1]　　Begin by reading the biblical selection and reviewing your notes on it.

[2]　　Then, focus on this specific time and place as you allow all other concerns to fall away before considering the people and place of this moment of prayer.

• Allow an image of Columba to emerge in your imagination, noting his physical characteristics and mannerisms. Look at what he is wearing or carrying. Make a note of whether he is sitting, standing, or walking. Ponder this mental image, allowing any other observations about Columba to form in your mind.

• Look at Columba's disciples, observing where they are standing and how they behave toward Columba. Look at the men and women in the crowd, noting their attitudes and behaviors toward Columba. Observe whether the people are sitting, standing, or walking. Take a moment to ponder this mental image, allowing other impressions of these men and women to form. Become familiar with the men and women you will encounter during your prayer as well as their behavior.

• Allow yourself to become aware of the location of this moment of prayer. Observe whether it is inside or outside, paying attention to its physical characteristics and the arrangement of the people in it. Look around the place and notice more details about it – if it in dim or bright light, if it is still and silent or filled with noise, if it has an unusual smell or not, etc. Become familiar with the location of your upcoming prayer.

• Take a moment to remain in this place with these men and women before allowing these images to fade from your consciousness.

[3]　　After you become still, become aware of your desires during this moment of prayer. Remember your desire to experience the divine presence all around you and to trust in God's plan for you, asking that you may feel gladness fully and rejoice intensely over the great glory and joy of Christ our Risen Lord. Recall your desire that, in this day or week of prayer, to understand how you might fully participate in the ongoing redemption of God's creation.

233

As these desires fill your consciousness, let all other concerns fall aside as you focus on this time and place of prayer.

[4]   Allow the image of Saint Columba and the crowd to reemerge in your imagination.

• Watch as the group assembles around Columba, either from a distance or as a participant. Listen to the sounds of this moment and become comfortable as you prepare to hear Columba speak. Feel the anticipation of the people around you and share in that enthusiasm.

• Ask God to help you share in this moment – either by joining it or by listening quietly to it. Focus your attention on Saint Columba, noting his physical appearance and his demeanor.

• Then, see and hear Columba present the passage from Paul's letter to the Philippians. You may want to quietly read the passage while remaining prayerfully aware of your mental image of Columba or you may choose to stay completely within the imagined realm of your prayer. Whichever you choose, know that God will offer you the words from the biblical passage that you need to hear – even if only in fragments.

• Afterward, watch and listen as Columba recites his prayer, "Helper of All Workers" (see page 305). Again, read the prayer while retaining your mental image of being with Columba and his disciples. As you read the prayer, allow its words to evoke images and feelings from the days or weeks of this retreat – as well as from your life before it and your hopes after it is ended.

• After Saint Columba finishes speaking, allow this image to fade from your imagination as you become aware of the phrases and images from this moment which touched you most deeply. Recall the emotions and memories – including any sounds or smells – evoked during your prayer. Allow these seminal aspects of your meditation to linger on your mind and in your heart, noting any special feelings evoked by them.

[5]   When you are ready, become aware of the risen Jesus' presence with you in this moment and have an open and informal conversation about this prayer period and how the passage from Paul's epistle expresses your own needs or desires – giving space for Jesus to respond or to highlight different aspects from the biblical account and your experiences during this contemplation. Then, gradually allow your thoughts to recede as you focus on the risen Jesus' continuing presence in your life and in the world around you.

[6]   Conclude by offering this prayer:

Confirm me in your love divine,
Smooth for my feet life's rugged way;
My will with yours entwine,
Lest evil lead my steps astray.
Be with my still as guard and guide,
Keep me in holy sanctity,
Let my firm faith on you abide,
From fraud and error hold me free. Amen.

[7]   Afterward, take 10-15 minutes in a quiet space to reflect on the most significant moments from this time of prayer and record your reflections in your journal.

[1]   Become aware of your prayerful desires during this day or week. Bring to mind your desire to feel gladness fully and rejoice intensely over the great glory and joy of Christ our Risen Lord. Ask also that you may understand how you might fully participate in the ongoing redemption of God's creation.

[2]   Call to mind the various prayers of the preceding day or days. Allow the images and words of these prayers to linger and then slowly fade from your consciousness.

• Remember your contemplation of the fourth part of The Contemplation to Attain Love from *The Spiritual Exercises of Saint Ignatius* before reviewing it in the same manner as your earlier prayers.

• Recall your imaginative contemplation of Acts 1:3-9. Consider the images and feelings evoked in you during your prayer, feeling God's presence in these memories and becoming aware of the specific sensations associated with each image.

• Review your imaginative contemplation of Acts 9:1-22, considering it in the same way as your memories of Matthew 28.

• Revisit your meditation on Philippians 3:12-21 (including Columba's prayer at its conclusion) in the same manner as the previous prayers.

Make a mental note of which senses are most active. You may see an image or a color, hear a sound or a phrase, or smell a scent or a fragrance. You may even taste a flavor or feel a sensation on your skin.

[3]   Then, relax and allow these various memories and experiences to quietly enter and leave your consciousness. Linger on the sensory images and memories being evoked in you – noticing any images or colors, any sounds or phrases, any scents or fragrances, any flavors or physical sensations associated with each prayer.

[4]   When you are ready, become completely still and clear your mind of all thoughts and concerns. Allow an image of a special personal space to form in your imagination. Then, watch as God enters that place and forms a small image or object for you that expresses the thought or awareness that you most need to carry with you into your life.

Reverently pick up the object or image, a reflection of the most important gift you have been given during this time of prayer. Look at it carefully and become aware of the divine presence contained within it. Register what it looks like and how it feels in your hand. Then, feel the joy and confidence that comes from touching the presence of God as you accept this gift, offering a short prayer of gratitude while you relax into the pleasure of this moment.

[5]   Then, conclude by offering this prayer:

> *Confirm me in your love divine,*
> *Smooth for my feet life's rugged way;*
> *My will with yours entwine,*
> *Lest evil lead my steps astray.*
> *Be with my still as guard and guide,*
> *Keep me in holy sanctity,*
> *Let my firm faith on you abide,*
> *From fraud and error hold me free. Amen.*

[6]   While your experiences are still fresh in your mind, record the most significant impressions or sensations from this time of prayer in your journal.

[1]   Remember your desires during the preceding day or week of prayer. Become aware of the divine presence all around you, offering you inner knowledge of Jesus Christ who became human for you so you may better love and follow him. Recall your desire to understand how you might fully participate in the ongoing redemption of God's creation.

After bringing these thoughts and desires into your consciousness, ask God once again to fulfill these desires in your own life and in your interactions with others.

[2]   Then, take a moment to allow the words, thoughts, and feelings from your prayers during the last day or week to linger – on your mind and in your heart – before asking God to reveal the fulfillment of your deepest desires in these various memories.

• Think about the prayer sequence at the beginning of this day or week. Make a mental note of any words, insights or images that remain particularly significant or meaningful to you.

• Ponder the story, "Columba's Mother Has a Vision". Note any words, insights, or images from them that remain particularly significant or meaningful to you.

• Remember your contemplation of the fourth part of "The Contemplation to Attain Love" from *The Spiritual Exercises of Saint Ignatius* before reviewing it in the same manner as your earlier prayers.

• Recall your imaginative contemplation of Jesus' ascension in Acts 1:3-9.

–Consider the most powerful images, phrases, or feelings from your prayer. Ask yourself what gifts God gave to you through these moments, perhaps offering you new insights or perhaps affirming an important aspect of your faith. Ask yourself how God may be calling you to change through these moments, being as specific as possible.

– Examine your disposition as you prayed, noting whether prayer came easily or with resistance. Recall the easiest moments in your prayer and any moments of joy you may have experienced. Remember also if you encountered any difficulty opening yourself to God or if you felt any sadness as you prayed. Ask God to help you understand why these feelings surfaced.

– Bring to mind any moments when you added personal elements (e.g., familiar places or people from your life) or connected your prayers to other scriptures or spiritual writings. Ask yourself how these additions helped or hindered you as you prayed. Again, if you do not know why this happened, ask God to help you understand.

• Review your imaginative contemplation of Acts 9:1-22, considering it in the same way as your memories of Matthew 28.

• Revisit your meditation on Philippians 3:12-21 (and Columba's prayer at its conclusion) in the same manner as the previous prayers.

• Reflect on the ebb and flow of sensory impressions and feelings that marked your application of the senses. Isolate the most memorable moments and sensory impressions from your prayer and reflect on how God used these moments to give you a particular gift, perhaps offering you new insights or changing you in some way.

[3]   Finally, ponder the times when images or feelings from the readings of this day or week surfaced outside these prayer periods. Consider those moments or events in which God's presence or guidance was especially strong as well as any moments when you were struggling. Think about the most memorable aspects of these experiences, asking God to explain their significance.

[4]   Take a moment to allow the words, thoughts, and feelings of these prayers to linger on your mind and in your heart. Finally, conclude by offering this prayer

> O God, I believe in you; strengthen my belief.
> I trust in you; confirm my trust.
> I love you; double my love.
> I repent that I angered you,
> Increase my repentance.
> Fill you my heart with awe without despair;
> With hope, without over-confidence;
> With piety without infatuation;
> And with joy without excess.
> My God, consent to guide me by your wisdom;
> To constrain me by your right;
> To comfort me by your mercy;
> And to protect me by your power. Amen.

[5]   After finishing these prayers, summarize your reflections on the gifts or graces you received during the prayers of this last day or week and record these thoughts in your journal.

Magis and the Pilgrimage into the Unknown

During these last days or weeks, as well as during your spiritual journeys through *From Loss to Love* and *From Disciple to Friend*, you made a pilgrimage of prayer into the unknown. Strengthened by God's forgiveness and grace, you confronted your own sinfulness and offered to walk with Jesus as his friend. At every stage of this journey, you discovered new dimensions of God's unconditional love for you – experiencing with each new revelation what Saint Ignatius called *"magis"* (or *"more"*), the unfolding recognition of new and greater opportunities to love and serve God through Jesus Christ. The gratitude you experienced in these moments gradually transformed from recompense for God's actions into reciprocal expressions of love.

As you conclude this journey of prayer, you will soon discover you have been invited to a new expression of *magis*. Your experiences in prayer are not intentioned to be hoarded away in private. Instead, your journey from being a abject sinner into being an intimate friend of Jesus Christ challenges you to share your experiences – both those which are sorrowful and painful as well as those which are joyful and liberating – with others as instrument of God's love. You should not hide or disguise the gifts you received during your travels with Jesus. Instead, in the words of Matthew 5:16, "Let your light shine before others, so that they may see your good works and give glory to your Father in heaven."

This will be a journey of faith shaped by the desires planted in your heart during your previous pilgrimage of prayer and by continuing companionship of Jesus Christ. As a Christian, your call to emulate and repeat the journey of Christ during his earthly ministry as part of the ongoing cosmic battle between God's desires and those forces that would diminish or deny them. So, like Jesus in his earthly ministry, you will experience moments of joy and elation while loving and serving others as well as opposition and even persecution for your choices. Yet, your experiences of God's love and presence will empower you to endure the pain of your own Passion as you arrive and experience your own place of Resurrection.

Among the ancient Celtic saints, there was an acute awareness of the veil separating material and spiritual realms of life so they actively sought out those "thin places" where the boundary between these realms was most diaphanous. Through holy wondering or pilgrimage, they abandoned the world they knew – with all its comforts and securities – in order to seek out the presence of God in new and unknown realms. It was an inherently challenging and even threatening choice, but it was transformed into a demonstration of faith before God and others when it was accepted as an act of love and trust. They knew they did not walk alone but traveled into the unknown with the assurance that God was walking with them.

Through your direct experience of God's presence in and around you, your life has become one of those "thin places" and makes your own pilgrimage of loving service to God through others possible. Through prayerful discernment, each day will offer you new opportunities to express the love of God to those in need – with each encounter inviting you to a new expression of *magis* through which you participate in the ongoing redemption of creation. Through your experience of God's love and your desire to reciprocate that love, you acquire courage to become a living instrument of God's redemptive activity in the world around you.

This fulfills the prayerful promise you offered at the conclusion of your spiritual journey through Saint Ignatius' *Spiritual Exercises* when you said, "Take Lord and receive all my liberty, my memory, my understanding and my entire will, all that I have and possess (*Sp.Ex.* #234)". This was in oblation of your own love in response to the love you have been shown by God, but it also was an expression of your willingness to seek new possibilities for *magis* as you embarked upon a new pilgrimage of service in realms known only to God – a choice made possible only if you have the assurance God's continuing guidance and protection. So, remember God's promise made through the prophet Jeremiah:

> For surely I know the plans I have for you, says the Lord, plans for your welfare and not for harm, to give you a future with hope. Then when you call upon me and come and pray to me, I will hear you. When you search for me, you will find me if you seek me with all your heart.
>
> (Jeremiah 29:11-13)

Abiding in the Domains of Love

Introduction

Just as you did after your previous retreats in *From Loss to Love* and *From Disciple to Friend*, you should take some time after this retreat to review the spiritual gifts you received during it. Remember once again that you are being transformed into an instrument of God's love and that this transformation requires time and further prayer to become fully realized in your life. Remember also that the challenges and demands of daily life may impede your ability to sustain or realize the holy desires that emerged during your retreat.

Nourishing the Gifts of the Retreat

Therefore, once again, you need to remain aware of God's loving activity in your life – nourishing the received during your recent retreat and nourishing the holy desires evoked in you during this period of intense prayer. Again, as with your earlier retreats, you need to maintain the spirit of generosity that you displayed during your recent retreat while also being careful to remain vigilant for any distractions or temptations which might undermine God's continuing activity in your life. So, once again, you spend the first three months after your retreat:

• Reviewing your thoughts and feelings by making at least one examen daily, paying particular attention to those moments in your day when you found yourself thinking about some aspect of your retreat.

• Repeating at least once every week a significant contemplation or meditation from your retreat.

• Considering once every week a specific "memento of grace" you received during the retreat – a particular moment of prayer or an insight that had a transformative effect on how you approached God and others.

Approach these prayers as an opportunity to re-engage the seminal aspects of your retreat. Remember they are opportunities for personal and spiritual growth, not a burden or obligation.

After three months of prayer, you may begin considering changes to your life that reflect the holy desires of your recent retreat. Remember to approach these spiritual leadings with the same spirit of generosity and openness that you displayed during your retreat, knowing you are being transformed into an instrument of God's love.

247

Resources for Prayer and Reflection

The resources in this section are designed to help you cultivate this holistic approach to your spiritual life by providing materials for prayer and reflection related to each of these aspects of spirituality. This includes reflections, prayer materials and spiritual exercises intended to foster but a deeper spiritual life that also embraces sacred citizenship and articulate witness.

The materials related to spiritual practices include:
•   A collection of traditional Irish prayers used in the development of the prayer sequences for this retreat and scriptural citations related to the themes of your most recent retreat.
•   "Writing a Personal Rule", an exercise designed to help you develop a set of guiding principles for your life that define and nurture your actions as an instrument of God's love in the world.

The resources related to sacred citizenship focus on the social dimensions of Saint Columba's life and ministry. This includes reflection questions on the readings concerning Saint Columba intended help you extend your own spiritual life outward towards others in the service of God's creation.

Finally, the materials focusing on articulate witness explore the process of achieving a unique voice in your public witness expressing God's special activity in and through you.

Spiritual Practices

The following early Christian hymns and traditional Irish prayers were woven into the fabric of the prayer sequences introducing the themes of your retreat. Individually, they offer a treasury of spiritual insight and devotion. By using them alone or by integrating them into your existing prayers, you should draw upon these ancestral voices to enrich and extend your spiritual vocabulary.

Short Prayers

Dear God of mercy and of power,
Bowed at your feet in prayer and love
I am; send down your heavenly dower,
The Spirit's largess, from above.
As you have filled my life with light,
And oped my heart to your grace,
So guide me ever in your might,
And fit me for your dwelling-place.

Source:
Early Christian Hymns

Let earth and heaven rejoice and sing
The supper of our Lord and King,
Who cleansed our souls from sin, and gave
The living bread to heal and save.
Let earth and heaven rejoice and sing
That supper of our Lord and King.
The Maker of the world, that night,
With wondrous mystery and might,
Brought to the soul her heavenly meat,
His blood to drink, his flesh to eat;
He cleansed our souls from sin and gave
The living bread to heal and save.

Source:
Early Christian Hymns, Series 2

O Christ, our everlasting Light,
You the glory of the starry sky,
Illume the darkness of our night,
Quicken our breasts and purify.
O, save us from insidious snares,
Protect us from the dangerous foe,
Guard, lest we stumble unawares,
And let our sleep no evil know.
Keep you our hearts forever pure,
Increase our faith, our will with you combine.
Be with us your protection sure,
Save by your power and love divine.

Source:
Early Christian Hymns, Series 2

Each sin I have sinned
From the day of my fall,
May the One Son of Mary
Forgive me them all!
May the child who was tortured,
God-man without stain,
Guide me safe through the torments
And shoutings of pain.

Source:
The Religious Songs of Connacht, Volume 1

I pray unto the Son, that He
Toward me be minded still,
His will is to redeem all,
I pray that He be of my will.
I pray unto the Father most high,
With the Holy Ghost, for safety.
They, together as three in one,
My life and salvation do guarantee.

Source:
The Religious Songs of Connacht, Volume 1

Be with us, Jesus, evermore,
Our paschal joy forever be;
Renew our lives, our hopes restore,

From sin and sorrow set us free.
For Christ, the King of love and might,
Has conquered death and broke the tomb;
He leads forth to heavenly light
The souls that long have pined in gloom.

Source:
Early Christian Hymns

Most clement Jesus, tender King,
Possess our souls that, all aglow,
The tongue may fitly say and sing
The love that unto you I owe.
Be with me evermore, O Lord,
And let your resurrection be
My paschal joy; from crimes abhorred,
In loving mercy make me free.

Source:
Early Christian Hymns

May you restrain from words of sin;
For bitter strife give calm within;
Veil from my eyes the garish light,
That lures the soul to darkest night.
Pure may my inmost heart remain
From evil thoughts and fancies vain;
And may I curb my flesh control,
That drags to earth the aspiring soul.

Source:
Hymns of the Early Church

Pure may my inmost heart remain
From evil thoughts and fancies vain;
And may the curb my flesh control,
That drags to earth the aspiring soul.
So, when the last stray beams of light
Shall fade before the return of night,
Kept in the path my feet have trod,
I shall give glory to our God.

Source:
Hymns of the Early Church

The light is yours, O Trinity, through all my years.
Your glory shines forth in the open day;
I come to you with songs and tears;
Lift up and guide my soul, I pray.
Cleanse me from stain of sinful pride,
And warm me in your living light;
You are my heavenly lamp, my guide;
Shine in your sweetness, clear and bright.

Source:
Early Christian Hymns

Long Prayers

Tell, my tongue, the glorious conflict,
Crowned with victory nobly won;
More than all the spoils of battle,
Praise the triumph of God's Son;
How by death the crown of conquest
Graced Him when the strife was done.
Grieving sore o'er Eden's sorrow
When our race in Adam fell;
And the fatal fruit he tasted,
Welcomed sin, and death, and hell;
God ordained a tree in Zion,
Eden's poison to dispel.
In the work of our Redemption
Wisdom met the tempter's foils;
On the ground he claimed, the Victor
Fought, and bore away the spoils;
And the bane became the blessing,
Freedom sprang amid his toils.
From the bosom of the Father,
Where He shared the regal crown,
At the time by God appointed,
Came the world's Creator down
God incarnate, born of a Virgin,

254

Shorn of glory and renown.

Source:
Hymns of the Early Church

Think of the cross of Christ each day,
Think how he suffered for all to view,
Think of the boon his passion gave,
Think of the grave that gapes for you.
Think of the Son of God, how He
Died on the tree our souls to save,
Think of the nails that pierced Him through,
Think of Him, too, in lowly grave.
Think of the spear the soldier bore,
Think how it tore His holy side,
Think of the bitter gall for drink,
Think of it, think for us He died.
Think upon Christ who gave His blood
Poured in a food our souls to win,
Think of tho mingled tide that gushed
Forth at the thrust to wash our sin.
Think of repentance timely made,
Think like a shade our time flits, too,
Think upon Death with poisoned dart
Piercing the heart and body through.

Source:
The Religious Songs of Connacht, Volume 1

You my Redeemer are, O Christ,
My heart's desire, my fervent love;
Creator of the world, you came
To wear our flesh, from heaven above.
'Twas love that brought you to our aid,
To bear the burden of our woe,
To bow the head in shameful death,
And life, immortal life, bestow.
Asunder burst the bands of hell,
The captives hailed your glorious day;
And by your mighty triumph crowned,
you are at God's right hand today.
O may your mercy still abound,

That, by the goodness of your grace,
We daily o'er our sin may rise,
And see the beauty of your face.
Spring of our joy, be you, O Christ;
Hereafter shall be our great reward;
And while the endless ages run,
Our praises shall we duly record.

Source:
Hymns of the Early Church

By death on the cross was the race restored,
For vain was our endeavour;
Henceforward blessed, O blessed Lord,
Be the Sign of the Cross for ever.
Rent were the rocks, tho sun did fade,
The darkening world did quiver,
When on the tree our Saviour made
The Sign of the Cross for ever.
Therefore I mourn for him whose heart
Shall neither shrink nor shiver,
Whose tears of sorrow refuse to start
At the Sign of the Cross for ever.
Swiftly we pass to the unknown land,
Down like an ebbing river,
But the devils themselves cannot withstand
The Sign of the Cross for ever.
When the hour shall come that shall make us dust,
When the soul and the body sever,
Fearful the fear if we may not trust
On the Sign of the Cross for ever.

Source:
The Religious Songs of Connacht, Volume 1

Writing a Personal Spiritual Rule

Spiritual rules have defined Western monasticism from its earliest days. These rules were intended to help a group of men or women (or a blended community of both) live together harmoniously. They reflected the seminal issues that originally shaped the beginning of that particular community by summarizing its ideals and providing specific behaviors that would make the achievement of those ideals possible (e.g. times for prayer, the preparation and consumption of meals, etc.). As such, spiritual rules were both a communal compact and a means for personal perfection.

In the Celtic tradition, the different abbeys (and their sub-abbeys) were shaped by the personality of the charismatic individual who gathered that community together at its beginning. For this reason, there were many different monastic rules in the Celtic Christian world and each of these was intrinsically personal in character – reflecting one person's vision that others came to embrace. This dynamic also led to the use of very different styles of writing and expression when composing the spiritual rules used among the Celtic Christians. It also empowered individuals to adapt these communal rules or prepare private rules better suited to their needs when they left the monastic community on pilgrimage or mission.

This phenomenon of individuals adapting or creating spiritual rules is not unique to the Celtic world. Various lay organizations were established during the history of the Christian Church to follow the rules of a particular religious community, such as the Benedictines or the Franciscans. Other individuals, such as Ignatius of Loyola, would develop their own individual rules to help them live a life of spiritual devotion and sanctity. Whichever of these paths were chosen, the goal was the same – to specify a set of physical behaviors and actions intended to bring an individual's life choices into harmony with God's desires.

Part 1

Before preparing your own personal spiritual rule, you will find it helpful to consider the purpose of this set of behavioral guidelines. As you know from your reflections in *From Loss to Love*, the Celtic

257

Christians developed a set of rules designed to mitigate against their sinful behaviors. These were the penitentials, which provided penalties and penances for specific sins with the purpose of correcting (and healing) sinful human tendencies. So, you may find it helpful to review the personal penitential that you prepared earlier.

> *Note: During this review, notice the language of your penitential and the manner in which it treats your negative (and sinful) behaviors. You may also find it useful to review the instructions for creating this penitential (Part 3 of "Preparing a Personal Penitential") in* From Loss to Love.

The tone and purpose of spiritual rules differs from those of the penitentials. While a penitential provides a summary of sinful actions and their correctives, a spiritual rule is a hopeful statement of spiritual desires. A spiritual rule focuses on the ability of an individual or community to live a life of faith consistent with God's desires for them and the world around them. As such, the behaviors and actions specified in these rules provide guidelines for remaining faithful to the promises men and women make to God in response to the many gifts they have received during their lives.

Still, it is important to recognize that spiritual rules and penitentials complement each other. Both serve to help men and women fulfill their desires to live a holy life consistent with God's desires, one offering guidelines for the future and the other correcting the mistakes of the past. So, as you begin to consider writing your own personal spiritual rule, it is important that you maintain a positive outlook toward your spiritual life and focus on the goals you hope to achieve rather than those areas of your life where you have fallen short in the past.

With this in mind you should answer the following questions:
- What are your most sinful tendencies in the past?
- What are the behaviors or actions that demonstrated these sinful tendencies?
- What behaviors or actions would contradict or eliminate these sinful tendencies?

<u>Part 2</u>

Before preparing your own personal spiritual rule, you also should contemplate the diversity of rules and the essential qualities they share. As noted earlier in this section, there were many different rules among the different communities of the ancient Celtic church and these were written in many different styles. Many, if not most, were lists (often presented numerically) of spiritual desires and corresponding actions. On the other hand, Columbanus presented ten virtues for his community with beautifully composed prose descriptions and directives for each. Yet, underlying this diversity, all of these spiritual rules provided guidelines for attaining spiritual perfection.

As you consider your own spiritual life and its needs, you should be encouraged by the diverse array of rules composed in the past. This empowers you to make the rules you compose in this section expressive of your own identity, desires, and personal style. It is important that you remember there is no correct way of writing a spiritual rule.

However, there are some qualities your spiritual rule(s) should demonstrate if they are to be an effective aid in your own spiritual development.
    • **Your spiritual rule(s) should be personal.** The rules you create should be reflect an awareness of your strengths and weaknesses as well as your own disposition, habits, and desires. Remember that these spiritual rule(s) are intended to be a tool for your own self-improvement, not other people or groups. Your unique relationship with God dictates the behaviors and actions shaping your rule(s), so anything too generic or related to the needs of others detracts from the efficacy of the rule(s) you write.
    • **Your spiritual rule(s) should be practical.** You should be able to implement the rules you create for yourself while, at the same time, be challenged by them. If the rules are too simple, they will become boring and unimportant to me. On the other hand, you will give up on trying to follow your rules if you cannot incorporate them into your life. The creation of your spiritual rule(s) becomes meaningless if it cannot be embodied in your day-to-day life.

• **Your spiritual rule(s) should be precise.** Being specific about the actions associated with each goal within your rule(s) will both make it clear what actions you think will improve your spiritual life and make it easier to assess your ability to implement them. Also, by using simple and direct language in the creation of your rule(s), you will be able to transfer the clarity you received in prayer to these directives for your life.

Also, as you prepare your rule(s), remember they shape a human life striving to respond to (and reciprocate) the many gifts and graces provided by a loving God. The ancient Celtic saints could be rigorous – even intimidating – in their spiritual practices but they never failed to maintain a healthy balance between the various aspects of human life. As an act of witness to others, they wanted the whole person to reflect the transformative power of God's love in them through tangible responses of love. Many centuries later, Ignatius of Loyola would echo this desire when he stated in his *Spiritual Exercises*, "Love ought to find its expression and deeds rather than words (*Sp.Ex.* #230)." Both of these sentiments should be intrinsic to the rule(s) you prepare.

Finally, remember that a spiritual rule usually addresses the behaviors and actions needed to achieve to a principle. So, before proceeding to the following exercises, take some time to consider the language you might use to connect an ideal with the practical action when preparing your own personal rule(s). Then, review the exercises presented in Parts 3-4 and decide which of the two types of rules would best serve your own spiritual needs before conducting that exercise.

Part 3

In this exercise, you will develop a rule based on the Seven Capital Virtues (the counterpoints to the Seven Deadly Sins): Humility, Generosity, Chastity, Meekness, Temperance, Kindness and Diligence.

1.   Begin by considering the Seven Capital Virtues. Reflect on your desires concerning each virtue and how you would like to manifest in your social and spiritual life.

- **Humility**, usually considered the greatest of the virtues, allows a person to come to God with the spirit of detachment from selfish desires.
- **Generosity** places a person's focus on others without a selfish desire for reward or renumeration.
- **Chastity** involves purity of heart and action. Although usually associated with sexuality, chastity also strives for unity between a person's body and their spiritual life.
- **Meekness**, sometimes referred to as Patience, mitigates against the sin of anger by inviting forgiveness of others (and ourselves, when necessary).
- **Temperance** demonstrates a well-ordered use of the material goods and social privileges received in a person's life.
- **Kindness**, sometimes referred to as **Brotherly Love**, strengthens a person's capacity to love his or her neighbor. It is often associated with comforting and caring for others, but it also counters the temptation to envy others.
- **Diligence** provides a person with the devotion to fulfill desires through actions and to move toward the fulfillment of God's desires in him or her.

2.   Consider the moral and spiritual effects of each virtue in your life and activities. Take time to reflect on the history of these virtues in your life. You have changed over the course of your life and one virtue may have risen to prominence in recent times or diminished insignificance. If necessary, use the "Rules for Discernment" proposed by Saint Ignatius during the second week of his *Spiritual Exercises* to examine this history.

3.   Consider the behaviors and actions that emerge from these virtues. Reflect on how they affect you, the people around you (both those you know and those you do not know), and the rest of nonhuman creation.

4.   Afterward, record these reflections in your workbook. Be as specific as possible in describing each of these virtues and their personal significance.

5.   Either in the order provided above or in their order of significance to you, write the virtue as a heading on the page dedicated

to it. Under each virtue, write a 1-2 sentence explanation of its meaning and importance to you (i.e., "Kindness involves...Through acts of kindness, I manifest God by..."). After each of these statements, right a promise to pray for better understanding of this virtue and its presence in your life on a particular day of each week.

6.   Then, after taking time to consider how you might incorporate these virtues into your daily life, write 6-8 short rules specifying actions you will take to manifest these virtues. Be certain to include at least one rule regarding your own self-improvement as well as one rule each concerning your behavior toward people you know, people you do not know and nonhuman creation.

      Note: Remember these rules may be revised in the future. You may decide to add or to replace rules as the requirements of your spiritual life change. As noted earlier in this section, these rules need to be practical so they do not become onerous and an impediment to your spiritual growth.

Part 4

In this exercise, you will develop a rule based on the "fruits of the spirit" listed in Saint Paul's Letter to the Galatians: love, joy, peace, patience, kindness, generosity, faithfulness, gentleness, and self-control.

1.   Begin by considering the behaviors listed by Saint Paul. Reflect on your desires concerning each virtue and how you would like to manifest in your social and spiritual life.
      • **Love**, demonstrated in concrete actions, allows a person to reflect the pure and unconditional love God offers all creation.
      • **Joy** involves the delight of fulfilling God's will, even through trials and tribulations.
      • **Peace** emerges when a person becomes aware of the Holy Spirit working in their hearts and minds to fulfill God's desires.
      • **Patience**, also called **Forbearance**, comes about when the Holy Spirit empowers a person to endure challenging situations with faith and perseverance.

• **Kindness** reflects moral integrity and loving concern for others in a person's actions.

• **Generosity** opens a person to God and to others through selfless actions and demonstrations of love that mirror God's own nature.

• **Faithfulness** indicates a person's dependability toward God and others based on the trust he or she has in God's own faithfulness.

• **Gentleness** conveys a person's submission to God and choice to act toward others with love and respect regardless of their actions.

• **Self-control** manifests a person's ability to control his or her sensual appetites and desires the power of the Holy Spirit.

2.   Consider the moral and spiritual effects of each ideal in your life and activities. Take time to reflect on the history of these ideals in your life. You have changed over the course of your life and one ideal may have risen to prominence in recent times or diminished insignificance. If necessary, use the "Rules for Discernment" proposed by Saint Ignatius during the second week of his *Spiritual Exercises* to examine this history.

3.   Consider the behaviors and actions that emerge from these ideals. Reflect on how they affect you, the people around you (both those you know and those you do not know), and the rest of nonhuman creation.

4.   Afterward, record these reflections in your workbook. Be as specific as possible in describing each of these ideals and their personal significance.

5.   Either in the order provided above or in their order of significance to you, write the ideal as a heading on the page dedicated to it. Under each ideal, write a 1-2 sentence explanation of its meaning and importance to you (i.e., "Patience involves...Through acts of patience, I manifest God by..."). After each of these statements, right a promise to pray regularly for better understanding of this ideal and its presence in your life. You may decide to combine two sets so you may pray for these ideals on a particular day of each week, or you may decide to cycle through the nine ideals presented by Saint Paul over the same number of days.

6.   Then, after taking time to consider how you might incorporate these ideals into your daily life, write 6-8 short rules specifying actions you will take to incarnate these ideals. Be certain to include at least one rule regarding your own self-improvement as well as one rule each concerning your behavior toward people you know, people you do not know and nonhuman creation.

    Note: Remember these rules may be revised in the future. You may decide to add or to replace rules as the requirements of your spiritual life change. As noted earlier in this section, these rules need to be practical so they do not become onerous and an impediment to your spiritual growth.

Part 5

Not all spiritual rules were intended to be comprehensive guidelines to the spiritual life. For example, Saint Ignatius includes a variety of more specific "micro-rules" in his *Spiritual Exercises*. These rules include the rules for discernment with which you are familiar as well as rules for alms-giving, the avoidance of scruples and thinking with the church. Saint Ignatius designed these rules to assist an individual with a specific issue or activity while the spiritual effects of his *Spiritual Exercises* transformed an individual.

1.   To write your own "micro-rule", begin by deciding which of the virtues or ideals in the previous exercise invites you into a deeper relationship with God. Consider which of these virtues or ideals provided you with the greatest sense of consolation. If necessary, use the "Rules for Discernment" proposed by Saint Ignatius during the second week of his *Spiritual Exercises* to examine this issue.

2.   Consider the behaviors and actions that emerge from this virtue or ideal. Reflect on how they affect you, the people around you (both those you know and those you do not know), and the rest of nonhuman creation. Record these reflections in your workbook, being as specific as possible.

3.   In your workbook, write a brief 1-3 sentence statement concerning the nature and dynamics of this virtue or ideal. This statement should include a description of the virtue or ideal, its benefits and the challenges in attaining it (i.e., "Generosity involves... Through acts of generosity, I demonstrate... However, while I strive for generosity, I can fall into patterns of...").

4.   Then, with the intention of sharing your insights with a close friend, write 8-10 rules describing how to recognize a trustworthy manifestation of the virtue or ideal you are describing. Using the "Rules for Discernment" presented by Saint Ignatius as a model, include at least four distinct rules for recognizing an untrustworthy demonstration of your virtue or ideal and four separate rules for recognizing a trustworthy manifestation of it.

     Note: Afterward, you should consider sharing this "micro-rule" with your spiritual director or soul friend. After listening to their response, make any revisions to your set of rules that bring you consolation and clarity using Saint Ignatius' "Rules for Discernment".

Part 6

Finally, you may find it useful to reflect on your spiritual rule and your penitential from time to time. Remember that they complement one another – correcting on the one hand your previous sinful behaviors and, on the other hand, providing a a map toward your future. Both tools connect you to God and offer you the opportunity to be transformed into an instrument of God's love. Still, you will falter and stumble along the way, so you must develop the habits of faith that allow you to seek forgiveness when needed as well as open yourself more fully to God's presence in you and in the world around you.

Over time and with God's guidance, the spiritual rules you develop for yourself will be written on your innermost being and flow naturally through you to good actions. However, before that occurs, you should consider ways to simplify and retain the essence of the spiritual rules by which you choose to live. For example, you might find it helpful to abbreviate each rule to a single sentence that can be easily remembered or reduce each rule to a maxim intended to remind you of the seminal desires at the heart of your spiritual life. Whichever method you find most helpful, you should make certain that it invites you into a deeper relationship with God by animating your deepest desires and aspirations.

Sacred Citizenship

In this excerpt from *A Passion for Justice: Social Ethics in the Celtic Tradition* (2008), Johnston McMaster explains the vision of the Beatitudes that shaped Columba's spiritual and community life.

These are literally the last words Columba is reputed to have spoken. It was just before midnight as 8 June 597 CE drew to its close. Columba had just been to the Sunday evening prayer vigil. He returned to his hut with his servant Diarmit and gave him one last message for the Iona monks.

These, O my children, are the last words I address to you – that you be at peace and have unfeigned charity among yourselves, and if you thus follow the example of the Holy Fathers, God, the Comforter of the good, will be your helper.

After speaking his final words, Columba lay in silence until the bell rang for midnight prayer. Dying as he was, he went to the church. The keynotes in the story, as it is told, are light and radiance. Columba's final vision was of the delight and joy in the community beyond. With that joyful vision he peacefully slept away. It was 9 June 597 CE.

It is said that Columba was eventually buried with Patrick and Brigid in Downpatrick. A piece of old verse has it:

> *His grace in Hy (Iona) without stain,*
> *and his soul in Derry;*
> *and his body under the flagstone*
> *under which are Brigid and Patrick.*

Wherever his final resting place, and Downpatrick has no historical basis, it is Columba's last words that live on and speak across the centuries. There is no authentic community in any age without peace and love. They are relational values, and Columba, true to the Celtic tradition, was thoroughly relational. That in turn was firmly rooted in the primary gospel metaphor of the kingdom.

The kingdom of God was the core idea and vision for Jesus. The Hebrew prophets before him and he himself never offered any precise definition of the kingdom. They painted various word pictures none of which by themselves could exhaust the meaning. Instead the metaphors, similes and parables provided Windows through which to see something of what God's kingdom or gracious activity in the world meant. Clues and signs are what the prophets and Jesus offered.

Whatever else the kingdom is about, there are enough windows, clues and signs to suggest that the kingdom is essentially about relationships and community. The essence of the kingdom for Jesus was in the Beatitudes (Matthew 5:1-12). Here is what it means to participate in God's kingdom and here is kingdom lifestyle. The core values of kingdom living are in the Sermon on the Mount and in the Beatitudes in particular.

None of the Beatitudes is about individualistic or private faith. They can only be lived in relationship and in community. They embody essential community values and are the core requirements for good community relationships. God is profoundly concerned for the quality of people's lives together and that means profound concern for the nature and quality of community life. It is in human and community relations that signs of the kingdom appear.

The blessedness of those who hunger and thirst actively for justice and peace making is a community experience. The peace and charity or love, which Columba wished for his Iona community are the basis of good relationships. Pieces total well-being, which in its Hebrew meaning is social, economic, political and therefore personal and relational. Love is only possible in relationship and in community. In public terms love is justice. Justice is about law and order, but it is much deeper and broader in its Hebrew and Christian meaning. It is about inequality of opportunity and access to power and resources. It is about fair play in social, economic and political relationships. Embodied by the Hebrew and Christian ideas of covenant and kingdom, peace and love, charity or justice are at the heart of a radical alternative vision for community.

Celtic Christianity and spirituality are community centered. In his longing for peace and unfeigned charity, Columba was expressing his community vision. Without such values and qualities, community disintegrates...

… Within our conflicting loyalties, our ancient hatreds and our deep divisions, Columba and the Celtic tradition still speak. There is a shared future, but only if we can practice his last words: "Be at peace and have unfeigned charity among yourselves."

Before proceeding to the next section, ask yourself the following questions:

1.   Does a particular part of this excerpt stand out for you? Why? Does it relate to a particular concern in your life or in your interactions with others?

2.   Does any aspect of the excerpt relate to your experiences of prayer during your retreat? If so, which?

3.   What does the excerpt tell you about Saint Columba? How does this help you in your own spiritual life? How does this challenge your beliefs about spirituality?

4.   How does this excerpt help you understand your calling to become a "citizen of heaven"?

These selections from *The Life of Saint Columba, founder of Hy* by Saint Adamnan (edited by William Reeves in 1874) illustrate the depth and breadth of Saint Columba's spiritual awareness and love.

After reading each of the following selections from Saint Adamnan's *The Life of Saint Columba*, ask yourself the following questions:

1.   What is the most important aspect of the selection? Why?
2.   Were there any parts of the selection that you found challenging?
3.   Were there any parts of the selection that you found comforting?
4.   How will you bring these challenging or comforting aspects of the selection before God in prayer?
5.   What is the grace you will ask from God in your prayer regarding these issues?
6.   How does the selection help you better understand your relationship with God and with others?
7.   What does this selection say to you about your life choices in the past?
8.   What does this selection say to you about your desires for the future?

In answering these questions, be specific in your responses and focus on the concrete actions you feel drawn to pursue either in the present or in the future. If a particular question provokes a significant response, record these insights in your retreat journal.

1.   How the Saint was favoured by God's grace with the power of distinguishing different presents.

About the same time Conall, bishop of Culerathin, collected almost countless presents from the people of the plain of Eilne on the Bann, to give a hospitable reception to the blessed man, and the vast multitude that accompanied him, on his return from the meeting of the kings mentioned above.

Many of these presents from the people were laid out in the paved court of the monastery, that the holy man might bless them on his arrival; and as he was giving the blessing he specially pointed out one present, the gift of a wealthy man. "The mercy of God," said he, "attendeth the man who gave this, for his charity to the poor and his munificence." Then he pointed out another of the many gifts, and said : "Of this wise and avaricious man's offering, I cannot partake until he repent sincerely of his sin of avarice." Now this saying was quickly circulated among the crowd, and soon reaching the ears of Columb, son of Aid, his conscience reproached him; and he ran immediately to the saint, and on bended knees repented of his sin, promising to forsake his former greedy habits, and to be liberal ever after, with amendment of life. The saint bade him rise: and from that moment he was cured of the fault of greediness, for he was truly a wise man, as was revealed to the saint through that present.

But the munificent rich man, called Brenden, of whose present mention was made above, hearing the words of the saint regarding himself, knelt down at his feet and besought him to pray for him to the Lord. When at the outset the saint reproved him for certain other sins of which he was guilty, he expressed his heartfelt sorrow, and purpose of amendment. And thus both these men were cured of the peculiar vices in which they were wont to indulge.

2. Of a Pestilential Cloud, and the curing of many.

At another time also, while the saint was living in the island of Hy (now Iona), and was sitting on the little hill which is called, in Latin, Munitio Magna, he saw in the north a dense rainy cloud rising from the sea on a clear day. As the saint saw it rising, he said to one of his monks, named Silnan, who was sitting beside him, "This cloud will be very baleful to man and beast, and after rapidly passing to day over a considerable part of Scotia (Ireland) namely, from the stream called Ailbine (Delvin, in Meath) as far as the Ford Clied (now Dublin) it will discharge in the evening a pestilential rain, which will raise large and putrid ulcers on the bodies of men and on the udders of cows; so that men and cattle shall sicken and die, worn out with that poisonous complaint. But we, in pity for their sufferings, ought to relieve them by the merciful aid of God; do thou therefore, Silnan, come down with me from this hill, and prepare for thy tomorrow's voyage. If God be willing and life spared to us, thou shalt receive from me some bread which has been blessed by the invocation of the name of God; this thou shalt dip in water, and on thy sprinkling therewith man and beast, they shall speedily recover their health." Why need we linger over it? On the next day, when all things necessary had been hastily got ready, Silnan received the blessed bread from the hands of the saint, and set out on his voyage in peace. As he was starting, the saint gave him these words of comfort, saying, "Be of good courage, my dear son, for thou shalt have fair and pleasant breezes day and night till thou come to that district in Meath, that thou mayest bring the more speedily relief with the healing bread to those who are there sick." Silnan, obeying the saint's words, had a quick and prosperous voyage, by the aid of God, and coming to the above-mentioned part of the district, found the people of whom the saint had been speaking destroyed by the pestilential rain falling down from the aforesaid cloud, which had passed rapidly on before him. In the first place, twice three men were found in the same house near the sea reduced to the agonies of approaching death, and when they were sprinkled by Silnan with the blessed water, were very happily healed that very day. The report of this sudden cure was soon carried through the whole country which was attacked by this most fatal disease, and drew all the sick people to St. Columba's messenger, who, according to the saint's orders, sprinkled man and beast with the water in which the blessed bread had been dipped, and immediately they were restored to perfect health; then the people finding themselves and their cattle healed, praised with the utmost expression of thankfulness Christ in St. Columba.

3. Of the Danger to the blessed man at Sea, and the sudden calm produced by his prayers.

At another time the holy man began to be in great danger at sea, for the whole vessel was violently tossed and shaken with the huge dashing waves, and a great storm of wind was raging on all hands. The sailors then chanced to say to the saint, as he was trying to help them to bale the vessel, "What thou art now doing is of little use to us in our present danger, thou shouldst rather pray for us as we are perishing." On hearing this he ceased to throw out the bitter waters of the green sea wave, and began to pour out a sweet and fervent prayer to the Lord. Wonderful to relate! The very moment the saint stood up at the prow, with his hands stretched out to heaven, and prayed to the Almighty, the whole storm of wind and the fury of the sea ceased more quickly than can be told, and a perfect calm instantly ensued. But those who were in the vessel were amazed, and giving thanks with great admiration, glorified the Lord in the holy and illustrious man.

4.   Concerning a certain other impious man, a persecutor of the Churches, who was called in Latin Manus Dextera.

On one occasion when the blessed man was living in the Hinba island, and set about excommunicating some destroyers of the churches, and amongst them the sons of Conall, one of their wicked associates was instigated by the devil to rush on the saint with a spear with the purpose to kill him. To prevent this, one of the brethren, named Findlugan, put on the saint's cowl and interposed, being ready to die for the holy man. But in a wonderful way the saint's garment served as a kind of strong and impenetrable fence which could not be pierced by the thrust of a very sharp spear though made by a powerful man, but remained untouched, and he who had it on was safe and uninjured under the protection of such a guard. But the ruffian who did this, whose name was Manus Dextera, retraced his steps thinking he had transfixed the saint with his spear. Exactly a year after wards, when the saint was staying in the island of Hy (now Iona), he said, "A year is just now elapsed since the day Manus did what he could to put Findlugan to death in my place; but he himself is slain, I believe, this very hour." And so it happened, at that very moment, according to the revelation of the saint, in the island which in Latin may be called Longa (Luing), where, in a battle fought between a number of men on both sides, this Manus Dextera alone was slain by Cronan, son of Baithene, with a dart, shot, it is said, in the name of St. Columba; and when he fell the battle ceased.

5.   Of yet another Oppressor of the innocent.

When the holy man (Columba), while yet a youth in deacon's orders, was living in the region of the Lagenians (Leinster), learning the divine wisdom, it happened one day that an unfeeling and pitiless oppressor of the innocent was pursuing a young girl who fled before him on a level plain. As she chanced to observe the aged Gemman, master of the foresaid young deacon, reading on the plain, she ran straight to him as fast as she could. Being alarmed at such an unexpected occurrence, he called on Columba, who was reading at some distance, that both together, to the best of their ability, might defend the girl from her pursuer; but he immediately came up, and without any regard to their presence, stabbed the girl with his lance under their very cloaks, and leaving her lying dead at their feet turned to go away back. Then the old man, in great affliction, turning to Columba, said: "How long, holy youth Columba, shall God, the just Judge, allow this horrid crime and this insult to us to go unpunished?" Then the saint at once pronounced this sentence on the perpetrator of the deed: "At the very instant the soul of this girl whom he hath murdered ascendeth into heaven, shall the soul of the murderer go down into hell." And scarcely had he spoken the words when the murderer of the innocent, like Ananias before Peter, fell down dead on the spot before the eyes of the holy youth.

6.   Of the Knife which the Saint blessed by signing it with the Lord's Cross.

At another time, a certain brother named Molua, came to the saint whilst he was writing, and said to him, "This knife which I hold in my hand I beseech thee to bless." The saint, without turning his face from the book out of which he was writing, extended his holy hand a little, with the pen in it, and blessed the knife by signing it. But when the foresaid brother had departed with the knife thus blessed, the saint asked, "What sort of a knife have I blessed for that brother?" Diarmit, the saint's faithful attendant, replied, "Thou hast blessed a knife for killing bulls or oxen." The saint then, on the contrary, said, "I trust in my Lord that the knife I have blessed will never wound men or cattle." This word of the holy man received the strongest confirmation the same hour; for the same brother went beyond the enclosure of the monastery and attempted to kill an ox, but, although he made three strong efforts with all his strength, yet he could not even cut the skin. When this came to the knowledge of the monks, they skilfully melted down the iron of the knife and applied a thin coating of it to all the iron tools used in the monastery. And such was the abiding virtue of the saint's blessing, that these tools could never afterwards inflict a wound on flesh.

7.   Concerning the illness with which the Druid Broichan was visited for his detention of a female slave, and his cure on her release.

About the same time the venerable man, from motives of humanity, besought Broichan the Druid to liberate a certain Scotic female slave, and when he very cruelly and obstinately refused to part with her, the saint then spoke to him to the following effect: "Know, O Broichan, and be assured that if thou refuse to set this captive free, as I desire thee, that .thou shalt die suddenly before I take my departure again from this province." Having said this in presence of Brude, the king, he departed from the royal palace and proceeded to the river Nesa; from this stream he took a white pebble, and showing it to his companions said to them: "Behold this white pebble by which God will effect the cure of many diseases among this heathen nation."

Having thus spoken, he instantly added, "Broichan is chastised grievously at this moment, for an angel being sent from heaven, and striking him severely, hath broken into many pieces the glass cup in his hand from which he was drinking, and hath left him gasping deeply for breath, and half dead. Let us await here a short time, for two of the king's messengers, who have been sent after us in haste, to request us to return quickly and help the dying Broichan, who, now that he is thus terribly punished, consenteth to set the girl free."

Whilst the saint was yet speaking, behold, there arrived, as he had predicted, two horsemen who were sent by the king, and who related all that had occurred to Broichan in the royal fortress, according to the prediction of the saint both the breaking of the drinking goblet, the punishment of the Druid, and his willingness to set his captive at liberty; they then added: "The king and his friends have sent us to thee to request that thou wouldst cure his foster-father Broichan, who lieth in a dying state."

Having heard these words of the messengers, St. Columba sent two of his companions to the king with the pebble which he had blessed, and said to them: "If Broichan shall first promise to set the maiden free, then at once immerse this little stone in water, and let him drink from it and he shall be instantly cured; but if he break his vow and refuse to liberate her, he shall die that instant."

The two persons, in obedience to the saint's instructions, proceeded to the palace, and announced to the king the words of the venerable man. When they were made known to the king and his tutor Broichan, they were so dismayed that they immediately liberated the captive and delivered her to the saint's messengers. The pebble was then immersed in water, and in a wonderful manner, contrary to the laws of nature, the stone floated on the water like a nut or an apple, nor, as it had been blessed by the holy man, could it be submerged. Broichan drank from the stone as it floated on the water, and instantly returning from the verge of death recovered his perfect health and soundness of body.

8. Of the sudden opening of the door of the royal fortress of its own accord.

At another time, when the saint made his first journey to King Brude, it happened that the king, elated by the pride of royalty, acted haughtily, and would not open his gates on the first arrival of the blessed man. When the man of God observed this, he approached the folding doors with his companions, and having first formed upon them the sign of the cross of our Lord, he then knocked at and laid his hand upon the gate, which instantly flew open of its own accord, the bolts having been driven back with great force. The saint and his companions then passed through the gate thus speedily opened. And when the king learned what had occurred, he and his councillors were filled with alarm, and immediately setting out from the palace, he advanced to meet with due respect the blessed man, whom he addressed in the most conciliating and respectful language. And ever after from that day, so long as he lived, the king held this holy and reverend man in very great honour, as was due.

9. Concerning a certain Peasant who was a beggar, for whom the Saint made and blessed a stake for killing wild beasts.

At another time there came to St. Columba a very poor peasant, who lived in the district which borders the shores of the lake called Lochaber. The blessed man, taking pity on the wretched man, who had not wherewithal to support his wife and family, gave him all the alms he could afford, and then said to him, "Poor man, take a branch from the neighbouring wood, and bring it to me quickly." The wretched man brought the branch as he was directed, and the saint, taking it in his own hand, sharpened it to a point like a stake, and, blessing it, gave it back to the destitute man, saying, "Preserve this stake with great care, and it, I believe, will never hurt men or cattle, but only wild beasts and fishes; and as long as thou preservest this stake thou shalt never be without abundance of venison in thy house."

The wretched beggar upon hearing this was greatly delighted, and returning home, fixed the stake in a remote place which was frequented by the wild beasts of the forest; and when that next night was past, he went at early morning dawn to see the stake, and found a stag of great size that had fallen upon it and been transfixed by it. Why should I mention more instances? Not a day could pass, so the tradition goes, in which he did not find a stag or hind or some other wild beast fixed upon the stake; and his whole house being thus filled with the flesh of the wild beasts, he sold to his neighbours all that remained after his own family was supplied. But, as in the case of Adam, the envy of the devil also found out this miserable man also through his wife, who, not as a prudent matron, but rather like one infatuated, thus spoke to her husband: "Remove the stake out of the earth, for if men, or cattle, perish on it, then thou and I and our children shall be put to death, or led into captivity." To these words her husband replied, "It will not be so, for when the holy man blessed the stake he said it would never injure men or cattle." Still the miserable man, after saying this, yielded to his wife, and taking the stake out of the earth, like a man deprived of his reason, brought it into the house and placed it against the wall. Soon after his house-dog fell upon it and was killed, and on its death his wife said to him, "One of thy children will fall upon it and be killed." At these words of his wife he removed the stake out of the house, and having carried it to a forest, placed it in the thickest brush wood, where, as he thought, no animal could be hurt by it; but upon his return the following day he found a roe had fallen upon it and perished. He then took it away and concealed it by thrusting it under the water in the edge of the river. On returning the next day he found transfixed, and still held by it, a salmon of extraordinary size, which he was scarcely able by himself to take from the river and carry home. At the same time, he took the stake again back with him from the water, and placed it outside on the top of his house, where a crow having soon after alighted, was instantly killed by the force of the fall. Upon this the miserable man, yielding again to the advice of his foolish wife, took down the stake from the house-top, and taking an axe cut it in many pieces, and threw them into the fire. Having thus deprived himself of this effectual means of alleviating his distress, he was again, as he deserved to be, reduced to beggary. This freedom from want was owing to the stake, so frequently mentioned above, which the blessed man had blest and given him, and which, so long as it was kept, could suffice for snares and nets, and every kind of fishing and hunting ; but when the stake was lost, the wretched peasant, though he had been enriched for the time, could only, when too late, lament over it with his whole family all the rest of his life.

10.   Of the brave fight of the Angels against the Demons, and how they opportunely assisted the Saint in the same conflict.

On another day while the holy man was living in the island of Hy (now Iona), he went to seek in the woods for a place more remote from men and fitting for prayer. And there when he began to pray, he suddenly beheld, as he afterwards told a few of the brethren, a very black host of demons fighting against him with iron darts. These wicked demons wished, as the Holy Spirit revealed to the saint, to attack his monastery and kill with the same spears many of the brethren. But he, single-handed, against innumerable foes of such a nature, fought with the utmost bravery, having received the armour of the apostle Paul. And thus the contest was maintained on both sides during the greater part of the day, nor could the demons, countless though they were, vanquish him, nor was he able, by himself, to drive them from his island, until the angels of God, as the saint afterwards told certain persons, and they few in number, came to his aid, when the demons in terror gave way. On the same day, when the saint was returning to his monastery, after he had driven the devils from his island, he spoke these words concerning the same hostile legions, saying, "Those deadly foes, who this day, through the mercy of God and the assistance of his angels, have been put to flight from this small track of land, have fled to the land of Tiree, and there as savage invaders they will attack the monasteries of the brethren, and cause pestilential diseases, of which many will be grievously ill and die." All this came to pass in those days, as the blessed man had foreseen. And two days after he thus spake from the revelation of the Holy Ghost, "Baithen hath managed wisely, with God s help, that the congregation of the church over which he hath been appointed by God to preside, in the plain of Lunge in Tiree, should be defended by fasts and prayers against the attacks of the demons, and but one person shall die on this occasion." The whole

280

took place as was foretold ; for whilst many in the other monasteries of the same island fell victims to that disease, none except the one of whom the saint spoke died in the congregation which was under the charge of Baithen.

Articulate Witness

Like the notes of a musical chord, each expression of articulate witness retains its own uniqueness while blending harmoniously with other testimonies in an announcement of the fullness of God's love for the world. Still, just as discordant notes can disrupt a musical performance, acts of witness that are not clear or fully articulated may confuse others – creating a need to continuously examine the passions emerging from a person's experience of God's love and the tools used to express that encounter. So, the call to articulate witness is also an invitation to ongoing discernment and self-disclosure.

Slowly and deliberately, consider the words of Isaiah 61:1-7:
> The spirit of the Lord God is upon me,
>> because the Lord has anointed me;
> he has sent me to bring good news to the oppressed,
>> to bind up the broken-hearted,
> to proclaim liberty to the captives,
>> and release to the prisoners;
> to proclaim the year of the Lord's favour,
>> and the day of vengeance of our God;
>> to comfort all who mourn;
> to provide for those who mourn in Zion–
>> to give them a garland instead of ashes,
> the oil of gladness instead of mourning,
>> the mantle of praise instead of a faint spirit.
> They will be called oaks of righteousness,
>> the planting of the Lord, to display his glory.
> They shall build up the ancient ruins,
>> they shall raise up the former devastations;
> they shall repair the ruined cities,
>> the devastations of many generations.
> Strangers shall stand and feed your flocks,
>> foreigners shall till your land and dress your vines;
> but you shall be called priests of the Lord,
>> you shall be named ministers of our God;
> you shall enjoy the wealth of the nations,
>> and in their riches you shall glory.
> Because their shame was double,
>> and dishonour was proclaimed as their lot,

> therefore they shall possess a double portion;
> everlasting joy shall be theirs.

Now, ask yourself the following questions:

1. Do you feel anointed by God follow a particular path of service and articulate witness?

>•How do you know that this vocation comes from God?

>•What are the activities and attributes of this path of service and witness?

2. How does your vocation proclaim redemptive desires of God expressed through Isaiah 61?

>•Which verses from Isaiah 61 speak most strongly to you? Why?

>•What feelings do the verses from Isaiah 61 evoke in you?

>•What actions do the verses from Isaiah 61 evoke in you?

>•How do these feelings and actions relate to your personal vocation of service and articulate witness?

3. Does your personal vocation connect you to God's redemptive activity in the world?

>•How does your chosen form of articulate witness proclaim God's love for all of creation?

>•How does your form of witness seek to liberate others? From what?

>•How does your form of witness console those who are suffering?

>•How does your form of witness build a joyful future and restore God's creation?

>•How does your form of witness nourish others?

4. What are the redemptive relationships you need to fulfill your personal vocation of service and articulate witness?

>•What aspects of your vocation rely upon you alone?

>•What aspects of your vocation require the participation of others? How and why?

>•How might these relationships change during the evolution of your vocation?

>•How will you know when these changes become necessary?

After answering these questions, review your responses in detail. Initially, focus on the questions which generated the strongest emotional responses. Carefully consider the reasons why these questions affected you so strongly. Also, take some time to observe which questions provided you with the greatest creative or intellectual clarity, observing patterns of thought or feeling that helped you better understand your specific type of articulate witness. Then, record these reflections in your workbook.

Part 1

Over time, through your exploration of your passions and your style of action, you facilitate a gradual blending of these elements into a form of self-expression that is unique to you. You recognize that even though others use the same tools as you do – perhaps even in a similar manner – no one else uses these tools or expresses the same ideas as you do. You also come to realize that God's loving presence flows through you easily and without any hesitation in all your words and actions. This is the moment when you discover your voice and achieve in intimacy with God that fills you with confidence, hope and love.

> *Note: It is important to recognize that this discovery of your voice does not necessarily suggest a path to fame or social stature – or the need to make grand gestures of faith. There are many famous saints but there are many more saints whose transformative activities in the world remain anonymous. A single person – working in food bank or a homeless shelter or reading scripture in a prayer service with passion and clarity, or faithfully writing letters of concern to governmental authorities – transforms the lives of many people without ever being acknowledged or recognized beyond a small circle of acquaintances. Each serves as an essential instrument of God's love through their faithful contributions to the building of God's kingdom.*

It is important that you remain faithful and consistent in discerning the God-given nature of your passions and your choices of style as you seek to make your articulate witness.

•Use the "Rules for Discernment" presented in *The Spiritual Exercises of St. Ignatius* to maintain your awareness of the activity of God in the passions you experience and in the choices of style you make when expressing your thoughts, feelings, or concerns – whether in acts of creative expression or social engagement. Remember that it is most helpful to use the rules Ignatius proposed during the first week of his *Spiritual Exercises* when engaging a new idea and to use the rules suggested during the second while examining the history of your choices and actions.

•Challenge yourself to expand the scope and range of your actions until your process of self-exploration reveals the place and type of activity God desires of you. Until you discover your voice, you also may find it helpful to revisit various experiments from your past to determine whether you see them in a different way than you did in your past.

•Engage increasingly challenging groups of people until God reveals to you the community or social group to which you are meant to minister. Again, this might involve revisiting groups that were initially unsupportive of your activities if you feel a spiritual leading in this direction.

However, it is very important to remember that your form of witness will flow naturally from you as you discover the various aspects of it. The discernment shaping your form of articulate witness will gain greater certainty and clarity over time, so it is important to include a recognition of this internal momentum in your discernment process. One highly useful tool in this effort is known as the "action-observation-reflection" method.

•This reflective process involves the consideration of an action you have taken to consider your future choices. Since this involves a consideration of a history, this method may be used in conjunction with the "Rules for Discernment" proposed by Saint Ignatius during the second week of his *Spiritual Exercises*.

•With this in mind, you should develop a framework for examining your actions based on Ignatius' set of eight rules. When considering your previous action, begin by revisiting the motivations for that action before reviewing the effects (on you and others) of your action using the rules proposed during the second week of this *Spiritual Exercises*. Make certain that you keep each aspect of this review distinct and separate from the others, using one rule at a time.

•When you are finished, compare the results of these separate reviews to determine which facets of your behavior reflected God's desires and which did not. Then, beginning with those aspects of your actions which inhibited or impeded God's presence, determine how you would amend these shortcomings in the future. Afterward, repeat this process with those aspects of your actions which heightened or strengthen the activity of God through you and decide how you would strengthen these choices.

•Then, take these observations to prayer and ask God to reveal the correct path forward before deciding how to proceed in the future with an awareness that these choices eventually will be evaluated using this same method.

Note: While the "action-observation-reflection" model appears to be cyclical, it creates a spiral of activity that acquires momentum with each completion of the circuit as it expands the range of possible actions to accommodate new opportunities.

Part 2

When you discover your voice, you will recognize both the personal history that has led you in that moment and the gift of God's grace it represents. The closer you come to the discovery of your voice, the more clarity you have regarding the passions and stylistic choices shaping your unique form of witness. In your discernment process, you will find that most of your choices offer you a sense of certainty that they are divinely inspired. You are becoming an instrument of God's love and you are increasingly familiar with God's presence in you and in your actions. This is both a gift and a challenge.

When you discover your voice, you must remain on guard against pride and other sins that might lead you away from God's presence and desires. In his *Spiritual Exercises*, Saint Ignatius points out that greater generosity of heart also makes a person more vulnerable to a desolating spirit. So, it is very important that you remain steadfast in your ongoing efforts to discern God's activity in and through you.

With this in mind, you may find it useful to stop randomly during your day to briefly consider a choice or contemplate God's activity around you. Use your knowledge of discernment and of the patterns of God's presence to remain both vigilant to the guile of the desolating spirit and trustworthy in your witness to God's love.

Part 3

As with the earlier explorations of your passions and style, take your insights and concerns to prayer on a regular basis. Imagine yourself sitting with Jesus in a comfortable space and tell him about your most intimate experiences of God and how you feel they lead to specific forms of public witness.

Listen as Jesus asks you questions about these matters and make mental notes about your reactions to Jesus' questions and observations. Then, explain both your willingness and your reluctance to share these experiences with others in some way. Again, listen to Jesus' response before asking for his continued support as you move forward.

Afterward, take some time to answer the following questions:
  • What aspects of your voice excite you and leave you without any doubt about using it?
  • What emotions make you uncertain about your personal voice?
  • What are you willing to sacrifice as God asks you to share your deepest spiritual experiences with others?

Part 4

After you discover your voice as a witness to God's presence and love in the world, you should never be afraid to change or adapt when receiving new insights into the nature of God.

Your prayer will reveal God's desires for and through you, but you should not exclude or ignore the human voices speaking to you. Once you have come to the recognition of your unique voice you may find that your passions and the styles of expression you employ may change with time. However, your voice – the earthly expression of your special relationship with God's creation – will remain constant and consistent.

In this way, the discovery of your personal voice and your vocation to articulate witness becomes both the achievement of a new state of being and an invitation to new forms of service. Trust in yourself and in God as you remember the words of John 14:17, "You know him, because he abides with you, and he will be in you."

Textual Resources

Excerpts from *The Spiritual Exercises of Saint Ignatius of Loyola*, edited by Charles Seager.

A Contemplation of the Kingdom of Jesus Christ (91-98)

91.   A contemplation of the kingdom of Jesus Christ, from the likeness of an earthly king calling out his subjects to war…

The first prelude for the construction of the place will now be, to imagine that we see the synagogues, villages, and towns, through which Christ passed preaching; and so concerning other places.

The second, relating to the obtaining of grace, will here be, to ask of God that we may not be deaf when Christ calls us; but be ready to follow and obey.

92.   Let the first point be, to place before my eyes a human king, chosen of God, whom all Christian princes and people are bound to reverence and obey.

93.   The second, to imagine that I hear that king speaking to all his subjects: I propose to subject to my power all the countries of the unbelievers. Whosoever, therefore, chooses to follow me, let him be prepared to use no other food, clothing, or other things, than what he sees me use.

He must also persevere in the same labours, watchings, arid other difficulties with me, that each may partake of the victory and felicity in proportion as he shall have been a companion of the labours and troubles;

94.   The third is, to consider what his faithful subjects ought to answer this most loving and liberal king, and how promptly to offer themselves prepared for all his will. And, on the other hand, if any one did not hearken, of how great reproach he would be worthy among all men, and how worthless a soldier he would have to be accounted.

95.   The second part of this exercise, consists in drawing a comparison between the said king and our Lord Jesus Christ, concerning these three points:

First, we shall thus apply the example: if that earthly king, with his warlike calling forth, is worthy to receive attention and obedience, how much more worthy is Christ, the Eternal King, and conspicuous to the whole world, Who invites each to Himself in these words: "This is My most just will, to claim to Myself the dominion of the whole world, to conquer all My enemies, and so to enter into My Father's glory.

Whoever then desires to come thither with Me, he must needs labour with Me; for the reward will be according to the labour."

96.   The second, we shall reason, that there will be no one of a sound mind, who will not most eagerly offer and dedicate himself entire to the service of Christ.

97.   Thirdly, it must be judged, that they who shall think good to be altogether subjected to the obedience of Him, will offer, not merely themselves for the endurance of labours, but also some greater and more illustrious offerings, conquering the rebellion of the flesh, of the senses, and of the love of self and the world whence each; will answer to the following effect:

98.   "Behold, Supreme King and Lord of all things, I, though most unworthy, yet, relying on Thy grace and help, offer myself altogether to Thee, and submit to Thy will all that is mine; testifying before Thine infinite goodness, as also in the sight of Thy glorious Virgin Mother, and of the whole court of heaven, that this is my mind, this my desire, this my most certain determination, that (so it turn to the greater advancement of Thy praise and my obedience) I may follow Thee as closely as possible, and imitate Thee in bearing all injuries and adversities with the true poverty, both of spirit, and also of goods; if (I say) it please Thy most holy Majesty to choose and receive me to such a state of life."

A Colloquy before Jesus on the Cross (53-54)

53.   The colloquy will be made by imagining Jesus Christ to be present before me, fixed on the cross. Let me, therefore, inquire with myself the reason why He, the infinite Creator, vouchsafed to become a creature, and from eternal life to come to temporary death because of my sins. Let me also call myself to account, inquiring what worthy of mention I have hitherto done for Christ, what I am doing now or ought to do. And, looking upon Him thus affixed to the cross, let me give utterance to such things as my mind arid affection shall suggest.

54.   Moreover, it is the property of the colloquy to be made similarly to the language of a friend to a friend, or of a servant to his Lord; now by asking some favour, now by accusing myself of some fault; sometimes by communicating my own affairs of any kind, and asking counsel or help concerning them.

A Consideration of Personal Sins (55-60)

55.   A meditation concerning sins; comprehending, after the preparatory prayer and two preludes, five articles or points, with a colloquy at the end [asking that we seek] intense grief concerning sins, with abundant weeping.

56.   Let the first point be, a certain inquest by which the sins of one's whole life are recalled into the memory, the person going through, step by step, and examining the several years and spaces of time. In which thing we are assisted by a threefold summing up, by considering, that is to say, the places where we have lived, the various modes of intercourse we have had with others, and the different kinds of offices or occupations in which we have been engaged.

57.   The second is, to weigh the sins themselves, how great is the foulness and wickedness of each on account of its own nature, even though it had not been prohibited.

58.   The third is, to consider myself, who or of what kind I am, adding comparisons which may bring me to a greater contempt of myself; as if I reflect how little I am when compared with all men; then what the whole multitude of mortals is, as compared with the Angels and all the Blessed: after these things I must consider what, in fact, all creation is in comparison with God the Creator Himself: what, now, can I, one mere human being, be? Lastly, let me look at the corruption of my whole self, the wickedness of rny soul, and the pollution of my body; and account myself to be a kind of ulcer or boil, from which so great and foul a flood of sins, so great a pestilence of vices, has flowed down.

59.   The fourth is, to consider what God is, Whom I have thus offended, collecting the perfections which are God s peculiar attributes and comparing them with my opposite vices and defects; comparing, that is to say, His supreme power, wisdom, goodness, and justice, with my extreme weakness, ignorance, wickedness, and iniquity.

60.   The fifth, to break forth into exclamation, from a vehement commotion of the feelings, admiring greatly how all creatures (going over them severally) have borne with me so long, and even to this time preserved me alive; how the angels, bearing the sword of the divine justice, have patiently borne with me, guarded me, and even assisted me with their prayers; how the saints have interceded for me; how the sky, the sun, the moon, and the other heavenly bodies, the elements, and all kinds of animals and productions of the earth, in place of the vengeance due, have served me; how, lastly, the earth has not opened

and swallowed me up, unbarring a thousand hells, in which I might suffer everlasting punishments.

The Contemplation to Attain Love (230-237)

230.   In the first place, two things must be noted.

The first, that love itself turns more on deeds than on words.

231.   The second, that love consists in the mutual communication of powers, possessions, and works; as of knowledge, riches, honour, and good of whatever kind.

The prayer is placed at the beginning as usual.

232.   The first prelude is, to see myself standing before the Lord, the Angels, and all the Saints, they being propitious to me.

233.   The second, to intreat the grace of God, whereby, perceiving the greatness of His benefits conferred upon me, I may spend my whole self in the love, worship, and service of Him.

234.   Let the first point be, to recall to memory the benefits of Creation and Redemption: in like manner to recount particular or private gifts, and to weigh over with the most inward affection, how much our most benignant Lord has done and borne for my sake; how much He has given me from His treasures; and that accord ing to His own divine decree and good pleasure, He desires to give me Himself, so far as He can. Which things having been very well considered, let me turn to myself, and examine with myself what my duty is, what it is equitable and just that I should offer and present to the Divine Majesty. Certainly it is not doubtful that I ought to offer all I have, and myself also, with the greatest affection, and with words after this, or the like, manner:

"Receive, Lord, my whole liberty. Accept my memory, understanding, and whole will. Whatsoever I have, or possess, Thou hast given me: this all I restore to Thee, and to Thy will altogether deliver up to be governed. Give me only the love of Thee, with Thy grace, and I am rich enough, and desire nothing else beyond."

235.   The second will be, to contemplate God existing in each of His creatures; and to the elements indeed granting, to be; but to the plants, by vegetation also to live; to the animals, in addition, to perceive; to men and women, in the last place, to understand also. Among whom I too have received all these benefits – to be, to live, to perceive, and to understand; and He has been pleased to make me a kind of temple of Himself, created after His own image and likeness. From the admiration of all which things, returning into myself, let me do as in the first point,

or better if anything better shall occur; which same practice must be followed in order in the points which follow.

236.   The third is, to contemplate the same God and Lord working, and in a manner labouring, in His creatures, for my sake; inasmuch as He gives and preserves to them what they are, have, can, and do. All which things, as above, must be turned back to the consideration of myself.

237.   The fourth, to behold how all gifts and good things come down from heaven, such as are power, justice, goodness, knowledge, and every other human perfection, circumscribed by certain determined bounds, and from that boundless treasure of all good, are derived as light from the sun, and as water from a fountain. I must add, also, the aforesaid turn ing back to the consideration of myself.

A colloquy also will be made at the end, to be concluded with *Pater noster* [Our Father/The Lord's Prayer].

1.   A Description of Saint Columba from *Lives of Saints from The Book of Lismore*, edited by Whitley Stokes.

Now there never was born to the Gael offspring nobler or wiser, or of better kin than he. There hath not come of them another who was meeker, or humbler, or lowlier. Surely it was great lowliness in Columba that he himself used to take off his monks' sandals and wash their feet for them. He often used to carry his portion of corn on his back to the mill, and grind it, and bring it home to his house. He never used to put linen or wool against his skin. His side used to come against the bare mould. A pillarstone used to be under his head for a bolster, and he slept only so long as Diarmit his fosterling was chanting three chapters of the *Beatus*. He would rise up at once after that, and… would chant [the Psalms] on the sand of the shore before the sun would rise. In the day he attended to the Hours. He offered Christ's Body and His Blood. He preached the Gospel, he baptized, he consecrated. He healed the lepers, and the blind, and the halt, and folk of every other disease, and he raised the dead.

2.   Stories about Saint Columba from *Three Middle-Irish homilies on the lives of Saints Patrick, Brigit and Columba*, edited by Whitley Stokes.

<u>Columba Raises a Dead Cleric</u>
At another time, the cleric Cruithnechan went with the young Columba to watch by a sick person. As they were going through a wood, the cleric's foot slipt on the path and thereof he suddenly died. Columba put his cowl under the cleric's head, thinking that he was asleep, and began to rehearse his lesson, so that certain nuns heard him as far as their cell. The learned compute that there was a mile and a half between them, and the sound of his voice was often heard at that distance, as saith the poet:
> The sound of Columba's voice
> Great (was) its sweetness above every train,
> To the end of fifteen hundred paces,
> Though great the distance, it was clear.

Then came the nuns and found the cleric dead before them, and they told Columba to bring the cleric back to life for them. Straightway went he to bring the cleric to life. The cleric arose out of death at Columba's word even as if he had been asleep. Thereafter Columba offered (himself) to the Lord of the Elements, and begged three boons of Him, to wit, chastity and wisdom and pilgrimage. The three were fully granted him.

Columba and the Miracle of the Feast
At another time, Boethin left Columba cooking a cow for the reapers. They had with them an old whilom-hero of the men of Ireland, Maeluma. Columba asked him, how much was his meal when he was a young warrior? Saith Maeluma, "When I was a young warrior I used to eat a fat cow to my full meal." Columba commanded him to eat his fill. Maeluma did that for him, and ate the whole cow. Thereafter Boethin came and asked if what should be eaten were ready. So Columba ordered Maeluma to gather all the bones of the cow into one place, and so it was done. Columba then blessed the bones, and their own flesh was upon them after that, and they were given to the reapers to eat their fill.

Columba Nears Death
One day in the month of May, Columba went to see the plowmen in the north of the island. He was comforting and teaching them. "Well now," saith he, "at the Easter that went into the month of April, then was I fain to have gone to heaven, but I did not wish you to have grief or sorrow after your toil, wherefore I have stayed with you to comfort you from Easter to Pentecost."

When the monks heard these words they were sorrowful exceedingly. He then turned his face westwards, and blessed the the island with its indwellers, and banished toads and snakes out of it.

When he had blessed the island he then came to his cell and not long after came the ends of the sabbath and the beginning of the Sunday. And when he raised his eyes on high there came a great glow to his countenance and to his face, and the brethren beheld that. An angel of God, moreover, tarried above him then.

Columba and the Mourning Nag
Thereafter he went to bless the barn, and he said to his servant Diarmit that on Sunday night he would depart unto heaven. After that the venerable old man, Columba, sat down on the edge of the path, for weariness had come to him, though his wayfaring had been but short;

seventy-seven years was his age at that time. Then came unto him the nag which the monks had in the island, and weeps in the breast of the cleric, so that his raiment became wet. The servant, Diarmit, sought to drive the nag away from him. "Let him be, O Diarmit," saith Columba, "until he sufficeth himself with tears and sorrow in lamenting me."

The Miraculous Cowl of Aed Slane

Columba once went to Aed Slane, and made a prophesy for him, and said that he would be long-lived, unless he were parricidal. If, however, he should commit parricide he was to live but four years after. So Columba hallowed a cowl for him and said that he would not be wounded while that cowl was on him. However, Aed Slane did commit parricide, against the word of Columba, on Suibne (son of Colman). At the end of four years after, he went upon a foray and he forgot his cowl so that he was killed on that day.

Columba and the Miracle of the Barley

Once upon a time he sends his monks into the wood to cut wattling for building a church for him. Where the wattling was cut was in a certain warrior's land which lay near the cell. Now he was vexed that the timber was cut in his land without his own consent. So when Columba heard of that he said to his household: "Take him," saith he, "the price of his wood in barley-grain, and put it into the earth." Now at that time it had passed midsummer. The grain, however, was brought to the warrior. He cast it into the ground, and it grew and was ripe shortly thereafter.

Columba Arrives at Hy (Iona)

Columba fared then in happy mood till he came to the stead which to-day is named Hy (Iona) of Columba. On the night of Pentecost he reached it. Two bishops who were biding in the island came to cast him out of it. But God revealed to Columba that in truth they were not bishops, whereupon they left the island to him when he told of them their story and what they ought to perform.

Then said Columba to his household, "It is well for us that our roots should go under earth here;" and he said to them, "It is permitted to you that some one of you go under the mould of this island to consecrate it." Odran rose up readily, and this he said: "If thou wouldst accept me," saith he, "I am ready for that." "O Odran," saith Columba, "thereof shalt thou have the reward, namely, to none shall his request be granted at my grave, unless he shall seek it first of thee." Odran then fared to heaven.

Columba then founded the church of Hy. Thrice fifty monks had he therein for meditation and sixty for active life, as said the poet:

Wondrous the warriors who abode in Hy,
Thrice fifty in monastic rule,
With their boats along the sea,
Three score men a-rowing.

After Columba had founded Hy, he fared on his preaching round throughout Scotland and Britons and Saxons; and he brought them to faith and belief after many miracles had been wrought by him, after bringing the dead to life out of death.

Columba Raises Two People from the Dead

Now there was biding in the country a certain man to whom Columba had preached, and he, with all his household, believed in the Lord. The devil was envious of that thing, so he smote the son of this man with a sore disease, whereof he died. Then the heathen were reviling Christ and Columba, whereupon he made fervent prayer to God, and awoke the dead son out of death.

As Columba was on a certain day preaching to the hosts, a certain man fared from them over the river which was near them, so that he should not be listening to the word of God. The snake strikes him in the water and killed him forthwith. His body was brought into Columba's presence, and he makes a cross with his crozier over his (the dead man's) breast, whereupon he at once arose.

Columba's Mother Has a Vision

Even as Columba's birth was foretold by Ireland's elders, so was it figured in visions and in dreams. Even so it was figured in the vision which appeared to his mother, namely, that a great cloak was given her which spanned across Ireland and the sea to the east, and of hues there was not a hue that was not therein. And a youth perceived the radiant vesture and took away from her the cloak into the air, and Ethne (Columba's mother) was sorrowful thereat, and her-seemed that the same youth came again unto her and said unto her: "O good woman," said the youth, "thou hast no need to grieve, but meeter for thee were joyance and delight, for what this cloak portendeth is that thou wilt bear a son, and Ireland and Scotland will be full of his teaching."

3.   "Helper of All Workers" (*Adiutor Laborantium*), translated by T. M. Moore.

Ah! Helper of all workers and
Blessed Ruler of all good; You stand
Continuous guard throughout the land,
Defending every faithful man,
Extending lowly ones Your hand,
Frustrating those who in pride stand;
Great Ruler of the faithful and
Hosts who in sin prefer to stand;
In justice ruling every man,
Condemning sin by Your command;
Cascading light on every hand,
Light of the Father of lights, and
Magnificent throughout the land;
No one will You Your helping hand
Or strength deny, who in hope stand:
Please, Lord – though I am little and
Quail wretchedly before Your hand,
Resisting stormy tempests and
Strong tumults and temptations grand –
That Jesus may reach out His hand
Unto me, I implore – His land,
Verdant and lovely, be my land!
Yes, make my life a hymn to stand
Zealous against those You withstand.
Please grant that paradise my land
In Jesus Christ by grace may be,
Both now and in eternity.

About the Author

A former Jesuit, **Timothy J. Ray** brings a diverse background in creative writing, cultural studies, theology, and the history of ideas to his work in spiritual direction and formation. He received his Bachelor of Arts, *magna cum laude*, in a multi-disciplinary program focused on the cultural history of law, economics and politics from Niagara University before earning, with distinction, both his Master of Fine Arts in Dramaturgy and Dramatic Criticism from Yale University and his Master of Letters in Theology from the University of Saint Andrews.

In addition to this Celtic journey through *The Spiritual Exercises of Saint Ignatius of Loyola*, he has published *The Carmichael Prayerbook, A Journey to the Land of the Saints* and *A Pilgrimage to the Land of the Saints, Nurturing the Courage of Pilgrims* and *Seeking our Place of Resurrection*.

For more information about Timothy and his activities, please visit http://www.silentheron.net.

Printed in Great Britain
by Amazon